REVISITING CHRISTIANITY

This book presents a view of Christianity and Christian thinking that draws on some key thinkers from Plato to Wittgenstein and represents a thoughtful 'common sense' theology offered as an alternative to the anti-intellectualism of many contemporary Christians and to the distortions of Christianity provided by some of the most vocal critics.

Seeking to make accessible some traditional Christian thinking and practices that are rooted in the desire to make the most of life, Felderhof highlights the additional Platonic corollary that unless we have learned to live well, we shall not properly understand, thus presuming the mutual interdependence of theory and practice.

Felderhof portrays how Christian theology has to do with making sense of what Christians do and how generally we are best advised to live. This is an invaluable introduction to key themes for students and a wide range of readers.

For my family

Revisiting Christianity
Theological Reflections

MARIUS C. FELDERHOF
University of Birmingham, UK

LONDON AND NEW YORK

First published 2011 by Ashgate Publishing

Published 2016 by Routledge
2 Park Square, Milton Park, Abingdon, Oxon OX14 4RN
711 Third Avenue, New York, NY 10017, USA

Routledge is an imprint of the Taylor & Francis Group, an informa business

Copyright © 2011 Marius C. Felderhof

Marius C. Felderhof has asserted his right under the Copyright, Designs and Patents Act, 1988, to be identified as the author of this work.

All rights reserved. No part of this book may be reprinted or reproduced or utilised in any form or by any electronic, mechanical, or other means, now known or hereafter invented, including photocopying and recording, or in any information storage or retrieval system, without permission in writing from the publishers.

Notice:
Product or corporate names may be trademarks or registered trademarks, and are used only for identification and explanation without intent to infringe.

British Library Cataloguing in Publication Data
Felderhof, M. C.
   Revisiting Christianity : theological reflections.
   1. Theology–Miscellanea. 2. Christian life–Miscellanea.
   I. Title
   230'.002-dc22

Library of Congress Cataloging-in-Publication Data
Felderhof, M. C.
   Revisiting Christianity : theological reflections / Marius C. Felderhof.
     p. cm.
   Includes bibliographical references (p.   ) and index.
   ISBN 978-1-4094-0672-3 (hardcover : alk. paper) – ISBN 978-1-4094-0673-0
   (pbk. : alk. paper) 1. Theology–Miscellanea. I. Title.
   BR96.F45 2011
   230–dc22
                                                                    2011014285

ISBN 9781409406723 (hbk)
ISBN 9781409406730 (pbk)

Contents

Preface   *vii*
Acknowledgements   *xi*

Introduction: On Revisiting Christian Faith   1

PART I: CLARIFYING WHAT CHRISTIANS DO

1	Eternal Life	15
2	Worship	29
3	Prayer	41
4	Sacraments	53
5	Human Beings	65
6	Living Well	75
7	Sin	87
8	Forgiveness	99
9	Church	109
10	Relating to Different Faiths	119

PART II: CLARIFYING TO WHAT CHRISTIANS ARE COMMITTED

11	Believing in the Spirit	131
12	The Work of Christ	139
13	The Person of Christ	145
14	On Speaking about the God	155
15	Revelation	167
16	Scripture and Tradition	175
17	Rhetoric and Hermeneutics	185
18	Defining Theology	195

Appendix: Christological Glossary   *203*
Bibliography   *207*
Index   *217*

Preface

This book has come from my experience of teaching Christian theology to first year students in higher education who came from all backgrounds, religious and non-religious, Christian and non-Christian faiths, including Muslims, Jews, Sikhs and Hindus, amongst others. This audience makes the experience of teaching somewhat different from the delivery of theological discourses in theological colleges where the students represent a more selected group in society. With such a diverse audience it is useful to be reminded of a common starting point that all people have. I took this to be that everyone has an interest in living well, in effect, in living life to the full. The problem is that we do not all know what that might mean; the additional problem to face in living well is that we only ever have one go at life or, at least, that is what most ordinary people believe in the West. We cannot do better next time round. 'There are no classes in life for beginners, always what is hardest is demanded of you right away' (Rilke, 2008, p. 65). A further difficulty in living well is that we are unable to undo the past; we may be able to overcome the mistakes and failures from the past but we cannot undo them.

Within Christian faith the experience and practice of forgiveness is, of course, an important element in being reconciled to our personal and collective past. Such experiences liberate us for the future because our past has a habit of getting in our way and limiting our future.

Most religious traditions have an orientation to the future which induces us to ask what should we do or what ought we to do to live well? At least some of these traditions go further – they project us forward into the future to the very end of time and backward to its very beginning so that we are forced to consider our personal life and human life generally in their entirety, and to ask what made that valuable and worthwhile. This final, or 'last', judgment on transient life may lead people either to despair or to discern something of intrinsic worth untouched by passing time. It is characteristic of religion to provide this overarching frame to life. For lack of a better term, I will refer to life's intrinsic worth, which does not depend on how things go, as our eternal good. Faith is the expectation that we may paradoxically encounter this eternal good in our time-bound life. Religious practice is 'designed' to give one the confidence to live from it and for it.

Perhaps because we only have one go at life and there is only one history, we look to the experiences of others. We read histories, biographies and autobiographies; we consider what has been handed on to us (tradition). It does not relieve us of making our own judgments but it would be foolish not to be informed by the faith of our fathers and mothers, by what they discerned to be the eternal good and the practices they used to engage with it. The different religious traditions offer some characteristic perceptions and disciplines for life, usually informed by (an) impressive root experience(s), preserved in texts and represented in ritual or simply shared in a form of life. Christianity is one such set of practices and forms of life. These may be unfamiliar to many in a secularised world, but before turning our backs on Christian traditions, we should at least give them some attention because they lie at the roots of Western culture and one option *not* open to us is to escape giving form to our life. The only option confronting us is which form of life is it to be? If we must choose, then clearly it is better to do so reflectively and self-consciously rather than to be moulded into one unwittingly. In this sense it is better on the advice of Socrates to embrace an examined rather than an unexamined life. Even a cursory examination will show that some forms of life are shallow and others are deeper and more profound. Doing theology should help in the endeavour of showing and deciding which is which.

There are various tasks in theology and different ways of accomplishing them. In a secular and religiously plural society, theology has become increasingly difficult because there are significant disagreements on what really matters and no assured methods of gaining agreement. We can try to show the nature of the disagreements and to provide reminders about the character of our life and to recall why it took the form it did or show why people once thought them important. In the midst of the many possibilities open to us now, one of the current theological challenges in a globalised world is to understand how, having been formed by one tradition and thought world, we can relate to and incorporate the valued insights of other traditions.

What is offered here is *a* view of the Christian faith; it is not *the* view, not least because Christianity takes so many different guises. My students were always reminded that there are many theological books with the Christian faith as their subject matter; getting alternative views from different places and different times is part of the process of getting an education. However, in the course of this volume the goal is not just to support a developed view *about* life. The purpose of good theology is to help with the examination of our life and to enable us to live more confidently. In this context it is equally helpful to be reminded of what kind of tool theology is and what its limitations are, but not without first trying to do some theology, for we must not lose sight of its primary purpose of aiding us to live well.

In eliciting opinions from students the response is often cast in terms of 'I feel that'. Perhaps this is just a careless modern expression in place of 'I think that', but when dealing with matters of the deepest concern to us we need to draw on more than intellect. In the goal of understanding what we have to do to live well, the whole person comes into play: intellect, affections and will. Sometimes the obstacles to understanding a matter lie in our feelings or lack of them. We may be too hard-hearted to grasp the point or too sentimental to see clearly. Traditionally too, Christianity located the problems of understanding in the will. We are too stubborn or too weak-willed to pursue the issues properly. Alternatively, our wills are seldom free enough from a concern with self to understand rightly. Failures in life and thought are never solely the result of a lack of logic or reason; frequently it is due to a lack of passion (eros or love) or due to the lack of purity of heart that comes from a single-minded commitment to the eternal good.

It would be foolish to claim that we have succeeded where others have failed, but it is important to observe the complexities and difficulties in any understanding pursued in the adventure of living well. In the face of the fragility and transience of life, this is a very modest contribution in the endeavour to keep alive the discussion in the public square of what should truly matter to us.

Marius C. Felderhof
University of Birmingham

Acknowledgements

'To teach is to learn' was the motto of one of the institutions in which I taught. In this sense I owe a deep debt of gratitude to all my former students, whether at the University of St Andrews, Westhill College or the University of Birmingham. There is no greater privilege than to be allowed the opportunity to engage with lively, young and enquiring persons. Teaching them was a great stimulus and I trust they did not find me too slow a learner. I certainly would not blame all the inadequacies of what follows on them.

The Classics Department of Dalhousie University, Canada, first introduced me to the Pre-Socratics, to Plato, Aristotle, the Stoics and the other Greek thinkers, nor did they neglect the Church Fathers. It made me aware of just how much the Christian faith owes to this ancient thought world – indeed, much would be unintelligible without it. Whenever I returned to it, I deemed myself richly rewarded. In comparison, much modern philosophy struck me as relatively sterile with respect to understanding the depths of religious life until I encountered the writings of D. Z. Phillips and L. Wittgenstein. They opened philosophical windows which encouraged me to persist in the quest to make sense of Christian faith and the forms of life it spawned.

Over the course of time I have had the benefit of many outstanding teachers and colleagues both in philosophy and theology. It would be invidious to name and identify some whilst omitting others, except possibly Dr Mario von der Ruhr and Dr Ieuan Lloyd, who originally advised me on my doctoral studies and have remained friends and conversation partners ever since. I also very much appreciated Open End, a colloquium group, meeting in private homes initiated by Professors John Hick and Michael Goulder.

The greatest debt I owe to my extended family, but especially to my wife, Jennifer, and our sons and daughter, Stephen, Jeremy, Catriona and Ben. They have never stopped teaching me what life offers and demands.

Introduction:
On Revisiting Christian Faith

> We cannot keep our minds open forever; we have to start forming an opinion somewhere.[1]

What is the point of revisiting generally?

For those who take an aesthetic approach[2] to life, the challenge is to maximise what life has to offer and always to do and to experience something new and different. In such a case, 'revisiting' will be seen as going over the same old ground and just a waste of valuable time.

Another position might be to see that the world in which we live is always changing, whether we like it or not. As one of the ancient Greeks observed, one cannot step into the same river twice. There are no genuine constants. Even when we think we have a firm intellectual grip on something, we know that the meaning of the object of our attention is held fast by what surrounds it. As the surroundings change, so does the object itself.[3] In fact Christianity is, and has been, profoundly changed by the world which surrounds it, i.e. by the culture in which it is located. Its sense never remains exactly the same, even when we seek to be faithful to its original vision and impetus.

How has Christianity changed?

A deep gulf exists between the modern Western world and the religious world which was once the norm. Nothing shows this more clearly than that once upon a time people were prepared to die for their 'faith' – whatever was meant by that. With some notable exceptions it is now hard for people in the 'enlightened' West to imagine what would be worth dying for.[4] And these exceptions do not normally

---

[1] Midgley, 1992, p. 50.

[2] See what S. Kierkegaard has to say about the aesthetic life, for example, in *Either-Or* (Kierkegaard, 1987).

[3] The modern study of human perception of colours reveals that the colour of an object can change according to its surroundings, so that whatever is grey in one setting becomes brown in another.

[4] Students will confess that they would die for their children or their family, which shows that they might die for what they love rather than for what they think. Soldiers are prepared to die for the security of their nation. There is always a nagging question as to whether the nation is worthy of such a sacrifice.

include religious doctrines or for that matter any other set of ideas. Further, at one point the characteristically religious life was a deeply, but certainly not exclusively, intellectual passion. The ultimate goal of religious life was a beatific vision. This beatific vision, though primarily intellectual, was the culmination of a deep-seated love, an eros of the mind. It integrated action, passion and thought in praise of the Divine.

In any case in the modern world, religious life appears to be associated more and more with emotion and affection, and less and less with thought. Possibly it is associated with action, but not often with action driven by intellect. A tentative reason for the suspicion under which the intellect is held in religious life is the implicit disengagement from life found in reflective theorising and in the sheer provisionality of all intellectual conclusions.[5] In Plato's dialogues, his discussions frequently end in 'aporia', which is a kind of indecisiveness. This outcome in turn leads to a paralysis of will. Religious life generally demands actions, and actions require a degree of real assurance to warrant the commitment to doing anything. Yet unquestioning certainty is seldom available in intellectual life. The lack of any final certainty is absent even in the realm of science; in fact, according to one philosopher of science, the growth of knowledge only proceeds from those occasions where our ideas are falsified (Popper, 1959), where we discover that we have gone wrong. Intellectual life offers no final certainties.[6]

So, on the whole, for many in the sphere of religious life, intellectual endeavour is put aside for failing to deliver where it counts, namely, in the business of living.[7] Instead, it is much easier to rely on 'feelings' for the impetus to actions – and acting or living is something which unavoidably we must do – so if intellect cannot help

---

[5] This is one of the reasons why Nietzsche considered Socrates to be a decadent. Intellectuals like Socrates appeared to question the value of life with their dialectics. They did not, first and foremost, get on with the task of living. Nietzsche comments: 'One must reach out and try to grasp this astonishing *finesse, that the value of life cannot be estimated.* Not by a living man, because he is party to the dispute, indeed its object, and not the judge of it; not by a dead one, for another reason' (Nietzsche, 1990a, p. 40, emphasis in original).

[6] Someone like St Augustine accepted this. In relation to a religious doctrine, he stated that 'no-one should affirm any of these theories rashly' (Augustine, 2010, p. 113), but he did not allow this uncertainty to detract from an ultimate commitment to the truth and the good.

[7] To illustrate this point we might consider a little scenario devised by Kierkegaard (1975, p. 641):

'The scene of the last judgement: Our Lord, a professor of theology

Our Lord: "Did you seek first the Kingdom of God?"

The professor: "No, that I cannot say. But 'seek first the Kingdom of God', that I know in seven languages: 1. In Danish, 2. In German, 3. In French, 4. In Greek, 5. In Hebrew, 6. In Latin, 7. In Arabic, 8. In Aramaic, 9. In Phoenician … but I notice that I know it in nine languages, two more than I had promised."

Our Lord turns his back on him while the professor goes on: "It is simply that I have put all my effort into investigation and research, day and night."

us, then 'feelings' must[8]. In short, the call to revisit Christianity comes from the perception that Christian religious life is undergoing continual transformations. For better or worse, 'Christians' appear to be abandoning their traditional faith simply by failing to think and finding their motivation and consolation in emotions.

What can revisiting do, or achieve?

In the field of education, teachers 'revisit' topics regularly. They do so to enlarge the enquiry, to raise new questions and to reinforce with additional details what has been learned at an earlier stage. By placing what has been learnt in a wider context, by adding new perspectives and by raising different questions, and to some extent by un-learning, the understanding of the enquirer is thought to grow and deepen, even though we may be in territory that is already deemed all too familiar. Unfortunately, too many 'Christians' and 'non-Christians' believe religious life to be familiar and known when in fact they are misinformed.

For the sake of an integrated life it would help to restore the role and place of intellect in religious life. We need a new model. The expectation of intellectual certainty before acting is itself unrealistic. The pressure of getting on with the task of living[9] frequently commits us to positions that are far from finally resolved. Life cannot be kept on hold whilst uncertainties are eliminated. This is true for believer and unbeliever alike and is the case in many spheres of life. On the other hand, the urgent task of living does not mean that there is now no further need to reflect and to address the uncertainties. We need to introduce the notion of a spiral curriculum for life. In the idea of a 'spiral curriculum', there is a presumption of prior knowledge and belief that is constantly revised and developed; there is a provisional place to stand whilst being open to new possibilities. In other words, we can, and must, live confidently, doing so on the basis of what we know whilst admitting a significant degree of 'provisionality' to our knowledge. In fact, it is the accepted and 'provisionally' constructed world that provides the means for revising our understanding in the face of new information and fresh perspectives.

The spiral curriculum is also a strategy that maintains a careful balance between practice and theory. There is no pretence of ignorance (e.g. in Socratic questioning) or of starting from scratch at every point in life (e.g. with R. Descartes' proposal

---

It is here that the angel Gabriel interrupts him with a boot that knocks him for a million miles.'

Kierkegaard reminds us that religion has to do with how we live, but that we can so conceive our intellectual activities that as intellectuals we become spectators and, in doing so, we successfully abstract ourselves from the business of life itself.

[8] For L. Feuerbach (1986, p. 55), it is feelings that show you what is real. Feelings are trusted and appear to inform a statement with a degree of authority.

[9] As Aristotle expressed his priority in *Magna Moralia* (1935): 'We do not wish to know what ... justice is but to be just ... Anyone who knows the essence of justice is not forthwith just.'

of beginning philosophical reflection by radically doubting everything). Instead, we are self-evidently already in the midst of life before we begin to learn to think more seriously about it. There is an existing 'tacit knowledge' (Polanyi, 1956) and a given experience of life with all its demands and failings. As noted, it is frequently this presumed knowledge that provides the occasion and the means for questioning and fresh thought. This complex interactive relationship between practice and theoretical (or reflective) enquiry was once put on the theological agenda by St Augustine at the outset of his *Confessions*, Bk. 1, ch. 1. There, he asks which comes first: 1) 'praising God' (an active religious practice),[10] 2) 'calling on God' (a tentative approach) or 3) 'knowing God, intellectually believing in God'? Following a certain Pauline logic that is quite contemporary in its force, he initially suggests that 3) comes first, 2) second and 1) last, but then he raises the reverse possibility: namely, in reality the religious practice of praising leads to the tentative calling on God and lastly to a knowledge of God. A major reason for his view is that he supposes that in order to know the God intellectually, it must already be present to us in some significant way. We can conclude that there is a complex interrelationship between knowledge and practice, the horizons of the one appearing to dictate the horizons of the other.

What happens if we do not bother to revisit Christianity?

In the Western world at least, most people know, or think they know, what Christian faith is and what Christianity is about. But unless this generates renewed questioning and attention, this knowledge is doomed to become increasingly shallow. Without taking the time to revisit initial impressions, we are left with a juvenile grasp of the matter. In itself this might have been tolerable, for possibly we do not all need sophisticated and detailed views on every topic in life to live well, just as we do not need to have a sophisticated understanding of how a car works to drive it. So, this tolerance of intellectual innocence might have been passable, except for the subtle impact of a changing context. A juvenile grasp of one field of knowledge is increasingly distorted by the developed knowledge in other fields which surround it. Without a progressive spiral of learning, we do not simply stand still, we regress.

For the impact of context, consider the example of language. In language, context and location clearly matter. Shout 'fire' in a theatre or shout 'fire' standing by a firing squad and the word 'fire' will have very different meanings and very different consequences. Change context and location, and the meaning of a text (or set of words) changes even when the physical text remains the same. With language the reality of constant change has a bearing on our capacity to communicate clearly. The impact of a changing context also applies to Christian faith. As its surrounding culture changes, Christian faith and our grasp of it may change for better or for worse. The impact is on our capacity to live well and to

---

[10] Comments in parenthesis are mine.

secure an 'eternal' happiness, since the essence of Christian faith is to serve that goal.

To give an obvious example of the impact of change on Christianity: when we live from a complement of stories that embody a certain understanding of life, we may in fact live well. Surround the same stories, for example, the Genesis creation narratives, with sophisticated and complex scientific theories of biological or geological development, and the sense of the old stories is soon misrepresented or altered. Unless we have a good appreciation of why narrative thought is central to human life and how the stories functioned in their original context, we will misread the meaning of the stories. So it is that the Genesis narratives take on meanings they originally never had when they are set alongside some modern Darwinian theory and treated as competitors. The problem lies not with the stories in themselves but in their location as (scientific) explanations. It is as if they were bodies captured by the gravitational pull of a sun that changes them and catapults them into directions they were never wont to go. As such, with these ancient narratives a new location alters their meaning, as a result of which their original sense is lost.

Without re-engaging in the conversation about Christianity and generating new questions, the weight and depth of Christian thought is lost and with it the confidence in the life it may offer and support. Since the character of our life is at stake, this is a serious matter. In the end it is not so much the label 'Christian' or Christianity which counts, but the overarching endeavour to live well.[11]

Who is in a position to make the enquiry or to do the revisiting?

The quick answer is everyone can, but obviously not everyone does!

Whether we do will depend on whether we have an *interest* in it. The interest may be aroused because we happen to see something in Christian faith which, on the face of it, appears to have something of value in it. To some, Christian faith will be no more than something with historical curiosity value. To others, Christian faith is something worthy of being resisted and opposed, and therefore worth testing and challenging, or else the interest in Christianity may just be an occasion for good sport. To yet others, Christian faith is life-inspiring and therefore deserves attention.

In principle, Christian faith is open to being questioned by everyone, insiders or outsiders, academics or simple folk, clergy or laity, men or women, black or white, rulers or ruled, rich or poor, young or old. With respect to the world of faith, a basic human equality exists that is seldom found elsewhere. This enables the

---

[11] Concerning Dante's *Divine Comedy*, 'The aim of the whole as of the part is to remove those living in this life from a state of misery and to lead them to a state of happiness' (cited by Reynolds, 2006, pp. 101f). There could be no better aim, whether literary or theological.

questioning to take place out in the open, in the public square, where everyone[12] can have a piece of the action. Differences quickly appear because not everyone sees the same things[13] and this condition invigorates the discussion.

Are there any who object to this open scrutiny and questioning that is undertaken by nearly everyone with an interest in Christianity?

There have always been some who object to Christian faith being so amenable to being studied and questioned by nearly everyone. For them Christianity is a treasured possession. Others will not necessarily treat it with due respect or approach it with the right will[14] or affection. Why throw pearls before swine, one might think. So invariably there are 'lovers' of Christianity who wish to exclude others by imposing unacceptable conditions on their participation in discussion. There is much talk of so-called 'insiders' and 'outsiders', for example. This distinction supposes that Christianity will be understood differently depending on whether we are inside Christian faith or outside it.[15] Then the argument becomes: who understands it better? Each of the parties, at some time or another, has made a claim to being uniquely favoured or qualified to undertake the analysis and evaluation of Christian faith. The 'other', they say, can only participate by giving up their status. Religious insiders have not infrequently stated that 'you must believe in order to understand', 'you need the inspiration of the Holy Spirit to really understand' or 'you need first to be taught by the God'! The believers, of course, presumptuously assume that only they, as insiders, possess the Spirit and have been taught by the God, and so only they can truly understand! The outsiders, they claim, will never understand unless they too start to believe.

The secular outsiders, on the other hand, have countered that only they can be truly 'objective'. By having a stake in the religious enterprise, believers corrupt their judgment, preventing a fair assessment. From the position of the secular outsider perspective, if 'insiders' are to have a go at trying to understand Christian faith, they will just have to imagine themselves as outsiders, or as spectators, as best they can.

Adjudicating the squabble between insiders and outsiders is complicated, as both positions contain half-truths. The dispute between insiders and outsiders is

---

[12] K. E. Kirk claims that 'The vision of God is open to all men' (and presumably women) but then qualifies it by saying 'not perhaps equally (that may depend upon temperamental conditions), but at all events adequately' (Kirk, 1932, p. 243)!

[13] This insight was fundamental to the writings of S. Kierkegaard, who adopted different authorial identities with which to explore the world. Kierkegaard ranks with Augustine, Aquinas and others as one of the great Christian thinkers.

[14] See Augustine, *On the Free Choice of the Will* (2010), where the divided will is identified as the obstacle to understanding and living well.

[15] S. Kierkegaard explores this in *Philosophical Fragments* (1985) when he asks how does one become a Christian from a non-Christian point of view?

really a part of a more general debate which we may encounter in anthropology. For example, being an insider to a culture gives you a degree of familiarity with practices, traditions and the moves made in the 'language-game'[16] that defines the meaning of words. The position of an insider can give one significant advantages. Outsiders can make the most appalling mistakes simply because they are insufficiently knowledgeable of the culture to appreciate all the nuances and complexity of human activity and language. But outsiders claim the advantage of distance by being impartial observers. Anthropologists have tried to overcome the dispute by becoming what they call 'participant observers', thus claiming the advantages of being both an insider and an outsider all at once and supposedly without the disadvantages of either.

We can see something of what is at stake in other comparable cases as well. For example, consider the case of linguistic competence. Those who learn a language as a foreigner, as an outsider, will often make mistakes that a native speaker, as an insider, would never make. Yet there is nothing inevitable about that. It is true that native speakers of English have an initial advantage. But at least some foreigners are known to learn the language to a level of competence that far outshines those who have English as their mother tongue. Religiously, the same is true. As James observed (2:19): 'You believe there is one God? You do well, the devils also believe and tremble.' On this issue, the devils are the pre-eminent outsider and yet they understand full well (that is why they tremble – would that some believers knew enough to do the same!). Biblically, this is a case of having good understanding without the outsiders being, or becoming, genuine insiders.

Against insiders, it should be said that having a deep involvement in some enterprise can affect one's judgment adversely. Insiders should be reminded of the popular observation that little Johnny can do no wrong in the eyes of his mother even though he is out of step with all the others. The close relationship between mother and son prevents her from making accurate assessments about her offspring and his achievements. For a different example, one might ask why it is that people sometimes go to counsellors. The answer quite simply is that there are times when 'others know us better than we know ourselves'. Being on the inside is in some cases a distinct disadvantage.

Whether we are so-called 'insiders' or 'outsiders', the objective is much the same: namely, to understand correctly, to discern what is true, just and beautiful, but also to feel rightly and deeply, to act courageously and temperately, in brief, to learn how to live well and perhaps to die well. To that end each of us has to learn to be self-critical, to listen to others, to question, to care enough about ultimate goals to be willing to change our minds in order to be true to them.[17] In the matters of

---

[16] A term coined by L. Wittgenstein.

[17] In *The Need for Roots* (1952), Simone Weil wrote: '... for religious feelings to emanate from the spirit of truth, one should be absolutely prepared to abandon one's religion, even if that should mean losing all motive for living, if it should turn out to be anything other than the truth. In this state of mind alone it is possible to discern whether

life and death we are really all insiders even if we are outsiders to a specific faith or philosophy of life. There is in important respects an agenda in which we all share: life. Religiously speaking, in life 'before God' we are all insiders (though we do not always know it), which is in part why theologians speak of the ubiquity (the every-where-ness) of God.

If theology is the name we give to this activity of questioning the faith by which people live and die, everyone is on the inside and everyone can be a theologian.

Where should we begin with our revisiting of Christianity?

If we take the Apostle's Creed as a brief guide to what Christian faith is about, then I am proposing that we start our enquiry at the end.[18] In doing so, we will be examining Christian faith in the reverse order from the way in which it is usually presented. It is like reading a good detective story. Do you want to avoid being puzzled and know what is going on? You can resolve it by checking how it is all going to end first. However, from the point of view of entertainment, this may be a mistake!

Traditionally, theological questioning has followed the order of the creed. St Thomas Aquinas (1224–1274), in his *Summa Theologiae*, is a typical example. He begins with the existence of God and ends by considering human life and the task of living well. On the other hand, John Calvin (1509–1564), in *Institutes, the Christian Religion*, is less sure about God being the best starting point, for he states that one could begin with either God or man. In the end he resolves it by saying it is more worthy to begin with God, but does so without giving a reason. He just happened to have a rather low opinion of human beings (in his view there was nothing in human life that was not distorted or touched by 'sin'). There are, however, some modern departures from this traditional pattern of starting with 'God'. Friedrich D. E. Schleiermacher (1768–1834), in *The Christian Faith*, essentially begins with the world supposedly familiar to us – with creation and Christian life. T. Haering, in his *The Christian Faith, a System of Dogmatics* (1915), has a brief preamble about theology itself but essentially begins with religion and its specifically Christian form. P. Tillich begins his *Systematic Theology* (1953) with a detailed discussion about theology and philosophy. We can conclude that the starting point for theological questioning could be: 1) God, 2) human life, 3) religion or possibly 4) the nature of theology itself. In the case of the latter, we ask what are we doing when we are questioning these matters?

We can see from the historical trend that theology has become a problem to itself. The initial subject matter of theology may well be 'God' or alternatively human beings and their religious life, with their ultimate concerns. But *how* the

---

there is truth in it. Otherwise one does not venture even to propound the problem in all its rigour.'

[18] See N. Lash in *Believing Three Ways in One God* (1992). He begins his work with a chapter on Amen, a word that normally concludes Christian prayer, i.e. he starts at the end.

God or the characteristically religious dimension of human beings could be topics, together with the possibility and manner of discussing them, have become issues in themselves. Theology, in other words, has become increasingly self-absorbed. Not unlike Cartesian philosophy, it likes to examine itself and its own methods so as to provide secure foundations for its supposed edifice of knowledge.

One of my reasons for starting at the end is to preclude any sophistical navel-gazing on the part of theology. In my judgment we can best show what theology is simply by doing it. This approach also avoids a problem highlighted in the nineteenth century, namely, of treating theology as if it were a form of intellectual system building. This too creates a problem. If we first need to understand fully before we can make decisions to 'believe' (or, better, to live),[19] we may never get around to the task of living. S. Kierkegaard criticised the philosopher G. W. F. Hegel for precisely this in the first half of the nineteenth century. He saw Hegel (who claimed to provide *the* intellectual understanding implicit in Christianity) as being engaged in building a fantastic intellectual castle whilst actually living in a hovel nearby (Kierkegaard, 1980, pp. 43f.). As Kierkegaard feared, the intellectual system will never be completed in a satisfactory way or at least not in a manner that gains general agreement, and so we might never, in a manner of speaking, be authorised to live – the presumption being that one has *to know* what is true *before* one can act on it. The reverse strategy to this approach is simply to live and, through the life we live and the actions we take, come to discover what is and is not true, worthy or beautiful. This can be learning the hard way, but it is effective for all that.

Experience has found that it is better to start from the life that we, and others, are actually engaged upon, and to question and reflect on that. Yet this approach to related intellectual issues and ideas has its own problems, especially when it comes to the Christian faith. Unfortunately, in our secularised world (or for that matter within the modern church) when we seek to understand the Christian concept of 'God', a serious acquaintance with, or appreciation of, a deep practice of *Christian* life can no longer be presumed, even amongst some academic theologians. Yet it is the life in which the concept of 'God' is embedded that defines its meaning. And in starting with the general notion of 'religious' life, it is difficult to know where to draw the limits. Even where there is some intimate knowledge of Christian life, most have to admit to the lack of a deep acquaintance with the full range of human religiosity. We may know our own traditions but are ignorant of those of others. In short, at the present time we are culturally located in such a manner that

---

[19] Traditionally faith was analysed as consisting of three components: *notitia, assensus* and *fiducia*. This can be taken as a temporally ordered development: taking note of what is proposed, giving one's agreement and finally trusting the assertions as demonstrated in one's life. Another way of looking at this is that this is not a temporal ordering but a logical ordering; logically the one leads to the other, but in fact they may be learned in a different order. We learn how to live, then we begin to understand what is assumed in our life and finally we begin to formulate the 'belief' or doctrine.

practically and intellectually, a deeper understanding of religious faith remains virtually inaccessible to most people in the West.

A consequence of this ignorance is that we have to make a serious effort to exercise our imagination and attend with some care to how people once lived. When we do this, we observe an important feature – but one rather alien to modern minds – notably, people once lived with *eternity* in view. The concept of gaining *eternal happiness* (bliss) had common currency. But what precisely did they mean by this? Only by unpacking this idea can we begin to understand religious life. As such, one of the central tenets I wish to maintain is that only with the quality of a life lived *sub specie aeternitatis* (under the category of the eternal)[20] and only by keeping eternity in view can we actually begin to deal with *the* distinctive features of the religious life. So, if we wish to grasp the main thrust of religious life and its concepts, it makes sense to start with what an eternal life might mean.

The idea of beginning our study with eternal life has the added advantage of providing a link to *other* religious traditions, since neither the concept of eternity nor its related practices are uniquely Christian.[21] Nevertheless, eternal life is a rather alien idea to what is normally accepted in the secular Western world[22] as the most sensible way to live, so it needs to be carefully unpacked. This is one of the main tasks of theology. But in order to discuss this we need at least a preliminary conception of what theology is as an intellectual discipline.

What is Christian theology? How is it organised?

An initial working definition of theology is that it is a conversation or a dialogue[23] that questions and leads specifically to the clarification of religious life. To be more precise, *Christian* theology is the set of conversations that leads to the

---

[20] See e.g. S. R. Sutherland, *God, Jesus and Belief*, 1984, chs 6 and 7, who has a somewhat similar starting point.

[21] Some maintain that belief in immortality is intuitive: see e.g. J. L. Barrett, *Why Would Anyone Believe in God?*, 2004, p. 77 'Developmental psychologists continue to find evidence that the godly properties of ... immortality are quite intuitive, at least for young children.'

[22] There are consequences from the failure of belief in immortality. F. Nietzsche comments: 'With tragedy the Greeks had given up the belief in immortality: not only the belief in an ideal past, but also the belief in an ideal future. The words of the infamous epitaph "inconstant and frivolous in old age" apply equally well to the last phase of Hellenism. Its supreme deities are wit, whim, caprice, the pleasure of the moment. The fifth estate, that of the slaves, comes into its own, at least in the point of attitude, and if it is possible at all now to speak of Greek serenity, then it must be the serenity of the slave, who has no responsibilities, no high aims, and to whom nothing, past or future, is of greater value than the present ... This womanish escape from all seriousness and awe, this smug embracing of easy pleasure, seemed to them [the church fathers] not only contemptible but the truly anti-Christian frame of mind' (Nietzsche, 1993, p. 72).

[23] This was a preferred medium of Augustine.

clarification of *Christian* religious life. A Jewish theology clarifies Jewish life, and so on. Apart from the specifically tradition bound labels, it is also possible to classify these theological conversations under a different set of headings. For example, the traditional branches of Christian theology are:

a. *Dogmatics*: this aims to question and set out the key signposts for a *coherent* life marked by Christian faith, its direction and character.

   In dogmatics there are two subdivisions: (i) *formal dogmatics*, which deals with the originating basis of Christian life, e.g. revelation and the presence of the God; and (ii) *material dogmatics*, which deals with substantive matters that are implied in this life and which provide guidance on how we might reasonably live. Thus, material dogmatics touches on the meaning of God, Christ, sin, forgiveness, etc.

b. *Apologetics*: literally this means 'defence', as in Plato's dialogue, *Apology*, in which Socrates defended himself in court against the accusations of atheism and the corruption of the young. Apologetics seeks to set out the sense of Christian faith in relation to other conceptions of life. Christian theology will try to set out the sense of Christian faith to those who live differently, who have a different history and who employ quite different concepts. Thus, it consciously seeks to engage in dialogue with those living the secular life and with those who belong to another religious tradition. In this sense theology must always be a genuinely public discourse.

Some add as a separate field of enquiry:

c. *Ethics*: but since Dogmatics and Apologetics are about the direction and character of the life lived with (Christian) faith, these must, by definition, be concerned with the ethical. Dogmatics and apologetics cannot be separate branches of discussion from those which enquire into the various goods of life and indeed into the *summum bonum* (highest good) of human life.

This brief classification shows that the proposed treatment of *eternal life* here probably belongs to both dogmatics and apologetics, the latter because conversations seeking to elucidate the meaning of eternal life engage the Christian and non-Christian alike. At the same time, the topic also seems to permeate the whole of dogmatics – for example, we cannot sensibly speak of the God, sin, etc. without some reference to eternity.

PART I
Clarifying What Christians Do

Chapter 1

Eternal Life

What is the role and significance of the idea of eternal life?[1]

Many people plan their lives according to a carefully ordered timetable of sequential steps recorded in CVs, that is to say, most people live in a fundamentally temporal way with a past, present and future. With this familiar pattern in mind, people are led into the preconception that eternity means 'time without end', an ongoing time, a movement of time without limit and that, consequently, eternal life is taken to mean a life that never ceases but goes on forever and ever. This conclusion may be natural but it should not be presumed. To take for granted the assumption that eternal life is like *this* life, only indefinitely more of it, i.e. that it is *quantitatively* more, actually discounts any potentially 'spiritual' meaning it may have. The term 'spiritual' here signals a *qualitative* rather than quantitative difference in life, one which truly distinguishes the spiritual from the materialistic. Similarly, we should explore the notion that the Eternal differs from the temporal *qualitatively*, just as the infinite is qualitatively different from the finite.

If a materialistic (some would say 'naturalistic') rather than a spiritual understanding of the world is taken for granted and one assumes this is the *only* way to think, asking what it means to live with eternity in view will inevitably seem rather strange and esoteric. Normally, our life cannot plausibly be described as going on forever without end; physically we die; our brains die; our mental processes cease. So how and where does the idea of an eternal life arise and have its application?

To open up other possibilities we should note that to confine ourselves to the material world could blind us to questions, for example, about its *significance and value*. If we are essentially located in time and space, we might take a 'position' beyond the boundaries of those considerations by asking what is the *meaning* of this existence?[2] What is the point of life in its totality when it is so obvious that our life begins and ends in nothingness? As human beings with a pressing awareness of our mortality,[3] we are often struck and overcome by feelings of pointlessness, especially when confronted by the death of the young and the innocent. A kind

---

[1] As a category for identifying what is characteristically religious, it is not the only candidate for consideration. An alternative, holiness, was canvassed by R. Otto in *The Idea of the Holy* (1959) (Jones, 1961; Webster, 2003). A further possibility is the idea of perfection: see Blamires, 2003.

[2] Sometimes this is done in and through literature.

[3] Of course, the idea of life going on forever does not of itself guarantee meaningfulness, as Samuel Beckett explored in his play *Waiting for Godot* (Beckett, 1965).

of nihilism takes hold of us and we reason that if life ends in nothingness, it is essentially meaningless and consequently we may lose the will to live.

Yet from the same imaginative vantage point of overviewing the totality of life, we are encouraged when we suspect that regardless of passing time and death, there are occasional intimations of *enduring* worth. These we are equally quick to observe and eager to acknowledge in everyday life, for example, at a Remembrance Day service where we recall all *those who do not grow old*. It is these intimations of enduring worth which are seized upon by faith, for above all faith is a kind of confidence that there is, or that there must be, a sense to life that is untouched by the passing of time, untouched by death. The challenge is not only to identify where the source and ground for this confidence lies but also how to talk about it and how to cultivate it in life. What we do not want is self-deception and false consolation.[4]

How can the confidence of faith, which sets aside the limits of time, be justified?

Firstly, faith generally resists the satisfaction of explanations offered by accounts that are wholly confined to location and movement in space and time, to connected causal relations, for example, the world as described in a materialistic philosophy. By 'materialistic' I do not mean having an overriding interest in money, but the view that everything ultimately boils down to a matter of physics or chemistry.[5] Materialism is basically a rather mechanistic view of the world, which is at its most reductive when it holds that everything can ultimately, in principle at least, be accounted for through the investigations of the causal connections offered by these two disciplines alone. Naturally, this reductionism eliminates the Eternal from any serious consideration for the obvious reason that the physical universe is clearly temporal in character. In fact, many cosmologists claim that the physical universe had a beginning some 15 billion years or so ago. There is no reason to doubt or quarrel with their claim on theological grounds. Theologians as theologians are not in a position to contradict the evidence of the natural sciences in this regard. What they do dispute is the sense of reductionism[6] and the assumption that the pursuit of the unity of knowledge requires it.

Simple successiveness can also be meaningless by being 'just one damn thing after another' which goes nowhere and ends nowhere.

[4] According to P. Byrne, 'almost anything which consoles is fake' (Byrne, 1998, p. 111), but if there is no consolation, then we are faced with nihilism as the only alternative. Of course, he does say 'almost anything', so presumably there must be something which he believes does truly console (Murdoch, 1970, p. 59)!

[5] See the criticisms of A. N. Whitehead (1929) or W. Barrett (1986, p. 7); more recently on the reductive tendencies of scientism, see J. Haldane (2010, pp. 37f.).

[6] To some extent at least, the atheist Richard Dawkins shares this view as his explanations, specifically those of life, are not found in physics and chemistry but in genes. But why stop there in resisting the reductionism? On the other hand, if biology resists a

Especially at issue is the claim that there can be no other meaning or any other forms of understanding than the materialistic one with its interest in causal connections. For the theologian, reductionism is seen to be a kind of imperialistic embargo as if the only thing we care about is restricted to the limits defined by space and temporality. But why should we accept such imperialistic moves? Most disciplines add their own unique insights into the multi-dimensional reality that is our world, highlighting features which cannot be explained by physics and chemistry. By resisting reductionism, we open up our perceived world to different possibilities which are in part generated by what we care about, i.e. by our differing interests. Basically we cannot come to know what does not interest us.

Do our interests need to be justified and how do they relate to each other?

Although the concern for eternal life may appear to characterise the religious life above all,[7] it is in fact an *interest* that most or, at least, many people share in one form or another. As a line of thought it is not solely confined to the ostensibly religious. It may first make its appearance as a general anxiety about the limits of life. Crudely children may ask what happens to people when they die. The question posed like this can only lead to agnosticism. Or, better, we might say nothing *happens* to them for they have ceased to be. If anything can be said to happen, it is that a person's identity is fixed and the possibility of change is removed; on the point of death we quite simply and unchangeably become what we once were. This may be a terrifying thought to some. The absence of a future, the inability to change or to be free from the past is deeply worrying. The midlife crisis some people experience may be an echo of feelings of being circumscribed, a point at which we are unable to live for something better or to become something better. We would like to begin life over again, to start afresh. With an increasing awareness of the limits of our life we are beset by the fear that we may be missing out on something we know not what. The confidence of faith is the obverse of an anxiety experienced in life.

---

reductionism to physical and chemical causation and requires other kinds of concepts (e.g. genes) and, through them, makes a contribution to human understanding, why not still others? From the perspective of theology, a critical difference comes into play when we change from the perspective of a spectator to the 'world' to that of an actor in the 'world'.

[7] For example, A. Nygren states: 'The necessary conditions for religion are lacking unless this present world of sense is set over against the world of eternity, and unless this life of ours is viewed *sub specie aeternitatis,* in the light of eternity. It need hardly be said that the idea of eternity as used here to indicate the basic factor in religion, has nothing to do with the popular notion of that which lies before or after time. Eternity is not an extension of time backwards and forwards, but an abolition and breaking through of time. It represents a life which knows that it is not subject merely to the conditions of finitude' (Nygren, 1960, p. 28). Perhaps he protests too much by claiming it has 'nothing to do with the popular notion'! The intellectual distancing may even be unnecessary since popular notions are often misrepresented and oversimplified.

As hinted earlier, another way to begin to understand eternal life is to note that within *this* life people do have a positive interest in cultivating in their life various concerns that are not strictly time-bound; in other words, there are activities done for their own sake, such as sports and art. There are quite simply concerns *that do not depend on how things go*; one does not do them for the sake of something else. They are pursued for the 'now' and not for some future good. They are in a manner of speaking timeless. It is with the timeless concerns of life, I propose, that we begin to discern the meaning of eternal life.

The most obvious things to note here is that we are dealing with a very basic human interest that is not readily (if at all)[8] transposed into something else. And purely as an interest, the Eternal is just one of a number of very basic interests[9] that human beings happen to have. Temporal interests include economic ones, making money (in gospel language, 'building ever bigger barns') or the interest in satisfying bodily needs such as hunger, thirst or sex. As mentioned earlier, people have an interest in causal relations;[10] this manifests itself when they ask what *caused* the accident or what caused the explosion. Basically, interests are what people have when they begin to develop some serious pursuits. From a cognitive point of view (i.e. in what we can come to know and understand), the particular interests that we happen to have can certainly affect the character and the limits of the understanding we have of the world and of ourselves. If we have no *interest* in beauty, the understanding that we develop of the world is unlikely to have an aesthetic dimension.

In somewhat the same way that a scientist's interest in causal relationships is what drives the investigations of the natural sciences, it is my claim that the interest in 'eternal life' is *the* characteristic and constitutive passion of religious life.[11] We must not forget that human beings do have a range of *other* interests apart from the 'causal' and the 'eternal' just mentioned. For example, human beings, almost universally, have an interest in: 1) what is right and good (Murdoch, 1970) – it is

---

[8] To deny that one can transpose it into something else is what people mean when they describe it as *sui generis*, i.e. in a category of its own.

[9] We must not assume that human interests are automatically 'self-interests'. To suppose that they are leads atheistic critics to see something demeaning and corrupting in religion, namely, an egocentricity that knows no limits.

[10] One must remember that causal relations are not all of a piece. There are different kinds of causes, such as chemical causes or feelings of various kinds (Winch, 1990, pp. xii–xiii). The cause of an explosion could be semtex or terrorists moved by certain psychological and religious motivations; such causes are of a very different order

[11] Even atheistic critics of religion recognise this. D. Z. Phillips cites and evaluates the contribution of L. Feuerbach in *Religion and the Hermeneutics of Contemplation* (2001) where he considers Feuerbach's position: 'Religious belief is an expression of our desire to overcome our finitude. Therefore, religion must attempt to show how death can be overcome.' This is why Feuerbach is able to say (Feuerbach, 1968, p. 33): 'If a man did not die, if he lived forever, if there were no such thing as death, there would be no religion.' Indeed, he claims 'that man's tomb is the birth place of the gods' (ibid., p. 113).

the interest which is constitutive of *moral* life – and also in 2) the beautiful – it is the interest which is constitutive of the *aesthetic* life. There are two important points to observe at this juncture. The first is that these interests cannot be easily transposed. They are simply different. Secondly, one does not normally need to have *reasons* for such interests – people simply have them!

Do connections exist between the different interests that human beings have? Is this connectedness a reflection of the world we know?

Insofar as we may rightly long for an integrated view of our life, we may assume that the various interests that human beings have do actually relate, or are linked, to each other *in some way*. But not everyone thinks this is so! Such people live more compartmentalised lives. There are artists who glory in being reprobates. Art is done for art's sake, not because it has any moral value; creativity may be treated as counter-cultural, rejecting anything that the culture has previously believed to be true, good and beautiful. There do seem to be some select individuals who write great music or poetry and at the same time manifest all the qualities of being thoroughly dissolute.[12] In short, there are people who have separated the aesthetic from the moral. There cannot therefore be an absolutely necessary link between the beautiful and the good so that one cannot have one without the other.

On the other hand, there are those who justify the maintenance of museums and art galleries on public funds on the grounds that art is somehow edifying and humanising; similar arguments are used for the maintenance of orchestras, ballet companies, troupes of actors and theatres. They are all thought to be worthy of support from the taxpayer for the common *good*. In other words, they appear to presume a fundamental connection between aesthetic and moral life. As a consequence, the people who employ such arguments implicitly believe that our society would be shallower and more impoverished – *less good* –without these aesthetic forms of life.

Historically, Plato thought of the Good and the Beautiful as being Eternal and that together they are ultimately one. In other words, he made connections between the fundamental interests that human beings have.[13] There is – he

---

[12] For example, reputedly Lord Byron. G. Steiner (1997) was puzzled by the fact some Nazis could play Bach with great feeling in the evening and in the morning could go on to torture the innocents. Such puzzlement is grounded in the assumption of an internal link between the aesthetic and the moral. Adam Fox sees this link in the culture of ancient Greece, but concludes it is not our view. He comments on the Greek word for beauty: '*Kalos* certainly means beautiful, but it also means good, also honourable; and sometimes satisfactory, or even successful, is as near to it as anything. For the Greeks nothing could be beautiful without being good, nothing good without being beautiful. Just our idea of morality was not theirs' (Fox, 1957, p. 14).

[13] Plotinus made similar connections; see the sixth tractate of his *Enneads* where he connects beauty to goodness (Plotinus, 1956).

supposed – an underlying unity in all reality. If this is true, it could explain the deep relationship that has been presumed to exist in Western cultural history prior to the Enlightenment: 1) between religion (with its interest in eternity) and morals, and 2) between religion and art.

The relationship that may exist between the interests in beauty, goodness and the Eternal on the one hand and the causal interest that scientists have on the other hand is much more complex. Indications that a relationship *does* exist may be gathered from scientists who speak of a particular theory being 'elegant' and 'beautiful', as if these aesthetic considerations are important criteria for preferring a particular scientific theory to potential rivals. We can only conclude that aesthetic judgments matter in science, even if we are not sure why.

The relationship between science and the moral is even more problematic. It has certainly been asserted by more than one scientist that science is strictly speaking amoral. Science, it is said, is concerned with whether something is true, not whether it is good. But the claim that science is strictly amoral has been profoundly worrying to many, since it rather supposes that activities, such as the rightness or wrongness of dropping the atomic bomb, the adoption of programmes in eugenics and the experimentation on sentient animals, are outside the scope of the scientist qua scientist. It appears to suggest that scientists can engage in research, in searching for truth, ignoring all moral considerations and consequences. But where science is taken to be amoral, it appears all too often to pave the way for, and to be a precursor of, *im*morality.

However, even if science in itself is amoral, the scientists who pursue their science are human beings. As human beings they can be held accountable for the intentions and consequences of their scientific work. The same is true for any society that expends its energy and resources on whatever will destroy,[14] whilst neglecting the scientific research that will clearly promote and enhance the flourishing of human beings and their world. When people confidently say that an individual scientist and the society *will be subject* to moral judgment and *will be held* accountable (using the future tense), what in fact is meant is that *sub specie aeternitatis* people are inescapably subject to moral judgment. They may not in this place or in this point in time invoke moral considerations, but from a religious point of view they cannot, as human beings, ultimately escape moral judgment. Hence, religiously, there is such a thing as a *last* judgment made in eternity.

If there are relationships between different interests that people have, what is the precise relationship between 'religion' and 'science'?

The relationship between the interests in the 'eternal' and the 'causal' is much more problematic than that generated by the relationship between morality and

---

[14] What do people think about nations such as North Korea and Iran which will expend vast social resources on developing nuclear weapons whilst there is significant poverty and hunger amongst their population?

aesthetics or between science and morality. This could explain some of the difficulties encountered between religion and science that have dominated the modern world.

Part of the difficulty resides in the presumption in our 'scientific age' that *all* knowledge and understanding is about having 'causal explanations'. This presumption is evidently a mistake. Whilst *some* knowledge consists of seeing a law-like, causal relationship between events, this is not true for all. Other kinds of knowledge, such as in botany, take the form of *classification*, while others, such as philosophy and theology, arise out of the quest for *conceptual* clarity. The latter means being clear about the concepts we use and the logical connections between them, i.e. what in Wittgenstein's terms is called their (conceptual) 'grammar', effectively how they work as concepts.

Thus, from a philosophical perspective, a possible source of confusion in the relationship between 'religion' and 'science' is the quite different ways in which the word 'cause' is sometimes used. It does not have a single meaning but may refer to quite different concerns that we have in life. Aristotle, for example, had identified *four* different kinds of 'causes': 1) material, 2) formal, 3) efficient and 4) final cause. What we normally understand to be the interest of modern science is probably best associated with Aristotle's efficient cause. Religion, on the other hand, is more attuned to the purpose or point of something in and of itself, which seems to relate more closely to the Aristotelian idea of a 'final' cause. St Thomas Aquinas made yet another distinction in the concept of causation when he differentiated between first and secondary causes. For him, the former was associated with the God and the latter was the concern of science. Whether this Thomistic distinction can make much sense today remains to be seen, but they are intended to point to significant differences between the God as cause and other causes in the world whilst at the same time affirming a connection between them.[15]

How do we come to know about eternal life?

The reason for thinking about the relationship between the Eternal on the one hand and causal interests (the latter is normally temporal in character) on the other is that many human beings, including many intellectuals, have popularly

---

[15] Note J-F. Lyotard's distinction between scientific and narrative knowledge in *The Postmodern Condition: A Report on Knowledge* (1984). At pp. 26f. he writes: 'It is therefore impossible to judge the existence or validity of narrative knowledge on the basis of scientific knowledge and vice versa: the relevant criteria are different. All we can do is gaze in wonderment at the diversity of discursive species, just as we do at the diversity of plant or animal species. Lamenting the "loss of meaning" in postmodernity boils down to mourning the fact that knowledge is no longer principally narrative. Such a reaction does not necessarily follow. Neither does an attempt to derive or engender (using operators like development) scientific knowledge from narrative knowledge, as if the former contained the latter in an embryonic state.'

tended to locate (mistakenly, in my view) the interest in the Eternal within the framework of causal explanations. Thus, they look for phenomena, such as near-death experiences,[16] ghosts, telepathic communication, etc., that might enable one to propose a hypothesis that 'there is a life after death'. The phenomena are taken to be appropriate though possibly not decisive evidence. And 'life after death' is seen as the (causal) *explanation* for the phenomena. In effect, they look at the belief of 'life after death' as a theory and then look for the kind of phenomena or experiences that would function as evidence (Hick, 1976) which may be said to 'verify or falsify' the theory.

In contrast to this approach, the sense of the Eternal may only become clear to us if causal relationships cease to dominate our interests and if the Eternal is seen to belong to a different order of concerns. Such an awareness of a different way of thinking I believe happens when we think of our life in its totality, from birth to death, and ask 'what is the sense of it?' or, similarly, when we think of our universe in its totality, from its beginning to its end, and again ask about its sense. In these contexts a different quest for meaning becomes apparent. When we suspect that a different kind of meaning is at stake, the usual causal sphere may appear to be abrogated, suspended or simply not relevant to our enquiries. This abrogation of the causal nexus in our understanding of life may lead some people to invoke the concept of miracles; thus, on an occasion when a meaning presents itself which suspends the causal interest or which will not allow us to apply a causal explanation, we can speak of the miraculous. In brief, miracles are little more than occasions where there is a refusal to turn to causal explanation as *the* meaning of an event.

Admittedly, this definition of a miracle is quite at variance with that espoused by D. Hume[17] in the eighteenth century, for he defined miracle as 'the breaking of a law of nature on the volition of the deity or some other supernatural agent'. However, a miracle is defined much more simply and in keeping with a religious conception as the point at which we encounter an eternal sense in our temporal world. With this in mind, in Christian life the Mass or the Eucharist, for example, has been classically identified as '*the* miracle'; it is also a way of saying 'I don't care what happened, or how it happens *causally*, but what really matters is that now the "eternal" meaning, the risen Christ, is present'.

As an aside to this, theologians have themselves often contributed to confusion on the issue of how exactly the Eternal is present because they too cannot resist speculating about what makes this possible. On occasion they also mistakenly look for causal explanations. As such, the evolution of medieval theories of transubstantiation and consubstantiation about the Eucharist emerged. In essence, this 'explanation' came about by presupposing that things were made up of 'accidents' (properties) and of 'substance'; they could then 'explain' how the elements of the Mass *appeared* to be the same (for its properties were the same)

---

[16] See, for example, the *Journal of Near-Death Studies*.

[17] See his *Enquiry Concerning Human Understanding* (2000), section X.

whilst claiming that *in reality* its 'substance' had changed from that of bread and wine to that of the body and blood of Christ. Of course, in reality it explains nothing when we do not know what it *means* for us to say that Christ is present – all the talk of a changed substance will not clarify it for us. How could we begin to differentiate between those instances where the *substance* had changed from those occasions where it had not if the properties always remain the same?

So far the attempt to elucidate eternal life has taken a rather negative form by indicating what, credibly, it could not be. It is *not* showing how life *goes* but what life *is* and what it means once we remove our interests in temporal and caused changes. It is a mistake to treat eternal life as a hypothesis[18] about what might happen to us *after* death not just because the existing evidence happens to be scanty but because, in principle, such evidence for what comes *after* is not only non-existent but misleads us by wrongly directing our attention to something temporal. The Eternal is simply not temporal, and either it is a reality *now* or it does not exist at all, for in the realm of the Eternal there is no coming into being or passing away. To insist on looking for 'evidence' for what comes *after* is to make what some have called 'a category mistake'.

The sense of what happens to us eternally (alternatively, the sense of what, so to speak, happens to us metaphorically[19] 'after death') cannot be the same as having ideas about what life might be like for us tomorrow or the next year whilst we are still alive, or how our life could be caused to go. The very nature of our causal knowledge is strictly confined to the limits of our life. If this is indeed the case, then it follows that near-death experiences are more properly said to be the product of a dying brain and, as such, is evidence for the nature of our present world rather than of the 'next' world. On the other hand, the other important conclusion to be reached is that if the limits of our knowledge are confined to the limits of our world, then clearly it is in our *present* world that we must seek for what it means to speak of the Eternal.

Does the idea of a 'final cause' not force us to look to the future?

It is tempting to identify the Eternal with Aristotle's final cause, i.e. with the ultimate purpose of things. This is an orientation that apparently points us to the future. The future end (eschaton) and purpose are closely related because in human life it is often not until the end of the narrative that we can understand the full purpose of things. As such, it may be the case that eternal life comes into focus at the point of death or 'after' death, then comes the last judgment, when our true nature and destiny are disclosed. However, if there is a purpose in things, then it

---

[18] The problem is to see a religious understanding as if it were a *hypothesis*. As S. L. Frank noted: 'The existence of God is not 'the most likely hypothesis' for a rationalistic explanation of the world' (Frank, 1946, p. 16).

[19] It can only be a metaphor because the words 'happens' and 'after' implicitly suggests change and time.

could equally be present from the beginning. Indeed, many a creation myth is there precisely to tell us about how the world should be regarded; they are told in order to disclose to us the purpose and meaning of our current world. They are not about what happened in the past. Thus, clearly the notion of purpose is not dependent on a specific location in the temporal process; it may be equally evident at the beginning, middle or end.

What then do we mean by eternal?

The Eternal is traditionally understood in two radically different ways: 1) as everlasting, i.e. infinite time, or 2) as atemporal,[20] i.e. the negation of the category of time.[21] If it is the latter, it cannot be the case that the Eternal switches in on the point of death – it is either always present in life or it does not exist at all. The beginning of our life is as near the Eternal as its middle or end, since time has no bearing on it.

In contrast to this strange atemporal conception, the other concept of the Eternal we have before us (i.e. infinite time) also raises equally curious questions. What would we do in, and with, such infinite time? To echo the questions posed to Jesus: would we marry? Would we be married to the same person? And if in life we had married different people, who would be one's wife or husband 'eternally'? Satirical magazines might generate 'jokes', for example, by asking how we could possibly sustain our zest for life over such an infinite period of time. Are we not likely to fall foul of some eternal ennui?[22] (We might respond that perhaps

---

[20] 'Eternity is not infinite continuation in time which one would have to pass through from beginning to end (though it has neither beginning nor end) in order to be certain of it; eternity is an immediately recognisable *quality* of being' (Frank, 1946, p. 50). Hence, he can claim 'I know with complete certainty now, at any given moment of life, that I am eternal'. In a similar vein, Meister Eckhart wrote: 'In eternity there is neither "before" nor "after". For this reason what occurred a thousand years ago and what will happen a thousand years hence and what happens now, are all one in eternity. Therefore what God wrought a thousand years ago, what He will do in a thousand years and what He is doing now is nothing but one work' (Eckhart, 1963, 'A Sermon on the Just Man and Justice', p. 51).

[21] As D. Z. Phillips put it: 'Eternity is not an extension of this present life, but a mode of judging it. Eternity is not *more* life, but this life seen under certain moral and religious modes of thought. This is precisely what seeing this life *sub specie aeternitatis* would amount to' (Phillips, 1970, p. 49).

[22] See the comment by Rush Rhees in *On Religion and Philosophy* (1997), p. 361: 'Perhaps I think of it too unimaginatively – as though what were promised to those who are saved were an everlasting life: which, saving the irreverence, were a destiny to make me shudder, even on a "new earth".'

I think of the Sybil in the bottle as mentioned by Petronius. She had angered Apollo and in revenge he made it impossible for her to die. When Aeneas encountered her, all of her had withered away but her voice, which was preserved in a bottle. Aeneas asked her if there was anything she wanted. She answered *'apothanein thelo [I want to die]'*.

a heavenly entertainment committee with infinite resources will ensure that we do not become bored. Everything will be perfect. One is reminded of the fiery preacher who warned a sceptical member of his congregation when she showed her toothless gums with a grin [as he spoke of the weeping and gnashing of teeth in the hereafter], 'teeth will be provided'!) Of course, such a concern is itself based on a view of life in which the 'meaning' of life is only sustainable by always doing something new and different. Kierkegaard describes this as the despair of the aesthetic life. In contrast to this, a fundamental question persists: is there nothing that could satisfy us eternally and bestow on us an eternal happiness? This is the religious issue: does life offer or intimate anything of an eternal nature?

What did people in the classical past see as 'eternal' in this life?

There have been some suggestions rooted in our past. As mentioned earlier, the ancient world had identified truth, goodness and beauty as three candidates that might ideally be the bearers of eternity. Of course, they thought that in this life we only grasp them in a partial and inadequate way, but our current, inadequate and conditioned conceptions are the *symbols* of their ultimate source. Socrates, for example, had defined philosophy as practising dying[23] because through the

---

In Benedict XVI's papal encyclical *spe salvi* he observes: 'But then the question arises: do we really want this – to live eternally? Perhaps many people reject the faith today simply because they do not find the prospect of eternal life attractive. What they desire is not eternal life at all, but this present life, for which faith in eternal life seems something of an impediment. To continue living for ever – endlessly – appears more like a curse than a gift. Death, admittedly, one would wish to postpone for as long as possible. But to live always, without end – this, all things considered, can only be monotonous and ultimately unbearable. This is precisely the point made, for example, by Saint Ambrose, one of the Church Fathers, in the funeral discourse for his deceased brother Satyrus: "Death was not part of nature; it became part of nature. God did not decree death from the beginning; he prescribed it as a remedy. Human life, because of sin ... began to experience the burden of wretchedness in unremitting labour and unbearable sorrow. There had to be a limit to its evils; death had to restore what life had forfeited. Without the assistance of grace, immortality is more of a burden than a blessing". A little earlier, Ambrose had said: "Death is, then, no cause for mourning, for it is the cause of mankind's salvation". Para 10

Whatever precisely Saint Ambrose may have meant by these words, it is true that to eliminate death or to postpone it more or less indefinitely would place the earth and humanity in an impossible situation, and even for the individual would bring no benefit. Obviously there is a contradiction in our attitude, which points to an inner contradiction in our very existence. On the one hand, we do not want to die; above all, those who love us do not want us to die. Yet on the other hand, neither do we want to continue living indefinitely, nor was the earth created with that in view. So what do we really want? Our paradoxical attitude gives rise to a deeper question: what in fact is "life"? And what does "eternity" really mean?'

[23] See the *Phaedo*.

practice of philosophy he sought to overcome his *relative* ignorance – relative, that is, to the absolute, not to other people (compared to whom he was declared to be the wisest of men). Plato depicted him as dying willingly and without fear in the *Phaedo* because Socrates had cultivated and nurtured his eternal *psyche* (soul or self) with the pursuit of this absolute truth and goodness. By this means, he 'participates' in their eternal nature.

Earlier in the *Apology*, Plato had shown how Socrates had dismissed death as an important consideration in his life as he advised his judges to 'bear in mind this one truth, that no evil can come to a *good* man either in life or after death, nor does God neglect him'. Sir Thomas More expressed similar sentiments (Phillips, 2004, pp. 156ff.) when he wrote to his daughter, Margaret, in his final days that he could come to no harm even though he might lose his head. For those without any sense of the Eternal and whose existence is solely within the realm of the temporal, to lose one's head and one's life is to lose everything. Since the temporal only offers death in the end, it is what brings despair. Only the Eternal (if the Eternal is a genuine reality) could save and console.

Did Christians in the past identify anything in human life that they regarded as 'eternal'?

The Christian way of life identified 'love' with eternity, hence the declaration that God is Love. The essence of the Christian way of life[24] is to cultivate the love which is derived and dependent on this notion of an ideal, eternal love, one that is unconditional. The romantic love with which we are much more familiar is, of course, fickle, conditional and time-bound. However, we also sense that the shortcomings found in romantic love are due to a failing on our part. On the other hand, if romantic love[25] is so appealing to people today, it is largely because it expressly tries to emulate the 'unending', eternal love that in weddings we symbolise by a ring. As a Neo-Platonist, St Augustine, of course, integrated Love, Truth and Eternity, for how could love be anything else than truthful and how could truth be anything else but eternal[26] since for him truth was unchanging?

The Christian confidence in the face of death has this logic: if 1) God, the Eternal is in any sense real and if 2) God is love, then 3) He will see that His beloved will come to no harm and 4) since according to the gospel we are the beloved of God, then 5) we need not fear death, for we will come to no harm and can rest assured to share in His eternal life[27] (Baillie, 1941). Note that this is not

---

[24] As J. H. Newman observed: 'We believe because we love' (Newman, 1880, p. 236).

[25] In reality, romantic love tends to be an insecure basis in life because, of course, it is primarily based on feelings which are in themselves fickle and subject to change.

[26] What about eternal punishment? For a discussion, see Ramsey, 1963, Chapter 1. Need we fear death?: Augustine, 1963, Bk. XXI, ch. 9.

[27] '... it would be unwise to write with precision of detail about our future expectations' (Church of England, 1995, p. xii).

an explanatory theory but comes from the analysis of the meaning of love and ultimately from the life of Christ, which is thought to display or reveal an ultimate love.

Chapter 2

Worship

> Therefore, ... I implore you by God's mercy to offer your very selves to him a living sacrifice, dedicated and fit for his acceptance, for such is the worship which you, as rational creatures, should offer. Adapt yourselves no longer to the pattern of this present world, but let your minds be remade and your whole nature thus transformed. Then you will be able to discern the will of God, and to know what is good, acceptable and perfect.[1]

How can we briefly understand the impact of the interest that dominates religious life?

I have tried to identify the particular interest that permeates religious life and defined it as an interest in the *Eternal*, in contrast to other kinds of interests, for example, in *causal* relationships. I also suggested that the interest in the Eternal is not the same as, but is nevertheless closely related to, some other core human interests, namely, the interests in truth, the good and the beautiful. These latter interests were traditionally regarded by Plato as focusing on what is eternal and, following him, we might take our recognition of these interests as providing, or being, useful signals of the Eternal. Plato conceived of them as interconnected absolutes and as ultimately One, and referred to this One as *ho theos*, the God.

The Eternal is in some sense 'other-worldly' since the 'world' as we know it is bound to space and time. It follows that we never *directly* encounter the Eternal in life;[2] we could only ever meet it *indirectly*, i.e. the Eternal in its absolute form is unknowable and can exist for us only in a mediated way through the 'world', conditioned by space and time. There is, then, something fundamentally paradoxical about encountering the Eternal in our spatio-temporal world. Inevitably, religious life is centred on something profoundly puzzling. In this regard it is not unlike a life in the grip of certain ideals because the ideals we normally happen to hold usually take the form of tentative definitions seeking something higher. Whatever concrete or embodied form we give them, they can only function as pale shadows or mere approximations to their absolute form(s). Whatever we think of as good or beautiful can usually be surpassed with something better and more profound; we have but to use our imagination. Our ideals always have another worldly character whilst being expressed and recognised in this world.

---

[1] Romans 12:1–2 (New English Bible).
[2] To see God face to face is to die: Exodus 33:20.

The paradoxical presence of the Eternal in our world should make us cautious about making any overbearing claims in theology or in pretending to occupy invulnerable intellectual positions; on the contrary, the paradoxical presence of the Eternal ensures our theological conceptions will inevitably fall short and there will always be scope for learning and knowing more. At the heart of religious life, we are faced with unfathomable mysteries that theology can only conceive inadequately. There is in fact a serious risk of going badly wrong because the elusiveness of the Eternal may tempt us into abstractions and into the speculations of our imagination, into projections of our human wants and aspirations.[3] In reality, it is always necessary to return to the sphere of embodiment where alone one can meet the Eternal paradoxically in space and time. We need to keep our feet on the ground and avoid becoming self-indulgent.

The important question for us as individuals and collectively is as follows: is a relationship to the Eternal really possible? Should one strive for this? Can anything redeem us from the inevitably temporal character of our existence? Plato believed that it was possible for philosophers as lovers of wisdom to do so. In pursuit of the truth,[4] philosophers were practically cultivating this relationship to the Eternal, seen as practising dying – a kind of self-disciplining and self-emptying in favour of an eternal truth. This activity pursued to its logical end had important consequences. Taken to its ultimate goal, one was relieved of the fear of death, for the self can come to no harm when life is wholly devoted to the truth. Many philosophers, including Socrates, have found a good deal of consolation in this vision of life.[5] Christian religious life did not essentially reject this Platonic vision but, because of the experience of Christ, it modified this vision of the Eternal to include Love, or essentially defined the Eternal in terms of Love, which was at one and the same time truthful, good and beautiful. They are absorbed by Love and cultivate a love of Love.[6]

---

[3] This is the risk of idolatry. Calvin notes that 'men never distinguish so accurately between the worship of God and the creatures as not to transfer promiscuously to the creature that which belongs only to God' (*Institutes of the Christian Religion* [1899], Bk. 1, ch. 12, p. 106).

[4] Mythologically we do this through the act of recollection because if it is eternal, it is eternally present and we simply have to recognise it, i.e. literally to re-know it.

[5] See e.g. Boethius (c. 480–524 AD), *The Consolation of Philosophy*.

[6] Inevitably this can draw on very physical, even erotic, imagery as in Augustine's *City of God* (1963), where in Bk. X, ch. 18 he likens worship to union with God in which God 'inflames' the psalmist with spiritual love so that the psalmist 'yearned to cast himself' into God's 'ineffable and incorporeal embrace'.

How does this interest in the Eternal express itself in human life and what is the most characteristic practice of the religious life?

Whilst religion is characterised by a particular interest, i.e. an interest in the Eternal, this is expressed in specific practices. Religion is essentially a form of life, something that people do. Moreover, it is not just something that people do in private; it is essentially a social activity, something that people do together and which resonates in the innermost recesses of an individual's heart.

The primary activity that religious people engage in, and that one can observe, is often referred to as the *cultus*. How should we define this? There are a number of possibilities and observations to make:

1. '*Cultus* is the latin for worship (*colo*, to till the ground, cultivate, worship) … it is used especially of the rites and ceremonies of worship' (Richardson, 1961, p. 83).
   This definition recalls (a) the ancient connection of religion with pastoral life and, in that context, (b) of what it means to flourish – the importance of fertility and so on. The definition's emphasis is on *what human beings do* and hints at the *reasons* for doing it.
2. We have a radically different definition in another dictionary:

> Worship has three fundamental dimensions. First, the work of God in Christ towards man and creation, revealed finally and most completely in the ministry, death and resurrection of Jesus Christ: this is an action of total self-giving, reaching out towards man and creation. Secondly, the life of the church as embodying within itself God's action. Thirdly, the life of the church as representative of the world, where God is active in creation and redemption, and as pointing to this action. (Davies, 1972, p. 159)

This definition, couched in somewhat Barthian (i.e. echoing the writing of the theologian Karl Barth) jargon, stresses the *action of the God* as the essence of worship.[7] It suggests we attend worship to experience the activity of the God and more generally to learn to see with greater clarity the activity of the God in the world. The act of attending may be demanding, but the emphasis is on the activity of the Divine, leaving human beings relatively passive. Perhaps this definition of worship most reflects the Protestant tradition, with its emphasis on the Divine Word, hearing and heeding it or, at least, taking it to heart. The reasons

---

[7] According to K. E. Kirk: 'Wherever goodness has attracted the soul, it has evoked the spirit of worship; and it will continue to attract. We may resist, deny or betray; we may welcome, co-operate and adore; but we shall never be masters of the situation. Worship depends not upon our own activities, but upon the activities which God brings to bear upon us; to them we are forced to react as worshippers' (Kirk, 1932, p. 465).

for attending are intrinsic to the Divine Word; because of what it is, it fascinates and even compels attention.

If worship is an activity, whose activity is it really?

If it is possible to see worship as the activity of the God, worship might also be defined as those occasions where the God *appears*[8] (theophanies – the appearance is sometimes referred to as God's glory or the face of God), i.e. where the Eternal is made manifest. There are a number of examples of theophanies recorded in the Hebrew Scriptures (for example, Moses, Elijah, Isaiah and Ezekiel experienced them), together with a record of their impact and consequences. Miracles (if there are such events) might be classed as other examples of theophanies. On this definition it is always an action of the God, not under human control, and therefore unpredictable; if there is evidence of predictability, it is attributable to the faithfulness of the God. The trouble with theophanies is that they are often as much about where the God is hidden as about the appearance of the God. The precise sense of the occasion and what it means is not always clear or evident. The event is frequently pervaded by an element of ambiguity and paradox.

To think of the human side, we may see worship as the *human activity* of honouring, as suggested by the meaning of the Anglo-Saxon word 'weorthscipe'.[9] But why would we think it is important to acknowledge and honour the Eternal? The reasons we have for engaging in the activity of honouring are to be found in the claims made on us by the object(s) of our attention. Worship cannot be self-serving. In fact, according to Kirk, 'disinterestedness' is *the* test of worship as opposed to some other activity. 'Worship', he says, 'stands out as the only means by which service can be purged of a self-centredness which renders it all but unserviceable' (Kirk, 1932, p. 463).

We subvert the activity of worship by turning it into a means to some other end, for example, of instructing the young, of creating a sense of community or of promoting social stability and cohesion. Indirectly the act of worship can indeed serve other ends, such as those just mentioned, since all human actions can serve a number of purposes. However, one must not confuse what is primary with what is derivative; in worship the derivative is parasitic on its primary purpose of acknowledging (revering) and honouring the Eternal. Distortions creep in when

---

[8] The choice of 'appears' suggests a more meditative mood rather than an imperative mood, though the latter seldom takes long to emerge with the provision of instructions and the issuing of commands.

[9] Legally the notion of valuing or honouring is in my view not yet worship, despite some RE theorists who wish to ameliorate the requirement of the law, i.e. that there must be a daily act of worship in school. They do so by pretending that school worship is, or should be, the expression of *our* values. This could very easily turn into a form of narcissistic idolatry or self-deification.

one seeks other reasons for doing the honouring, using grounds distinct from the object of the devotion.

Perhaps the pressure to provide reasons for worshipping should be resisted altogether, thus countering the idea that the demand for reasons is itself always reasonable. We do many sensible things in life without giving reasons or having reasons for what we do, for example, loving our parents. To give reasons here might be invidious. Wittgenstein suggested that we do not always have to provide grounds for what we do. We reach a position where it makes no sense to give further justifications; here is 'where the spade is turned' and in this vein we can simply state about worship that 'this is what we do'. Theologically, we worship because it is what the existence of the Eternal evokes from us, i.e. the Eternal evokes reverence, and worship is our way of cultivating our sense of it. Note Augustine's observation that in seeking the God, He is already present, for how could we seek that of which we know nothing?[10]

How do we cultivate the Eternal, for example, truth and love, in our life?

One answer with respect to truth is through *scientific enquiry* with its disciplined commitment to find significant causal relationships in the world. The expression of this commitment is found in the conduct of the pursuit of this knowledge through the formulation of theories with a *rigorous disinterestedness* and through a reliance on *confirmation* (either verification or falsification) by others. Another answer to the question of how we can cultivate the truth, and the one favoured by Socrates, was through conceptual enquiry, i.e. through an investigation of the meaning of the concepts we use in the intellectual constructions of our world, which also requires *self-discipline* and *testing* with others in conversation. Both the scientist and the philosopher may be said to be 'obsessed' by the truth.

In Christian life the 'platonic' answer to the cultivation of the truth is developed in conjunction with the concept of love and since priority is given to the cultivation of Love,[11] truth takes on a slightly different hue. Firstly, Christian love echoes the disinterestedness of science when this love is described as a form of 'self-emptying' (Phillipians 2:5–11) and, secondly, this love echoes the confirmation of results looked for in science (a reference to the scientific community) by understanding love as that which builds up the community.

There are some important qualifications to make here. Disinterestedness does *not* mean being without any interest and self-emptying does not mean utter self-negation or simply absenting oneself, as suggested by some mystics.[12] Disinterestedness is having a serious interest that is uncorrupted by being self-serving; it means letting the truth dominate and it is a commitment to being

---

[10] Augustine, 1991, ch. 1

[11] Plato was not uninterested in the role of love, as his dialogue the *Symposium* makes evident.

[12] See the discussion on disinterestedness in Kirk, 1932, pp. 451ff.

impartial. Comparably, self-emptying is a self, seriously being with and for the other. The extreme antithesis of self-emptying is being self-indulgent, letting the needs, wants and desires of the self predominate and rule; corrupt forms of religious life usually show evidence of this kind of self-indulgence.

Confirmation in science does not mean automatic agreement but a collective process of investigating and testing the claims made; likewise, no community is built without a process of serious discussion of diverse perspectives within the framework of commitment to one another in which the unique identity of the other is acknowledged and accepted. There is no mere conformity. Any agreement about the shared project of human life is something towards which we must all work. A genuine community emerges from the activities true to the nature of both scientific and religious life. It is notable that this sense of community is motivated by a serious interest in Nature on the one hand and in whatever is strictly Other[13] on the other hand. Human nature is such that in both cases the interest in Nature and in the Other is also the source of profound pleasure and enjoyment.[14] This enjoyment can culminate in celebration; the collective celebration often takes the form of symbolic and expressive actions that make explicit the commitment not to a particular theory but the commitment evoked by the truth itself. When celebration focuses on Truth and Love as life's ultimate source and goal, it becomes worship, an act of acknowledging, valuing and revering the truth for truth's sake. In short, science, and learning generally, properly culminates in worship.

How do the reflections on the pursuit of truth and the cultivation of love illuminate religious life?

The practice of worshipping is universally characteristic of religious life. It is where the ultimate goal and value of the whole or totality of (our) life is acknowledged and valued. In brief, given our starting point in theology, the definition of worship, I propose, is straightforward. Worshipping is cherishing the Eternal. In traditional language, one might put it in the same way that the Shorter Catechism does when it asks: what is man's (humankind's) chief end? The answer to this is that man's chief end is to praise and glorify God and to enjoy Him forever. To express and declare one's love, to value the eternity of Love and to appreciate or to make explicit that one lives from this loving Eternal – this, I suggest, might approximate the meaning of this traditional language in the catechism. This, in my view, is also the very essence of worship, a human response to the active presence of the

---

[13] One could say here the Wholly Other, but one can only love God through loving creation and human beings who are a part of it: 1 John 4:20–21.

[14] If Augustine implied in *De Doctrina Christiana* that we are to use the things of this world and not to enjoy them, for only God is to be enjoyed, one might retort that one cannot enjoy God without enjoying His world. Calvin certainly suggested that we should take delight in the world. See Calvin, 1899, Bk. III, X, 2 and Bk. I, XIV, 20. The traditional *uti, non frui* (to use, not to enjoy) becomes *frui et uti* (to enjoy and use).

Divine. The connection of religious worship with the devotion to the truth in science becomes clearer when the connection between love and truth is explored.[15]

What is the most basic structure of Christian worship (liturgy, from the Greek leitourgia, *the act of service or ministry)?*

Inevitably, in this practice of worshipping there are two foci which are brought into a relationship with each other: 1) the Eternal and 2) human beings.

Since the Eternal is not wholly controllable by human beings ('The wind bloweth where it listeth': John 3:8), any relationship to the Eternal is controlled by 'It'. This leads people to speak of religious life in terms of 'submission' and 'obedience'. Even though we cannot control the Eternal, we can, to a degree, control the contribution of other human beings and of our own life to the relationship. As such, we can regard the practice of religious life as an attempt to discipline ourselves, to cultivate the relationship, for example, through a practised attentiveness in meditation; now the question becomes how should we cultivate the relationship to the Eternal in life, in our spatio-temporal existence? The structure of worship will reflect the dynamic relationship between the two foci – the active presence of the Eternal with us and the human response to this presence. This might characterise the whole of one's life but should be overtly evident in a ritualised expression of it. For a more detailed description of Christian acts of worship and the minor differences among the various denominations, see the entry for 'Liturgy' in Davies, 1972.

Why do we use ritual to worship?

In theory, everything in the 'world' (the spatio-temporal context of our existence) is equally near and equally distant from the Eternal. In practice, human historical and cultural experiences have taught us to set aside certain times and certain spaces as sacred. From a theoretical point of view, these times and spaces are largely arbitrary,[16] but practically speaking there are elements in our spatio-temporal world (including our cultural history) which appear to have evoked the Eternal for us so that we discipline ourselves with specific rites and practices to recall them. Acts of worship are the practices that are used to recollect, re-present or re-experience the Eternal.

---

[15] John 4:23–4.

[16] Note John Calvin's comments (Calvin, 1899, Bk. IV, ch. X, 31): 'It is of no consequence what the days and hours are, what the nature of the edifices, and what psalms are sung on each day. But it is proper that there should be certain days and stated hours, and a place fit for receiving all, if any regard is had to the preservation of peace. For what seedbed of quarrels will confusion in such matters be, if everyone is allowed at pleasure to alter what pertains to common order?' In other words, sacred times and places are merely a practical social issue.

The different religions have different historical and cultural traditions and have identified different occasions that became *momentous*[17] for the faithful. Judaism, Christianity and Islam, amongst others, are called *positive* religions precisely because they return to their own unique events of revelation (the Torah, Christ and the Qu'ran) which function as *the* source and criteria for their respective religious lives. The actual ritual practices are therefore by no means arbitrary because they are dependent on these events. The practices also tend to be very conservative in that nothing must change if one is to be confident or assured of re-living or of re-cognising the originating moment(s). At the very most, one changes only those things in the practices that enable one to continue to be true to that originating moment(s) or event(s), place, or text. As such, reformations always espouse a claim to be returning to the original source.

Are there alternatives to looking to the past or ancient texts for the symbolic presence of the Eternal?

There are religions that turn to nature and either do not rely on a specific history or go beyond their specific history. In Christian tradition those religions that rely *exclusively* on nature to evoke the Eternal and sacred are referred to as 'paganism'. In this case the religion tends to identify something in nature that is particularly impressive and which may point one beyond the spatio-temporal character of the 'world' to the sacred. Thus, typically one might identify a mountain, a large, old tree, a particularly powerful, fertile animal such as a bull, a particular time, for example, the 're-birth' of the sun or light, or a particularly beautiful scenery that attracts one back again and again. Such things become sacred to us because of their power to evoke or project our attention *beyond* the horizons of our 'world'. However, if they simply identify something *in* our world as something to be valued above all else as the absolute, then they are idols.

At this point it is important to note that the distinction between the Eternal, the God and idols is a very fine one. What for one is a god may be an idol to others; what may be a god for one person at one time may be an idol for that same person on another occasion. Idolatry confuses between the symbol and the symbolised, i.e. it merges the two categories of the created with the creator into one in which the 'world' or elements of the world are deified or where the Eternal is straightforwardly identified with some element of the spatio-temporal[18] reality.

What are the main features of Christian worship?

If we now look specifically at the character of Christian worship, we note that there is considerable variation. The Society of Friends (Quakers) worship in

---

[17] I.e. filled with meaning by conveying a sense of the Eternal.
[18] Pantheism is where the spatio-temporal as a totality is identified with the Eternal.

silence because nothing can be said that will truly capture for us the sense of the Eternal. If there is speech, it is whatever is evoked by this attentiveness to the Eternal in silence. Others focus on sacred text and as a result most of the practice of worship takes the form of prayer, scripture reading and studied commentary.[19] Still others focus on precise ritual actions which are deemed to render Christ present – Christ from a Christian perspective being the revealing 'word' or sense of the Eternal. Generally speaking, the major core of Christian practice is fairly consistent (Maxwell, 1936) in incorporating certain essential elements and which reflect a specific location of the Eternal in time and space.

What are the times that matter?

There are assigned 'sacred'[20] times,[21] i.e. there is a Christian year which sets aside a certain day for worship[22] and recognises certain festivals as providing a specific focus. Broadly speaking, a little over half of the Christian year traces and re-lives the key moments in the life of Christ, and in the remainder of the year the church seeks to direct our thinking, feeling and willing so as to see our life in the perspective of the Eternal. Thus (selectively), the highlights of the Christian calendar strictly begin with advent (originally 40 days) – the period of attentive anticipation, followed by Christmas – the birth of Christ in the world, epiphany – the manifestation of Christ to the world, followed by the discipline of Lent (40 days) – Christ's desert fast, Palm Sunday and passion week – Christ's suffering, Good Friday – Christ's crucifixion and death, Easter – Christ's resurrection, and Ascension Day (40 days after Easter) – Christ's 'physical' departure. The church's teaching cycle begins with Pentecost (50 days after Easter) – the giving of the Spirit, followed by Trinity Sunday, where teaching begins with God.

Some of these Christian celebrations reflect Jewish practice and commemorations. It is not irrelevant to the Christian community that Easter (generally) coincides with Passover, the commemoration of the exodus, or that Pentecost, the celebration of the giving of the spirit and constitution of the church,

---

[19] M. Hengel (1983, preface, p. xiii) observes that 'the important thing here is that all these writings [the whole of the New Testament] including the Gospels grew out of worship, the focal point of the earliest church, and were written to be used in worship [1 Thess. 15:22; 2 Thess. 2:15]. They have come down to us only because they were read in worship'. Scriptures arise out of a context of worship and become a stimulus for worship and attentiveness to the Eternal.

[20] The quotation marks are there to remind the reader that from a theoretical perspective, allocating *this* time rather than *that* time to the realm of the sacred is arbitrary.

[21] The reference here is to days or times of the year. Each day also has its moments. I will refer to these when discussing prayer.

[22] Saturday for those who are bound by Jewish tradition, the creation myth and the Ten Commandments; Sunday for those who took the first day of the week as the day when 'Christ rose', i.e. when the disciples began to recognise the Eternal in the life of Jesus.

coincides with the Jewish (Shavuot) harvest celebration and the giving of the Torah, establishing the covenantal relationship with the people of Israel. (In the Jewish festival the prescribed lection is Exodus 19–20:26.) It would be impossible to understand Jesus or the Christian life without reference to their Jewish roots.

Interspersed with this programme of recollection and reflection are numerous saint's days which seek to exhibit something about the conceived ideal of the good or religious life. Moreover, the Christian church does not entirely ignore the natural world as a source for our sense of the Eternal and so its liturgical calendar also includes, or intersperses into the calendar of 'memorable' events, the cycle of nature with its key points, such as harvest time.

Which spaces should one seek out?

There are also assigned 'sacred' spaces, i.e. spaces that have been set aside as sacred. There are only two places in Islam where one is not permitted to pray (or so I am told): one is in the toilet and the other is in the cemetery. The reasoning that seems to apply here is that as the sacred should be associated with purity in life, neither of the two places mentioned appear to convey this sense of purity to many people. Here Christianity differs in at least one important respect, in that it seems more than willing to worship and pray amongst the dead. Two main reasons for this suggest themselves: the first was one of *necessity*, in that the early Christian experience of persecution reputedly forced believers into the catacombs in Rome in order to meet in secret. Secondly, the Christian sense of the Eternal is associated with the suffering and *death* of Christ; it is at the tomb that the disciples first met the risen Christ. A possible third reason may be an element of 'ancestor' worship; the sense of the totality of life and unity with those who have gone before and those who might follow after may also evoke a sense of the Eternal. This is brought out later in the definition of the church.

How should 'sacred' space be organised?

The space of worship has often been so organised as to accommodate movement or procession, reflecting a journeying of life and point to the east, the destiny of life in the figurative eternal city of Jerusalem. Alternatively, the space may take the shape of a cross to remind one of the death of Christ, which evoked the sense of the Eternal. Worship can also occur in a secret space to reflect its character of inwardness, but mostly where worship is communal a public space is required and that is done by specifically designating a space to be sacred. The space may be highly decorated (for example, locally in Birmingham, one finds that in the Serbian Orthodox Church in Bournville, the walls and ceiling are covered with pictures) so as to remind one of significant people and events, or the space may be plain (as in most reformed churches) because simplicity has its own beauty. On the other hand, the reasoning may be not to distract the worshipper from the Eternal that stands over against our world.

What summarises the main features of Christian worship?

The format or order of worship has taken the form of a) instruction (the pursuit of truth and understanding) and b) celebration. There is a certain rhythm in the ritual actions and gestures that are representative of loving attentiveness. A hearing and responding, incorporating some of the key emotions and attitudes of life (thanksgiving, joy, remorse, etc.), whether expressed through words, music, art or worship, is associated with some basic elements of life such as water, bread and wine. Nevertheless, the total purpose of Christian worship is to experience and express eternal love, which it believes can only be done: 1) through acts of recollection of events that embody that love; 2) through a coming to oneself or by being honest with oneself; and 3) through a mediated love of others and concern for others that unifies humanity and ultimately the world.

Chapter 3
Prayer

Is there a view of prayer in Scripture?

There are various relevant texts, but here is one:

> Is any among you afflicted? Let him pray. Is any merry? Let him sing psalms. Is any sick among you? Let him call for the elders of the church; and let them pray over him, anointing him with oil in the name of the Lord: And the prayer of faith shall save the sick, and the Lord shall raise him up; and if he has committed sins, they shall be forgiven him. Confess your faults one to another, and pray for one another, that ye be healed. The effectual fervent prayer of a righteous man availeth much. Elias was a man subject to like passions as we are, and he prayed earnestly that it might not rain: and it rained not on the earth by the space of three years and six months. And he prayed again, and the heaven gave rain, and the earth brought forth her fruit. (James 5:13–18)

How should we read and understand such practices? Do they have a point or are they rooted in superstition?

But why should we attend to prayer?

We are trying to understand Christian religious life by looking, in the first instance, at what Christians do. Earlier we discussed worship as an activity that religious people universally and characteristically practised. In view of my identification of the religious interest as being an interest in the Eternal, worship was defined by me as 'cherishing the Eternal' or a 'waiting on God'. Whilst in theory everything in the spatio-temporal world might become an *occasion* for knowing and relating to the Eternal, in practice certain experiences, natural phenomenon and artefacts have traditionally signalled or become signposts to the transcendent; it is these that become the focus of worship in which one seeks to remember and re-experience or re-cognise the Eternal once again. And if worship is the mark of the religious life, then prayer is the core of worship.[1] But what is prayer and does it make any sense?

---

[1] Note the opening line of F. Heiler's classic study of prayer: 'Religious people, students of religion, theologians of all creeds and tendencies, agree in thinking that prayer is the central phenomenon of religion, the very hearthstone of all piety' (Heiler, 1958, p. xiii).

Do all (religious) people agree that prayer is an important practice?

Heiler in his classic study certainly thought it was central, but not everyone sees the point of prayer. The sense of prayer is undermined by criticisms originating from two quite different directions. The first comes from our understanding of the 'world' and the other from features of the religious perspective itself and its theology. The exploration of these two very different criticisms will begin to mark off the territory within which any deeper understanding of prayer must be found.

How does our understanding of the world affect our understanding of prayer?

The 'worldly' perspective is dominated by a *causal* interest and as a consequence it seeks to provide what may be taken to be an *explanation* for prayer. It does this by enquiring into a) what *causes* people to pray and, in turn, b) what, if anything, are the *results* of prayer. With these two questions (of cause and consequence) in mind, some obvious and simplistic answers have presented themselves.

With an explanation in mind, what do some intellectuals think causes people to pray?

One can easily propose answers that may all have some warrant. Some of the *explanations* offered are that people pray due to habit, tradition, peer pressure, culture, fear and anxiety, and hopes and dreams. These can all feature in the worldly or 'scientific' reply (Schleiermacher, 1987, p. 170) as to why people pray. The explanations, in effect, set out the social and psychological functions of prayer. Many religious people experience such explanations as a case of 'explaining away' prayer because they appear to ignore the religious force of prayer.

The status of such explanations becomes more evident when it is noted that the very same type of answer might feature in the response to the question as to what prevents or stops people from praying. So perhaps people do *not* pray because they have not developed the habit. And if prayer is a habit, and they come to see it as such, they may no longer pray or cease to pray because they have come to think it is *mere* habit. Similarly, tradition may come to be regarded as an empty tradition. Culture and peer pressure may equally serve to repress the activity of prayer as to encourage it, depending on whether we live in a religious or a secular and avowedly atheistic society. If prayer is the response to fears and anxiety or to hopes and dreams, we may come to see it as an irrational and ineffectual response to these psychological states, just as prayer may be seen as something to be done precisely because it meets the needs of these psychological states. Within the *causal* framework, all these sociological and psychological answers, whilst having some bite, appear to be indecisive as to the point of prayer because they can be used to argue the case both ways.

The problem with these sociological and psychological accounts of why people pray (or why they do *not* pray) is that they offer *explanations* without actually touching on the sense of prayer. In fact the sociological and psychological explanations of praying (or not praying) are fundamentally *external* to activity of prayer by not relating to any potential religious meaning. They appear to presuppose that the primary sense of prayer is to be found in its social and psychological function. Theologically, this seems to be more a prejudgment than the outcome of a careful look at the activity.

No progress can be made unless the sense of prayer is investigated through an analysis of the concept and activity itself, but before doing so perhaps we should reflect on what prayer is supposed to do.

Could it make more sense to look at the results of prayer rather than at the causes of prayer?

Perhaps the ambiguity and confusions generated by thinking about the *causes* of prayer can be resolved in another way. The 'right explanation' may be thought to hinge on what prayer is supposed to achieve or on what people believe it does, i.e. on its *effects*. Thus, some people may regard the practice as irrational because it is ineffectual, but presumably the obverse could hold for them, namely, it would be rational if it could be demonstrated to 'work'.

Is it possible to test whether prayer 'works'?

Some people do try to show that prayer works, or does not work, without first stopping to enquire into what prayer really is (Phillips, 1965). In short, they take (wrongly, in my view) an *experimental* approach to prayer. For example, in the nineteenth century Sir Francis Galton treated prayer as an activity, the effectiveness of which was *in principle* testable (Brummer, 1984). Accordingly, since one might observe that it is the norm for church people to pray for the health and well-being of the monarch, one might reasonably expect the current queen to have a longer life expectancy and better health than her subjects. If this proved not to be the case, then one might suppose to have genuine grounds to doubt the efficacy of prayer.

This way of treating prayer is not just one of the oddities of a previous century. From time to time one still reads of 'scientists' conducting a large-scale, double-blind experiment in which critically ill people are divided into two groups, one of which becomes the focus of prayer and the other not. This procedure imitates the research pattern of testing the efficacy of certain drugs where some patients are given a drug under investigation and others a placebo. In *Doctor*, 16 May 2002, there is a brief review of one of these 'experiments' in an article entitled: 'Can Praying for Ill People Improve their Health?' It concludes: 'There is not yet any firm scientific evidence that prayer can alter health outcomes in illness [note the 'not yet' as if empirical evidence might, in principle, be forthcoming in the future]

... but it may never be possible to prove or disprove possible benefits of prayer to ill people.' Presumably the doubt and uncertainty expressed by the author here has to do with the difficulties of constructing a truly critical experiment in this field *in practice*, which otherwise, *in principle*, would prove the case one way or the other once and for all. This way of seeing and evaluating the function of prayer is a mistake, as I shall try to argue.

There is something distinctly odd about handling the subject matter of prayer in this way; in fact it comes across as strikingly and profoundly irreligious. According to Schleiermacher, to have 'false conceptions of prayer's purpose' and the 'sad experience of its slightest advantages' can lead to disastrous consequences. Admittedly, the manipulative and objectionable way of looking at the matter in this way is deeply ingrained,[2] for there are similar experimental ways of treating the matter in the Scriptures themselves. See, for example, Elijah's approach in determining the power and identity of the true God in his conflict with the priests of Baal (1 Kings 18) or note Jacob's vow in Genesis 28:20–22: '*If* God will be with me, and will keep me in this way that I go, and will give me bread to eat, and raiment to put on, so that I come again to my father's house in peace; *then* shall the Lord be my God: And this stone, which I have set for a pillar, shall be God's house: and of all that thou shalt give me I will surely give the tenth unto thee.' The commitment to God here is conditional; it depends on how things go; an element of bargaining or manipulation creeps in with a human incentive scheme for God to come up with the goods! On this view we will only know whether it is worth

---

[2] M. Weber purports to see a development in religion from the mere magical to a more 'exemplary' type of religion. The former is reckoned to be manipulative coercion of the God in the service of man. Weber admits that: 'In these cases, religious behaviour is not worship of the god but rather coercion of the god, and the invocation is not prayer but rather the exercise of magical formula' (Weber, 1964, p. 412). But why does Weber think the exemplary type is a deeper form of religious life? Is it because the devotee has realised that the results are far from certain? He seems to be saying precisely that when he claims that 'the god becomes a great lord *who may fail on occasion* [emphasis added], and on whom one cannot approach with devices of magical compulsion, but only with entreaties and gifts' (1964, p. 414). But surely the magical practitioner must have realised this too! In the exemplary religion Weber claims: 'The pervasive and central theme is *do ut des* [I give in order that you give]. This aspect clings to the routine and mass religious behaviour of all people at all times and in all religions. The normal situation is that the burden of all prayers, even in the most other-worldly religions, is the aversion of the external evils of this world and the inducement of the external advantages of this world.' It seems that even in the exemplary religions it has not yet become apparent that the saying of prayers makes no external difference at all or that the rain falls on the just and on the unjust. Perhaps only in a rational secular age, of which Weber no doubt sees himself as one of its pre-eminent members, are we supposed to realise that! Whilst not denying that for some people religion takes precisely the form of *do ut des*, the deeper form of religion looks to internal benefits rather than external benefits, i.e. where prayer is valued for its religious meaning rather than for its external benefits.

praying or worth acknowledging and serving God *if* x, y or z follows.[3] Note also the 'temptations' of Jesus in Matthew 4 (and parallel gospel passages), where the relation of 'if ... then' is explored, or in the suffering of Jesus (Matthew 26:67–8) and at his crucifixion (Matthew 27:40, 42–3).

On the other hand, the assumption of the 'if ... then' relationship, which human beings might then test and exploit, is specifically rejected elsewhere in Scripture as a form of 'tempting God' (Matthew 4:7, Deuteronomy 6:16). 'Tempting God' is just another way of saying that this is an impious or irreligious[4] form of behaviour. Applied to prayer, an empirical approach misconstrues the nature of the human relationship to the Eternal and thus misconstrues the nature of prayer. In their defence, the 'empiricists' might argue that without this relationship of 'if ... then', religion becomes irrelevant to life, i.e. religion must be perceived to make a difference to life, because if it does not, why should one bother with it?

One way to overcome the prohibition of *not* putting God to the test in an empirical approach to prayer is to admit that, of course, one cannot devise critical experiments to test the effects on the 'world out there'. The real difference prayer makes is to the person who prays;[5] the practice *affects the self*.[6] The function of

---

[3] A. J. Twerski (1985, pp. 178f.) reports this story:

'Another time, the interaction between the Maggid and a supplicant took a different course.

A Man came to the Maggid and unburdened himself of his many worries and troubles. The Maggid listened sympathetically, then said, "Have faith in God, and He will certainly help you."

The man was not satisfied. "That is not what the holy *sidur* says," the man complained. "I *daven* everyday, and in my *sidur* it says that God helped the Israelites from the hands of the Egyptians, and the Israelites *then* had faith in God. First He must help, and *then* we believe."

The Maggid smiled. "You are right," he said. "Even the Almighty is obligated to follow what the holy *sidur* says. Your prayers will be answered."

The Maggid explained, "This man's piety was simple and sincere. He was not manipulating. He was not conniving. His relationship with God was open and without reservation. This trust warrants the Divine blessing."'

By way of commentary, one might observe that the initial advice appeared to advocate a form of life that is self-serving. This self-serving orientation is essentially irreligious and should not be confused with the observation that confidence in God can grow from seeing life's sense.

[4] Calvin, 1899, Bk. III, ch. XX, 51.

[5] This explanation may resemble but is also very different from the observation Kierkegaard made in *Purity of Heart* (1956, p. 51) when he writes: 'A hasty explanation could assert that to pray is a useless act, because a man's prayer does not alter the unalterable ... The true explanation is therefore at the same time the one most desired. The prayer does not change God, but it changes the one who offers it. It is the same with the substance of what is spoken. Not God, but you, the maker of confession, get to know something by your act of confession.' The benefits of which Kierkegaard speaks are not some material or physical goods but the spiritual benefit of becoming transparent to oneself.

[6] 'Even Comte, in his atheistic system of religion, prescribed for his disciples two hours of prayer a day, for the disciplinary effect which the mere act of kneeling down and

prayer is taken by some to be a form of self-exhortation and encouragement in the face of the challenges of life. It is said that meditative prayer, yoga, etc. may 'de-stress' one or make one more serene, more tolerant and more caring. This change of focus from effects in the outside world to effects within persons themselves does not, of course, remove it from the empirical or testing sphere. After all, as human beings we are also part of the objective world. We can equally well test for the physiological effects of prayer and for changes in the attitudinal differences made by prayer and other religious practices as for other, more obviously physical consequences in the 'world out there'. In fact, some people do claim that there is some empirical evidence showing, for example, that religious people live longer, that it stimulates certain regions of the brain or that religion has survival value (it is reputed that people with strong religious convictions, such as the Jehovah's Witnesses, lived slightly longer in the Nazi death camps than those who did not have strong convictions). All of these areligious effects are judged to commend religious life!

It might be noted that whether these effects of religious practice and belief are verified or not, they are quite independent of any assumptions about the Eternal or about the 'existence' and nature of the Divine. This also shows that they may have little to do with any seriously *religious* understanding of the activity of prayer. It is said of some people that they know the price of everything but the value of nothing; in brief, such people are accused of measuring by the wrong standards or using the wrong criteria to make sense of an activity. In this case they judge prayer by the wrong considerations, for they do not understand what prayer is. As Kierkegaard noted, the reality of inwardness is incommensurable with every external expression of it and every external consequence.[7] The interest in inwardness and human subjectivity provides a different standard from

---

praying had upon them' (Holmes, 1911, p. 35).

[7] See Kierkegaard, 1992, pp. 83f. In a footnote he relates:

'Let us try an experiment. Socrates stands and gazes into empty space. Two individuals pass by, one of whom says to the other: "What is that man doing?" The first man answers: "Nothing." Let us suppose, however, that one of them has a little more notion of inwardness, and gives to Socrates' behaviour a religious expression, saying: "He immerses himself in the Divine, he prays." But does he make use of any words, or is he perhaps voluble in prayer? No, Socrates has understood his God-relationship in such a manner that he dared not say anything at all, from fear of indulging in foolish prattle, and from fear of having a mistaken wish fulfilled, of which examples are supposed to have existed. As for instance when the oracle informed a man that all his sons would acquire fame and distinction, and the anxious father said: "And then I suppose they will all come to an unfortunate end?" The oracle replied: "This too will be granted to you." For the oracle was consistent enough to suppose that whoever consults it is a petitioner; whence the use of the word, granted – a sad irony for an anxious father.

Socrates does absolutely nothing. He does not even speak to God inwardly, and yet he realises the highest of human actions.'

the impact religious belief and practice (for example, prayer) might have on the objective world.

For example, K. E. Kirk (1932, pp. 203ff.) cites the positive contribution of monasticism to Christianity as what gave prayer 'primacy among Christian activities'. The key feature of prayer is taken by him to be 'self-forgetfulness'. If self-forgetfulness is the substance of prayer, we cannot then begin to think about what benefits the self may gain from the activity of prayer and then to test for these benefits experimentally to ensure that we are not wasting our efforts.

Are the empirical problems the only problems facing the practice of prayer?

No, in addition to the difficulties thrown up by an empirical approach, prayer can also encounter some strictly *theological* difficulties. See, for example:

a. Origen in the second to third centuries AD (in *De Oratione*)[8] articulated and tried to contend with an objection that over time many others have raised in the following way: if God is omniscient, good and omnipotent, then there is no need to pray. The logic is as follows: if He is omniscient, He will already know[9] all your needs and wishes, and if God is good and omnipotent, He will always be willing and able to do what is for your good and will do so without your intercession.

b. Yet another related line of thought that obviates prayer goes like this: if the God is eternal and, by virtue of this status, 'foreknows' all that could and will happen in our spatio-temporal 'world', then there is no point in prayer because 1) everything is foreknown and 2) already determined, so nothing that you say or do could change what has already been ordained by God.[10]

In short, the theological case for prayer is logically very difficult.

In addition, Meister Eckhart[11] expresses some *religious* reservations about prayer beautifully and along the same lines. Thus:

---

[8] *On Prayer* (Origen, 1954).

[9] Augustine writes: '... when the same apostle says, "let your requests be made known unto God," this is not to be understood as if thereby they become known to God, who certainly knew them before they were uttered, but in this sense, that they are to be made known to ourselves in the presence of God by patient waiting upon Him, not in the presence of men by ostentatious worship' (Augustine's letter to Proba, 412 AD [Schaff, 1979, p. 465]).Augustine saw prayer primarily as the effort to sustain one's desire for the Eternal and to see or know oneself in the light of *that* context.

[10] Kierkegaard writes in *The Sickness unto Death* (1980, p. 40): 'The fatalist's worship of God is at most an interjection, and essentially it is a muteness, a mute capitulation: he is unable to pray. To pray is also to breathe, and possibility is for the self what oxygen is for breathing.'

[11] A German mystic (1260–1327).

> Once someone asked a sick man why he did not pray to God to make him well. Then the man said that there were three reasons why he would be sorry to do that. The first was because he wanted to be sure that our loving God would never allow him to be sick, if that were not the best thing for him. The second reason was that if a man is good, he wants everything God wishes, and not that God should wish what he may want, for that would be wholly wrong ... The third reason why ... is because I do not wish to and I should not ask our mighty, loving and merciful God for so small a thing. (Eckhart, 1981 pp. 236f.)

(Firstly, can we be sure we know what constitutes our good? Secondly, all prayer should be about conforming to God's will rather than about realising our wishes and wills. Thirdly, the most significant goal in life is to be one with God; everything else is either subordinate or unimportant.) And again:

> But now I ask: 'What is the prayer of a heart that has detachment?' And to answer it I say that purity in detachment does not know how to pray, because if someone prays he asks God to get something for him, or he asks God to take something away from him. But a heart in detachment asks for nothing, nor has it anything of which it would gladly be free. So it is free from all prayer, and its prayer is nothing else than [a desire] for uniformity with God. That is all its prayer consists in. (Ibid., p. 292)

Kierkegaard stated: 'When prayer really becomes prayer, then it becomes silence.'[12] If the aim of religious life is a worldly, temporal detachment, then prayer itself may be an indication of spiritual ill health. These observations highlight some serious religious difficulties in the practice of prayer.

How can we summarise the problems facing the practice of praying?

There are three key points that need to be made:

1. Many of the difficulties with prayer stem from a misperception of the purpose of prayer and as a consequence also wrongly focus exclusively on a particular type of prayer, viz. impetratory prayer, in which we express our

---

[12] In this, Kierkegaard echoes St Augustine in *De Magistro*. Augustine, having established that talking has the two functions of teaching and reminding, sees prayer as an exception, since there is no need to teach or remind God. So he says to his son: 'It is for that reason (I'm sure you realise) that we are instructed to "pray in our inmost chambers", a term for our soul's deep recess – because when we ask what we most direly need, God is not waiting to be reminded or taught what that is. One who talks is varying conventional noises to signal the wants within him outward to others. But God is sought and prayed to precisely through our *unexpressed* [emphasis added] interior wants, by a call within, in the temple whose consecration he desires' (Wills, 2001, p. 134).

desires for some material gain or for how things should go for us. Whilst this prayer may be the most common, it is not the only or the deepest form of prayer. Any survey of religious practice will refer one to prayers of thanksgiving, prayers of confession, of blessing, of cursing, of complaint and of protest. If one then asks 'Does prayer work?', then one can only say that in making these prayers one achieves one's end in the very act of doing them. By expressing thanks in prayer we do actually give thanks. If the goal of prayer is to exist honestly before God with all our needs and wants, then by bringing our needs before God we do actually succeed by the very act of doing so.

2. Origen responded to the theological objections mentioned above by simply asserting that Christ commanded us to pray and that, moreover, to pray without ceasing. The sense of this approach was highlighted by Meister Eckhart where he shows the real point of prayer is to be detached from the world and united with the Eternal. If the fundamental nature of prayer were to ask for things in this world, then it would follow that true religiosity (which he characterised as detachment) is to be free from prayer. But if prayer is to turn to the Eternal and to will to exist *before God*, then in the very act of doing it, we realise our purpose. In this sense only, prayer may be said to work without fail. We might add that *before God*, from whom nothing is hidden, we can only express honestly what is in our souls to show what we already are.[13] There is no scope for deception, although such honesty with ourselves is difficult.[14] As D. Turner notes: 'Prayer is the process of discovering in ourselves that with which we can truly love God: that is our will, that is where our hearts are. For "you have made us for yourself, and our hearts will not rest until they rest in you".[15] For the same reasons as Augustine, Thomas Aquinas once said of prayer that it is *quodammodo interpretativa voluntatis humanae* – prayer is a kind of revelation to us of what our wills truly are, it is a kind of hermeneutic of the opaque text of desire' (Turner, 2002, p. 98). From the honest confession of

---

[13] Prayer is therefore a form of self-knowledge and the act of prayer is an act of becoming transparent to oneself. Perhaps there can be no true self-forgetfulness until we know who and what we are – only then can we commit ourselves into the embrace of the Eternal.

[14] Fénélon wrote in *The Inner Life*: 'TRUE prayer is only another name for the love of God. Its excellence does not consist in the multitude of our words; for our Father knoweth what things we have need of before we ask Him. The true prayer is that of the heart, and the heart prays only for what it desires. *To pray,* then is *to desire* – but to desire what God would have us desire. He who asks what he does not from the bottom of his heart desire, is mistaken in thinking that he prays. Let him spend days in reciting prayers, in meditation or in inciting himself to pious exercises, he prays not once truly, if he really desires not the things he pretends to ask' (ch. 4).

[15] Augustine, 1991, Bk. 1, ch. 1.

who we are, all the forms of prayer follow naturally. For example, we offer impetratory prayers because as human beings we are filled with desires and longing, and honesty requires us to present them. Prayers of protest are offered because there is much in life that offends us, morally or otherwise, and we are duty bound to express this, and so on. In prayer we seek to express what we are before the Eternal; perhaps we do not always know how to do this – if so, we must rely as Paul suggests in Romans 8:26 on the groanings of the spirit. Without this fundamental honesty about the self there can be no real self-forgetfulness.

3. The problem is can we separate prayer from actions with some more immediate end in view, an end which would bring it into the 'this-worldly' realm and thus into the realm of experimentation? For Kirk, some ostensibly self-forgetful action towards others will not suffice because they will 'fail to evoke the full disinterestedness'[16] (Kirk, 1932, pp. 92f.). For him only the God as the object of prayer can bring about true self-forgetfulness. Yet this state of self-forgetfulness must form the basis of a properly religious relationship with the things of this world.[17] Devising a different way of being in the world in the light of prayer is unavoidable – by their fruits you will know them, so perhaps sociologists are able to discern something of the sincerity and depth of our religious life. With the reality of self-forgetfulness, we might reasonably expect people of faith to be more community-minded and concerned for the well-being of the natural world.

We might conclude the discussion on prayer with S. L. Frank's observations:

> The spiritual realisation of faith coincides with what is usually called 'devotional life'. That conception, however, should not be understood in too narrow a sense. To begin with, prayer is not necessarily a supplication addressed to God – there is such a thing as the prayer of praise, and the prayer of submission, humility and trust ('Thy will be done!'). But even apart from this, devotional life need not take a verbal form at all. Although our communion with God, like our communion with human beings, finds its natural expression in speech it has a wider range. According to the unanimous testimony of mystical literature, at

---

[16] Kierkegaard supposed (in a Protestant context!) that the only true prayer and love was for the already dead, for only then could one be truly assured of being disinterested, since the dead can do nothing for you.

[17] In *The Inner Life*, Fénélon wrote: 'The first effect of a sincere love is an earnest desire to know all that we ought to do to gratify the object of our affection. Any other desire is a proof that we love ourselves under a pretence of loving God; that we are seeking an empty and deceitful consolation in Him; that we would use God as an instrument for our pleasure, instead of sacrificing that for his glory. God forbid that his children should so love Him! Cost what it may, we must both know and do without reservation what he requires of us.'

the heights of religious life prayer is replaced by contemplation and union; and something analogous to that is found even at ordinary, intermediate stages. Just as the most intimate loving communion with a human being is often silent and consists simply in the delight of nearness and in contemplation of the loved one's image enchanting to the lover, so intimate communion with God may consist in silently contemplating Him and absorbing His reality. The realisation of faith in the spiritual life may in its general form be defined as the effort of approaching God and possessing Him and find rest in Him, though our sense of doing so may be clear or dim, intense or feeble, completely actual or merely potential. (Frank, 1946, p. 226)

Chapter 4
Sacraments

What are the most notable features of religious life we have observed so far?

To recap, religion is first and foremost a form of life that arises from a particular interest that human beings normally have, namely, an interest in the Eternal. This form of life has certain distinctive practices. One of these is the practice of worship that I have defined as the acknowledgement and cherishing of the Eternal. Worship, in turn, is centred on 'prayer', an activity which is common but is by no means self-evidently sensible. It cannot be an activity of manipulating the Eternal.

Meister Eckhart's presupposition of religion as entailing a form of 'detachment' from the world (the spatio-temporal realm) raises an obvious problem for the activity of prayer. On his understanding of religion, impetratory prayer (i.e. prayer that asks for favour) is clearly misguided by virtue of the implicit and demonstrable attachments implicit in requests on behalf of a self that desires things in this world. Now, Eckhart may or may not have been right in supposing that existing *before God* or *the Eternal* requires 'detachment' from the world. Perhaps the religious life is better described as existing *in* the world before the Eternal. What one can say is that existing with a sense of the Eternal does *change* one's perception and relationship to the 'world' and that this should be taken into account in one's understanding of prayer. The most obvious change that takes place by existing before God is that the 'world' becomes of *penultimate* significance rather than of *ultimate* value in one's life (Bonhoeffer, 1971).

What is clear is that by existing before the God we become utterly transparent, so there is no scope for (self)-deception. A consequence of this is that we naturally set out in prayer all the fundamental human responses, feelings and aspirations that we have as a confession of what we are, not as a shopping list for the Eternal to meet. Thus, in religious life we can observe prayers of confession, thanksgiving, protest, supplication, meditation and reflection, etc. because all of these are fundamental human affections and aspirations without which we would not be fully human. Prayer essentially articulates the nature of the self and the human community before the God or in the context of the Eternal.

But is there not more to worship than prayer?

Of course! In addition to the key activity of prayer, religious people generally also engage in other characteristic forms about ritual expression. The most important of these within the Christian tradition are known as the '*sacraments*'. It is to these that we now turn.

What is a sacrament?

A sacrament[1] is a ritual action. Above all, the sacraments re-emphasise an important feature of religion, namely, religion is what people *do*. Theologians have often stated that what is *done* in the sacraments is what really matters rather than what is *said*.[2] The words are in some sense subordinate to the action, though words are still regarded as essential.[3] The sacraments are public, meaningful dramas that are declarative of a state of affairs with a consequential role in moral and religious formation.[4] So, religion is primarily what people do together in order to transform our collective life. Religion is essentially a shared activity and, only secondarily, what people do 'privately' or in 'secret'.[5] This contrasts starkly with what many people think of religion, namely, as holding a *set of beliefs* (quite often, moreover, as holding beliefs that are possibly unjustifiable or, at least, of a rather dubious nature, intellectually speaking).

Christians speak of 'celebrating' the sacraments, which fits in with the view of religion as a communal activity; celebrating as an isolated self does not make much sense. However, it is important to note that within the broad spectrum of Christian traditions there is no universal agreement on precisely what sacramental practices should be followed. As S. L. Frank observes, (1946, p. 233): '... a sensitive and religiously open mind ... approaches reality with reverence and wonder, feeling the presence of God's power and greatness in everything and through all. Such a mind will feel perplexed not by the recognition of sacraments, but by the restriction of the term to a small and specifically defined group of facts.' For Frank, in principle everything, and no doubt every action, could become sacramental, i.e. as an occasion for relating to the Eternal. Yet Christian tradition identifies some actions and some things as sacramental and not others. How is this decided? There

---

[1] According to C. Bigg (1905, footnote on p. 42) a '*Sacramentum* means especially, "the soldier's oath of allegiance," and its use in Latin theology as in Isis worship follows immediately from the conception of the believer as a soldier'.

[2] Thomas Aquinas speculates about the consequences of getting the words wrong either deliberately or by mistake. See Aquinas, 1989, Part 3, 60, 7–8.

[3] Aquinas maintains: 'The very notion of sacraments as signs requires words, since words have pride of place in our signifying: they can be formed in countless different ways to signify different mental ideas, and so can express much more distinctly what we are thinking about. To define the signification of sacraments more precisely, then, we need words as well as things: water by itself could be a sign of washing or cooling, but by saying *I baptize you* we show that in baptism we are using it to signify spiritual cleansing. Words and thing together make a unified sign in the sacraments, the thing providing a sort of material the meaning of which is formed and completed by words' (ibid., Part 3, 60, 6).

[4] 'The rites and practices of religion are modes of behaviour directed at transforming the will' (Barrett, 1978, p. 75).

[5] Read the account of Victorinus, an African intellectual who taught rhetoric in Rome in the time of Constantius, in Augustine's *Confessions* (1991, Bk. 8, 2, 4–5) and how he made public confession and received baptism.

is basically no fundamental agreement across the broad spectrum of the church on the nature or relevance of the sacraments as there would be, for example, on the importance of the practice of prayer. However, differences arise that relate to a) whether people should engage in any sacramental ritual practices whatsoever, but those who do, differ on b) the *range* of these practices and c) on what they *mean*. Thus, there are Christian communities, such as the Society of Friends (Quakers) and the Salvation Army, which are considered to be 'non-sacramental'. It is not the case that there are no rituals in these communities of any kind, but they do not share the rituals which are commonly called 'sacraments' in the wider Christian tradition. There are also major differences between the Protestant churches on the one hand and Roman Catholic and Orthodox churches on the other hand on the *number* of sacraments (two versus seven). Finally, there are differences of detail in what is done in the ritual and hence on what they supposedly signify.

Why do Christians bother with these actions?

The sacraments insofar as they are practised are not just 'empty' rituals. In other words, they are not just *actions simpliciter*; they are *intentionally meaningful actions*. They take the form of gestures, much like pointing with one's finger or shaking one's fist, which convey clear meanings even without words. Of course, without words, meanings are not always secure and the meanings of such gestures can be lost or become confused. When that happens, the actions may take on the appearance of being arbitrary and inconsequential. In the case of the sacraments, when this happens it is even possible to speak of the 'death of the sacraments' (Tillich, 1948, pp. 94–112).[6]

Tillich notes the rather ambiguous position that the sacraments have in Protestantism: for example, some Protestants went so far as to condemn the Mass (generally regarded as the most important Christian sacrament) as 'an accursed idolatry', and yet Martin Luther[7] personally held the sacraments in high regard. Tillich's anxiety about contemporary Protestantism is that in the modern world sacramental practices are under threat. He observes that: 'A complete disappearance of the sacramental element would lead to the disappearance of the cultus and, finally, to the dissolution of the visible church itself' (1957, p. 94). Thus, the whole existence of the institutional church is seen by him to depend on making sense of the sacraments and on their continuation as communal practices.

---

[6] Apart form the 'death of God', many things are reported to have died in the modern world: democracy, capitalism, communism, music and art. But as Hans Kung said about art, 'many artists ... live quite well on what they proclaim to be the "death of art", "the renunciation of art" and the "art of artlessness"' (Kung, 1981, p. 12).

[7] One of the major figures of the Protestant reformation in the sixteenth century.

How can we begin to make sense of sacramental actions?

To start making sense of the sacraments, one should see the role of ritual in human life more generally. No sense can be made of the specific character of the Christian sacraments unless one can first locate them within the wider proclivity of human beings for *ritual behaviour* and for what might be called the embodiment of knowledge. In oral cultures especially, knowledge is close to how life is lived – it is participatory. Learning takes place by *identifying with* human situations rather than by becoming 'objectively distanced' from them (Ong, 1982). In the modern world, possibly as a consequence of literacy and science, knowledge takes on a more abstract and a much less self-involving character, so the consequent attitude to ritual in contemporary society is somewhat ambiguous. Tillich's fear for the future of the institutionalisation of religion was fully justified.

A feature of the growing secularisation of society is that a general suspicion has arisen in our culture of any and all institutional and ritualised behaviour.[8] There is a degree of uneasiness about ritual behaviour for at least a couple of reasons: firstly, ritual tends to be rooted in habitual, repetitive behaviour, which gives it the appearance of being automatic, unthinking and uncreative. For a culture shaped by the Enlightenment, with its demand that everything should be rational, it is uncomfortable to be reminded that there are areas of human life which are not overtly rational but are governed by natural, affective responses. Suspicion of ritual behaviour deepens when we note that certain forms of insanity[9] are marked by repetitive behaviour. Secondly, ritual tends to be social and formal. In a culture that has become increasingly individualistic and informal, traditional ritual no longer appears to be at home in it.

Against these two points (in reverse order) it should be noted, firstly, that if our culture is more individualistic and informal, it could be the case that the rituals continue to thrive in our society in a different guise rather than that there are no rituals at all. It is not that difficult to observe in our individualistic world forms of habituated behaviour, behaviour to which one naturally inclines and to which one feels the need to conform. Think, for example, of how people behave at football matches or how people in Britain queue at bus stops and tills in shops. We believe that is how things should be done.

Secondly, to restrict rationality to what amounts to discursive discourse may itself be an impoverished view of rationality and understanding. Normally, rituals work because they are like gestures – *recognisable, physical actions that are loaded with meaning* – but the recognition of the meaning of gestures is in part dependent on their constant repetition. In this way, they become the fixed landmarks by which the surrounding world is held fast. Rituals, and the myths associated with them, are themselves ways of imposing a basic order and sense on a potentially

---

[8] One notes that in universities, ritual, such as graduation ceremonies, is alive and well.
[9] In *The Varieties of Religious Experience*, W. James noted a potential connection between religious genius and a psychological pathology (James, 1974, pp. 29ff.).

disordered world. Through them, a kind of understanding is forthcoming of which one could not otherwise avail oneself. The abnormality of the repetitive behaviour of the insane is itself an indication of a breakdown in habituated behaviour that in normal circumstances would lead to new ways of doing and living; instead, one gets stuck and one finds that like the needle that gets stuck in a groove of an old vinyl record, one can only go back to the beginning instead of carrying on. The more normal connection between ordered structures and creativity can be illustrated by any game. The same rules in chess will lead to an infinite variety of games and if it is the case that only the same moves were being made, then the game has clearly broken down. Rituals, like the rules of a game, should direct life in new ways for each individual in their own specific context.

Nevertheless, an unease about formal social rituals does exist in our society. Protestantism may be directly implicated in modern cultural trends with its suspicion of ritual. One can see from the very buildings used by Protestants how they have relegated the sacraments. Architecturally, many of the Reformed (that is, the Presbyterian and Calvinist churches of Hungary, the Netherlands, Scotland, Switzerland, etc.) Protestant churches reveal the subordinate role of the sacraments in their life by placing the spatial focus on the pulpit and the Bible, i.e. the emphasis in worship is on the reading, exposition and preaching of the 'Word'. It is then not surprising that religion becomes a matter of belief rather than practice. Having said this, Protestantism does attempt to re-introduce the sacraments theologically, and hence to maintain some sacramental practice, by speaking of the sacraments as the 'Word made visible'. This designation underscores the observation that the sacraments are not just actions but 'meaningful actions'.

How does one begin to identify the meaning of the sacraments?

The emphasis in Protestantism on the sacraments as the 'Word' made visible is an important key. The use of the 'Word' is not accidental because the 'Word' in the Christian theological tradition signifies the Divine Logos, the power that creates meaning, order and sense. Thus, the 'Word' is said to have 1) created the world, 2) provided the Torah, inspired the prophets and 3) become embodied or incarnate in Jesus Christ. In each case there is the sense of the Eternal that shows itself both rationally and at the same time concretely; the 'Word' shows itself 1) in the law-like ordering of the physical world, 2) in human words and laws, or 3) in the structured life of a human person. The sacraments therefore continue the supposition that a human relationship to the Eternal is both rational and importantly something constituted by, or comes to human beings through, the sensual, something that can be seen, heard, tasted, smelled and touched. They repudiate the view that religious life is essentially and solely in the realm of the mind as a set of abstract ideas. In principle, with the notion of the ubiquity of God, the Eternal, anything and everything might also become the vehicle for its manifestation.

That a relationship to the Eternal is mediated in this rather physical and concrete way becomes more comprehensible to us if we note that all deeper human relationships arise in precisely this way. Love expresses itself through, for example, a kiss, and by kissing we create and confirm a close relationship. A monarch's subjects manifest the authority of the monarch in the ritual of bowing to him or her. The physical action is redolent of meaning. This observation could mislead us into thinking that in reality the physical and concrete is the essence of the matter, i.e. that ritual is merely a matter of physicality. We may then try to explain it through the causal framework and thus to embrace a form of reductionism. To do this is to make a mistake.

It is the case that, philosophically, there are those who seek to 'explain' all human life as ultimately reducible to a function of the world as described by physics, chemistry et al. In their view, for example, thoughts are no more than electrical impulses of the brain, and love a gene survival strategy. There are, however, many others who challenge these reductionistic accounts and consider them to be profoundly misleading. Nevertheless, it is equally true that it is not generally thought possible for human beings to exist without also being a physical entity. In the context of discussions about eternal life, the observation about the intrinsic importance of the physical to the spiritual led some Christian theologians to insist that there must be a resurrection of (or something like) a body if there is to be any intelligible belief in a life after death – in other words, the survival of the mind or the soul of itself would not do. There is then the perception that in all aspects of human life, whether it has to do with the aesthetic, moral or religious life, there must be some relationship to the physical realm. Alternatively, one can express it the other way round; the physical has the power to become the bearer of aesthetic, moral and religious significance. This is an important discovery about our universe.

How can the physical world convey spiritual meaning?

The observation that phenomena in the physical world can come to have deeper meaning (for example, a moral meaning) is interpreted differently by various thinkers. Some take this meaning to be entirely *conventional* and thus contributed by human beings, while others see the deeper meaning as somehow necessary or inseparable from the physical reality. Consider some examples:

> Example 1: is a smile, meaning friendliness, a matter of convention or is it an integral part of the physical 'gesture'? One might come to think it is the latter, as it appears to be a gesture common to all human cultures. On the other hand, caretakers of primates have to be careful not to smile and show their teeth as that is taken to be a sign of aggression by other primates. One might conclude that a smile is a uniquely human gesture of friendship but is as natural to humans as tail-wagging is to dogs.

> Example 2: when a certain set of sound waves is not just a set of sound waves, but constitutes music and not a cacophony, is this because we

conventionally choose to regard it as music or is musicality an essential property of a set of sound waves? Evidence for the latter position may be found in the following: music in one key is conducive to cheering us up and in another key induces a mournful spirit. Alternatively, consider onomatopoeic words like 'bang!': the *sense* of the word appears to be given in its very nature as physical sound. Obviously, other words or sounds, such as 'table', have their meaning fixed solely by a linguistic tradition, i.e. the English language. These traditions are, of course, conventional and largely a matter of historical accident. One might nevertheless conclude that in the case of some things at least, there may be something compelling about the character of the physical features which endow these features with a deeper meaning that is by no means accidental. Admittedly, in other cases, the meaning of certain physical realities seems to be much more fluid and wholly dependant on human traditions and human determination.

The question that the foregoing reflections raise for us is as follows. Does the universe have an intrinsic sacramental meaning? In other words, is the universe normally capable of deeper meaning, one that is somehow an essential aspect of it and which we are bound to acknowledge, such as the beauty of a sunset? Or is the sacred something that human beings merely attribute to it? In other words, are sacred objects and sacred meanings of practices something that are assigned traditionally and conventionally to them by human beings? Perhaps this way of posing the problem is misleading. It suggests that *either* human beings are in control of the meaning *or* that the meaning might be discovered by dint of our investigations because it is somehow natural. The former leads one to say with Marx that 'man makes religion'. Human beings are the source, and are in control of, meaning for better or for worse. The latter position, that all religious perceptions and practices must be natural and therefore universal, undermines the distinctive contribution of any one form of religious life, for example, Muslim, Christian, etc.

Neither of these approaches will, I think, help us in understanding the sacraments or the significance of rituals and sacred objects. We need different categories; neither natural necessity nor human imposition or convention will do here. Theology draws on the category of grace and the transforming power of the Eternal. Whether the ritual action is meaningful then depends primarily on the activity of the Eternal Word. There is nothing automatic here; it is neither natural nor a human convention under human control. The real issue remains: is the Eternal disclosed in the action?

How can we be sure that a sacramental ritual is truly meaningful?

Can one be certain of meaning? With reference to the sacraments, there has always been a Protestant reaction to the Roman Catholic teaching of *ex opere operato*, i.e. through the action it is done, on the grounds that it suggests that it is mechanistic and automatic or alternatively conveys an element of the magical about it. Perhaps this Roman Catholic teaching expresses a religious confidence in the action and words and, as such, it is properly located in the faithfulness of God, with the implication that God always does His part if human beings do their part. These actions are 'means of grace' as promised by the God, and the God's promises may be trusted. To speak and argue like this is to show that we are in a realm here that is far removed from a mechanistic magic. On the other hand, the Protestant supposition that the sacraments are only 'means of grace' by virtue of the *faith* of the recipient does not seem right either. By making faith a condition of grace, it once again appears to place too much emphasis on human activity instead of on the meaning-endowing (creative) activity of the Eternal.

If the God is faithful, could sacraments ever lose their point?

Elsewhere in human life, rituals, like symbols, may grow and die. The reasons for this are always multi-factorial, both human and natural. There are two observations: a) simple repetition is not a guarantee of the vitality of ritual – in fact, some religious people turn to ritual and liturgy precisely at the point where religion as a vital force is spent and where their faith is in its death throes. The repetition and interest in the detail of what should be done takes on an air of desperation; b) as words depend on sound and the aesthetics of a picture depend on the oil paint, so physical actions are the effective medium of the *meaning* of rituals. The perception of the appropriateness of the physical to the meaning may well be due to conventional and natural factors. The connection between the physical and its meaning is essentially one of mutuality, if not a necessary relationship; love may lead to kissing and kissing may lead to love, but kissing can also be a form of betrayal, as in the case of Judas. The meaning is always open to dispute and can be betrayed. The key point remains that in these sacramental rituals the Christian tradition finds its relation to the Eternal and it is where this relationship is made a present reality. However, one may become deaf and blind to the Eternal by virtue of changes in our culture and in our physical world. And without the uncontrollable presence of the Eternal, the rituals will certainly become empty and meaningless.

In general terms Christian sacraments get their meaning from their association with the figure of Jesus Christ and the perception that the Eternal is present in him. If this perception is lost, then it follows that the sacraments will lose their power to convey the gift of the presence of the Eternal.

How many sacraments are there?

The *number* of rituals in human life is indefinite. If one asks how often or regularly one must repeat the actions, then there is no one, clear answer, other than to say as often as necessary to perform their function psychologically (individual and social) or as nature, culture, history or theology, etc. might demand. Of those rituals in Christianity which are deemed to convey the relationship to the Eternal, within Roman Catholicism and Orthodox Christianity the most significant of them are narrowed down to seven sacraments: 1) baptism, 2) confirmation or Chrismation, 3) The Eucharist, 4) penance, 5) unction (anointing with oil), 6) ordination and 7) marriage);[10] all other rituals become 'sacramental signs' (*sacramentalia*). Protestant Christianity restricts the essential sacraments to two – baptism and the Eucharist – because according to the Scriptures, only these two appear to have been instituted by Christ (as such, they are sometimes referred to as the 'Dominical' sacraments) and therefore only these two are reckoned to be required (note that the Eucharist is also referred to as the Mass, Communion and the Lord's Supper).

Why baptise?

A short answer might be because Christ commanded it. Though it is claimed that Christ instituted the rite of baptism, there is in fact no clear evidence that he actually did do so. The text often used as evidence, Matthew 28:19 ('Go ye therefore and make disciples of all the nations, baptizing them in the name of the Father and of the Son and of the Holy Spirit'), is in all likelihood a later Christian tradition and not to be ascribed to Christ himself.[11]

However, contrary to the supposition that Christ did not support the practice of baptism, D. M. Baillie (Baillie, 1957, pp. 76ff.) suggests four reasons why one should accept the sacrament as Dominical. Firstly, the New Testament throughout appears to regard baptism as uncontroversial, unlike, for example, Circumcision, which was at the heart of a dispute between St Paul and St Peter. This 'unquestioning unanimity', Baillie claims, suggests that the 'usage came from Jesus himself'. Secondly, the mission of John the Baptist was, as his name suggests, intimately associated with the rite. Jesus' own mission was closely connected with John's, as all the gospels show. Thirdly, Jesus was himself baptised by John in the river Jordan. Fourthly, Jesus refers to baptism at two key moments in his life and in that context his words appear to be more than passing metaphors (Mark 10:38; Luke 12:50), They intimately associate his baptism with his suffering and death, a connection which is repeated elsewhere in the New Testament. This should be enough to support its status as a practice within the Christian community. The close connection between Christ's baptism, suffering and death should also be borne in mind in trying to fathom its meaning.

---

[10] Thomas Aquinas writes: 'Our spiritual life resembles our bodily life in needing to be strengthened in us both as individuals and as members of the whole community in which we live as naturally social animals. Individually we are born [cf. baptism], we mature [cf. confirmation] and we must feed [cf. the Eucharist]; and since we also suffer disease and sin we need cure [cf. penitence] and recuperation [cf. last anointing]. In community as a whole, men share in government [cf. ordination] and engage in propagation of the species [cf. marriage]' (Aquinas, 1989, Part 3, 65, 1).

[11] If true, this would undermine the authoritative basis for the practice of baptism within Protestantism.

There are also other dimensions. Baptism is the ritual which effectively confirms the name of the child to the wider community. This sense of naming might follow from the scriptural view that God calls each one of us by name. In the end religious life is not only social but also intimate and personal, and directly appeals to an awareness of responsibility for what we are and do.

How is baptism done in the church?

The ritual of baptism is marked by considerable variation in the practice: Jesus himself appeared to have been baptised by immersion in the river Jordan and some churches to this day continue the practice of immersion;[12] others pour water from a jug over the head of the person to be baptised; still others sprinkle a little water with the fingers. Any judgment about whether this really matters may well hinge on what one takes its meaning to be. As suggested earlier, some theologians have emphasised the *actions* rather than the words as what really matters. One might then expect more uniformity of practice; however, it is also *symbolic* action and as such allows for some leeway. One notable feature about baptism as a symbolic action is that it is normally carried out only *once* in a lifetime, although during the Reformation there was one small group that diverged from this and who were known as Anabaptists (literally, re-baptisers).

But why use water and what does it mean? Water has three main associations: 1) *purity* – water is used for washing and cleansing; 2) *source of life* – it can make the deserts bloom, and without water one would quickly die; 3) *chaos and death* – water has no shape or form and can destroy as well as give life. In the dissolution of life we metaphorically pass over or through water according to many traditions; thus, we will cross over the river 'Jordan' or the river Styx (in Greek mythology) to 'the other side'.

1) Purity cannot simply refer to washing or cleansing, or we might otherwise wonder why there is such an insistence on its *once for all* character of baptism. The reference is to the purity of another life, a new beginning in the life of the spirit. In this sense baptism is an initiation ritual and so traditionally the baptismal font was at the west end of the church, i.e. at or near the entrance. Through it, one physically and metaphorically entered the church or community of faith and hence the spiritual life. 2) Its communication of the life of the spirit and its association with the Eternal leads it to be regarded as the source of true life and vitality – the 'living' water promised by Christ also echoes fresh, spring water that bubbles up in contrast to the stagnant water of ponds and cisterns. 3) Baptism was also seen as a dying of an old life and rising to a new life with Christ. Immersion in water signified a form of death; to come up from it was to come up into a new life.

Remembering that the sacraments in terms of their most general meaning are regarded as 'means of grace', we can find this illustrated in baptism because the

---

[12] R. L. Wilken claims: 'In the early church ... baptism was always by immersion, and one can see to this day the pools that were used' (Wilken, 2004, p. 59).

beginning of this new life is a gift that is mediated to the person through the symbolic action. However, in this description there is a certain ambiguity. What is the role of the individual and what is the role of the community with its clergy in all of this?

In taking the phrase 'means of grace' and by concentrating on the 'means', one can be led towards quite different interpretations and practices. Because it is believed that the individual must do something, for example, consciously have faith and profess it, the Baptist church insists on adult baptism only. And because it is believed that only by following the rules of a properly instituted community can the efficacy of the ritual be assured, it also follows that only the church[13] can give one access to grace. Both lead to a form of exclusivism on the one hand and to an element of Pelagianism – i.e. the ancient (so-called) heresy that salvation or the new life essentially comes through human effort – on the other hand.

By genuinely concentrating on the notion of 'grace', i.e. one where freedom and new life is always received as *a gift*, the element of human action and control fades into insignificance. For John Calvin, the life of the spirit was open to all, from the moment of conception (*ab ovum*), so for him the ritual action of baptism became a 'sign and seal' of what had *already* taken place (making infant baptism therefore appropriate). It is no longer a 'means' but a form of recognition. It is inclusive but, problematically, also apparently makes human beings into the *passive* recipients of a destiny already determined for them from eternity.

If baptism is truly a means of grace, then it is because of what the ritual communicates to human beings; if through its association with Christ it communicates the sense of the Eternal in the love of God, then it has succeeded – but not because human beings have made it so. Whether sacraments work or do not work is in the power of the Eternal and of what Christ has done, but human beings can destroy institutions and symbols through the life they live and through the culture that they create. Fortunately, there are limits to human destructive power (see Graham Greene's novel *The Power and the Glory*).

Why the Eucharist? And what does it mean?

Again the short answer is that Christ supposedly commanded it. Unlike baptism, there is more evidence that Christ instituted the Eucharist. The rite imitates the *actions* of Christ the night that he was betrayed when he took bread and wine, blessed it, broke it, poured it, shared it and said 'this do in remembrance of me' (see Matthew 26:26ff.; Mark 14:22ff.; Luke 22:17ff.; 1 Corinthians 11:10 and 23ff.). In this sense it is clearly a re-enacted drama that Christ himself began.

Over the centuries attention has been paid by some traditions to ensure the Eucharist's aesthetic appeal so that it is a colourful spectacle and by this means intend to do justice to its deepest meaning – that here we encounter the Eternal,

---

[13] This of course can lead to institutional abuse, because this supposed control leads to a bid for power and its misuse.

reconciled to all things worldly. Others prefer a simpler, more understated repetition of an action more fit to recollect the actions of a man who was by all accounts poor.

Theologically, the Christian sacraments are essentially only meaningful actions because of the 'Word' or sense that is revealed in them. The emphasis is therefore on their being instituted by Christ or their recalling of the manifestation of the Eternal in Christ. It relates Christians to that life and to that community which lives from the Eternal, as shown in the life known as 'Jesus Christ'. As such, there are theological discussions about the *real presence* of Christ in the Eucharist or whether Christ is only present symbolically. For Calvinists, the Eucharist is fundamentally an act of remembrance. For Roman Catholics, Christ is really and substantially there in the bread and wine.

Chapter 5

Human Beings

Why are human beings a topic for theology?

It may be said that the God (the Eternal) is the real object or the business of theology, not human beings. But the topics 'God' and 'human beings' are inextricably linked.[1] All knowledge with which we are familiar is human knowledge. It was a *human* interest in the Eternal that created religious activity, so we have in effect been thinking a good deal already about human beings. A man is what he does, so religious life is a part of what human beings are, perhaps something hard-wired through our genes.

So far we have tried to analyse the practices that are characteristically religious and have reflected on the kinds of puzzles and confusions that they generate, all in the light of the peculiar interest that creates religious life and all done in order to gain a better view of faith and the sacred – what it is or could be. Now we should look at the subject or the agent of that religious life. How does this characteristically religious interest and how do the religious practices affect human self-understanding?

We have already implicitly touched on some features of human self-understanding:

a. In the face of our *finitude* it was believed that a sense of eternity can remove the fear of death and provide consolation (from the discussion on immortality)
b. On the supposition of a human tendency towards being *self-enclosed* and self-serving, we noted that the key religious practices are intended to encourage a serious openness and responsiveness in human beings towards other things, other people and, additionally, being transparent to what is foundationally Other (from the discussions about worship and prayer).
c. A religious self-understanding challenges a false sense of *human ultimacy*, with its presumption that 'man is the measure of everything'. Everything

---

[1] See L. Feuerbach's comment in *Principles of the Philosophy of the Future,* #2 (1986), where he attributes this to Protestantism: 'The religious or practical form of this humanisation was Protestantism. The God who is man, the human God, namely, Christ – only this is the God of Protestantism. Protestantism is no longer concerned, as Catholicism is, about what God is in himself, but about what he is for man; it has, therefore, no longer a speculative or contemplative tendency, as is the case in Catholicism. It is no longer theology; it is essentially Christology, that is, religious anthropology.'

in this spatio-temporal realm within a religious perspective is declared to be penultimate and can be radically questioned. As a consequence, nothing in this realm (including the self of the human being) can function as the final reference point and serve as an absolute within the life of the religious person (from discussions about worship). When things in the spatio-temporal realm are treated as ultimate, they become idols.

d. On the other hand, for a religious human being everything in this spatio-temporal realm has the potential to become the bearer of a deeper meaning or may point beyond itself to what is eternal or to what is qualitatively different from the spatio-temporal realm (from the discussions about the sacraments).

We have in effect been making some important claims about human beings and their life. Can we be more systematic and can these peculiar claims about human beings be fully justified?

Is theology well placed to help us in the quest for human self-understanding?

In the previous discussions in this book, theology was operating very much within its own proper sphere, viz. the religious sphere, asking questions about the nature and meaning of a particular religious practice. Now turning specifically to 'human beings', the topic up for discussion is much more obviously a matter of common property; other disciplines have made human beings a subject for disciplined and systematic study. Anthropology, psychology, sociology, biology, genetics and others – all offer considered views of what human beings are. And if it is not enough for theology to be challenged by the perspectives of the human and social sciences, even the ordinary person on the street has views about what it means to be human that must somehow be taken into account and addressed. One can compare the situation to schooling. The teacher may regard it as his or her professional domain, but because everyone in this day and age is, or has been, a part of the schooling process, everyone also has a view of what schooling is or ought to be. Similarly, everyone has a stake in being human and so everyone has a more or less considered view of what it means to be human. In short, the topic 'human beings' is one in which the theologian jostles with others to be heard, and he or she frequently has to rely on the insights and contributions of others. In many respects the theologian is the amateur where others are professionals. Nevertheless, the theologian has a distinctive voice and a distinctive contribution to make, but it is not a contribution which goes unchallenged, particularly when it ventures beyond its own remit.

What are the problems for a specifically theological account?

The main challenges to the religious view of human beings are relatively modern – i.e. they come from post-Enlightenment thinking, though some have ancient roots.

The most essential challenge maintains that human beings can be wholly understood without reference to transcendence; indeed, it questions whether the transcendent should enter the discourse at all. Religion is discussed as a part of human efforts to understand themselves, and these religious efforts may prove to be distorting or even thought to be pathological (both Marx and Freud believed religion to have this kind of impact. Richard Dawkins offers a more recent example). As such, religious people are taken to be psychologically dysfunctional and, from the point of view of the functioning of society, religions are seen as obstacles or as forces resistant to change and thus as socially harmful, and furthermore religious people are seen to be subversive of intellectual life by short-circuiting rationally accepted processes of establishing claims to knowledge and understanding.

The consequence of such challenges is that theologians have had to be both more systematic and defensive, and perhaps more modest in their thinking and claims about human beings.

It is important to note that theological thinking about human beings is not just an accidental fact, as if it were a topic theologians might equally well ignore in culturally more friendly times or drop in the face of the first signs of hostility. Truly, to think about the God is to think about human beings; to think about the humanity of human beings is to think about the God. The ancients recognised this link, hence Xenophanes (b. c. 570 BC) made the observation that we are prone to make the gods in our own image and if we are to change or to change our society, we have to change our gods as well.

'Homer and Hesiod have ascribed to the gods all things that are a shame and a disgrace among mortals, stealing and adulteries and deceiving of another' (fr. 11). And this he held was due to the representation of the gods in human form. Men make gods in their own image; those of the Ethiopians are black and snub-nosed, those of the Thracians have blue eyes and red hair (fr. 16). If horses or oxen or lions had hands and could produce works of art, they too would represent the gods after their own fashion (fr. 15). All that must be swept away, along with the tales of Titans and Giants, those 'figments of an earlier day' (fr. 1) if social life is to be reformed.[2]

The link between understanding the God and understanding human beings has become increasingly evident during the last couple of centuries. The German theologian W. Pannenberg describes the theological developments as the 'anthropologisation of theology'. It characterises a form of thinking which begins (roughly) with the nineteenth century precisely because since that period theologians have been unable to do any theology without relating it to anthropological (in its theological sense of thinking about human beings) discussions. Generally speaking, the emergence of other disciplines and sciences could easily have been ignored by theologians, bar the implications these disciplines have, or appear to have, for human self-understanding. These implications, the spoken and unspoken claims about human beings, are frequently the focal point of the dispute between

---

[2] The Internet Encyclopaedia of Philosophy.

them – if there is a dispute. Thus, Copernicus' proposal for a heliocentric universe, Galileo's confirmation of it and Darwin's evolutionary theory might all have been ignored by theology. Theologians could have treated all these 'discoveries' as a bit of tinkering with the *Weltbild* (world-picture) people had of the world in which they lived. But the intellectual discoveries of the sciences could never be left as mere modelling of how the world is or works. Scientific theories can easily be seen to affect the *Weltanschauung* (world-view), i.e. the view people had of themselves and their relationship to the world in which they lived. It is this anthropological import of science that has a significant bearing on theological thinking.

In the past, especially in the classical world, such as that of Plato, it had simply been taken for granted that human beings were eternal souls with an eternal origin and destiny. Human beings stood in a hierarchical relationship to other creatures and objects in the world, thinking of themselves with their self-consciousness as the pinnacle of creation, and of their action or inaction as that which determined not only their own fate but also the very meaning of the universe itself. In this classical picture each person was a bearer of that meaning in the universe, each was, so to speak, a microcosm of the macrocosm.

The religious presumption of an intimate connection between the sense of human life and the meaning of the physical universe would ensure that the growth in scientific discoveries and the development of scientific thinking led to an inevitable tension with religious perceptions. The scientific picture that entailed a decentring of the earth from the universe in the fifteennth century foreshadowed a dethronement of mankind from its lofty pinnacle, unveiling the perceived high status of human beings as a form of self-aggrandisement. Later, human kinship with the animal world in evolutionary theory reinforced that dethronement, appearing to require a much more modest valuation of human beings, even though human beings continued to regard themselves as the culmination of a process that took aeons. (The latter position is a rather odd vestige of previous assumptions about the high status of human beings, since evolutionary theory does not of itself imply any judgments of the relative value of the species that survive[3] from one age to the next or about the species that temporarily dominate.) More recent discussions, such as those of Desmond Morris' *The Naked Ape*, Richard Dawkins' *The Selfish Gene* or John Gray's *Straw Dogs*, all give polemical accounts that seek fundamentally to exclude religious aspirations or religious accounts of human beings, and with them any remaining vestiges of human hubris.

The animal origins of human beings, or the genetic make-up of human beings, are scientifically seen to account for the entirety of human behaviour in a manner that would appear to make the religious account redundant. Or, in the case of Gray, the teleological (purposive) thinking that pervades the religious thought world is

---

[3] Dawkins is inclined to call a gene good because it is one that survives or persists, but why should we think that survival endows moral value?

'shown' on scientific grounds to be an illusion[4] of which human beings might best rid themselves.

The insights these accounts and explanations provide should not be dismissed lightly, since they are often illuminating. The main problem is that the subversion of human hubris, which in itself might have been welcomed by the theologian,[5] seems to go hand-in-hand with the suspicion that the scientific accounts and practices also in important respects dehumanise and undermine the dignity of human beings. Furthermore, the scientific accounts tend to be reductionist. This, as mentioned earlier, is a problem for theology, since there is no easy way to counter reductionistic explanations other than to say that all reductionistic claims unnecessarily exclude insights from other disciplines. Perhaps the theologian might take the line of a recent Booker Prize winner, Yann Martell, in his book *The Life of Pi* (which purports, fictionally speaking, to provide an unanswerable proof for God) and say that the religious story is simply a 'better' story than the more mundane one (the more so since it was the imaginative story that enabled Pi in the book to survive, with the implication that the religious story enables human beings to survive with their humanity intact). In resisting the reductionism or in preferring the 'better' and more imaginative story, theology seeks to preserve the 'humanity' of human beings.[6] At the core of the theological analysis is the observation that this 'humanity' of human beings is dependent on the relationship of human beings to the Eternal as the source of creative possibilities and freedom.

What are the key elements of the Christian account about human beings?

The Christian religious story is largely dominated by two biblical texts.

Psalm 8
Psalm 8:4–8 reads (in the King James version):

> What is man that Thou art mindful of him? And the son of man, that Thou visitest him? For Thou hast made him a little lower than the angels, and hast

---

[4] This claim is made contra other 'enlightenment thinkers', such as Immanuel Kant, who regarded the teleological character of the world an *a priori* intuition in his *Critique of Judgment* (2005).

[5] It has led to some re-reading of the Scriptures, in which the corporeality of human beings was stressed, Adam being made from the dust, the stuff of physical being. Human beings are first and foremost flesh and blood.

[6] Wittgenstein remarked in 1914: 'When we hear a Chinese, we are inclined to take his speech for an inarticulate gurgle. Someone who understands Chinese will recognise *language* in it. So I often cannot recognise a *human being* in a human being' (translation of *Vermischte Bemerkungen*, p. 11, cited by Bolton, 1979, p. 37). So it is that the nature of theology and its language is designed fundamentally to help the reader recognise the humanity in human beings.

crowned him with glory and honour. Thou madest him to have dominion over the works of Thy hands; Thou hast put all things under his feet: All sheep and oxen, yea, the beasts of the field; the fowl of the air, and the fish of the sea, and whatsoever passeth through the paths of the sea.

The creation narratives of Genesis

In a similar vein, the Genesis creation narratives depict human beings as being created on the sixth day, the same day as the other animals, thus locating them in that sphere of life. Yet they, unlike the other animals, were created in the image and likeness of God. The creation of human beings is declared to be good, indeed very good; human beings are given dominion over the animals and in the cool of the evening Adam, the paradigmatic man, walks (or communes) with the Divine.

Religiously, human beings are the in-between creatures who metaphorically have one foot on earth (they are flesh and blood, dust) and one foot in heaven; in other words, human beings have a status in their relationship to animals (dominion) and to the Divine (communion or friendship).

What do these religious narratives mean theologically?

Most traditional theological discussions have focused on the *imago dei*.[7] That is to say, most theological discussions explore the sense in which human beings may be thought to be decisively different[8] from the other animals, mainly in a manner that might manifest the Divine or the sense in which human beings relate to the Eternal as an integral part of their nature. When theologians do this to the exclusion of the other side of human beings – their relation to the physical and animal world – they really introduce a fundamental distortion. This other, secular dimension of the story should not be neglected, that is, it must show how human beings relate to animals and the physical world. An excuse for neglecting this aspect might be that the physicality or bodily nature of human beings is all too obvious; however, by neglecting it, theological accounts become one-sided in a way that the original religious narratives were not and, indeed, in the way the early church struggles were not, when, for example, the church sought to reject 'Gnosticism' together with its spiritualising tendencies. Instead, the church was inclined to treat physical nature as both real and valued, yet also as a constraint on our spiritual ambitions. According to the Gnostics, the physical was something from which one was to be liberated – *soma sema*, they declared – 'the body is a tomb', as if our physical nature was of no account and disposable; worse, that it was an obstacle. This view was rejected by the early church. In his *Animal Theology* and other writings,

---

[7] This is described by one theologian as 'that useful but dangerous concept, the image of God' (Gunton, 2002, p. 40).

[8] Mary Midgley in *Beast and Man* (1980) challenges the sense of this question, for how human beings differ or how they resemble other animals depends very much on the animal.

Andrew Linzey has provided an interesting antidote to the neglect of the animal nature of human beings in modern theology.

One notes that a failure to acknowledge human kinship with animals often leads to an exploitative relationship with them and to gross distortions of human nature and of human obligations.[9] In this respect Linzey's writings, and the secular equivalents of, for example, Desmond Morris, provide a long overdue balance in the exploration of human nature.

Do theological descriptions of human beings really matter?

The descriptions provided by the different disciplines inevitably imply evaluative judgments. It has often been presumed that to see a human kinship with animals or to see that human beings are physical beings is indirectly to *devalue* the human. The presumption could explain the fierceness of the resistance to the evolutionary theory of Darwin. On Darwin's views, it was believed that human beings were regarded as just another primate, and since monkeys were not rated very highly, neither could human beings. If in the end human beings are little more than dust and ashes, then it would seem that humans are not worth much. On the other hand, instead of devaluing human beings as a result of seeing their kinship with animals, one might as easily *revalue* the physical world and the animal kingdom. In other words, one could begin to see more clearly the *intrinsic worth* of the physical world and of animal life in it. The sheer complexity of the physical world and its biodiversity is truly awesome and, at the same time, fragile and precious.

The dethronement of human beings can teach us to appreciate and respect our physical habitat more. A logical consequence is that cruelty to animals and the carelessly destructive exploitation of the natural world can no longer be tolerated. Whether this also leads to vegetarianism, as it does for Linzey, is less clear. A reason for this is that the kinship to animals should not blind us to the presence of significant differences. For example, human language clearly has its roots in animal communication, but the difference in complexity is telling. The difference in the degree of complexity in 'language' eventually leads us to see a difference in kind (Lorenz, 1952). Likewise, we must not be so impressed with the work of geneticists, which purports to show human beings to be very similar to pigs genetically, that we fail to notice that these small genetic differences also make us very different – they are what set human beings apart. One cannot but conclude that in view of the differences, to understand human beings fully, different categories are needed.

No matter what all the similarities to animals may tell us about human beings, it does not exclude the possibility of additional categories that may be necessary

---

[9] In *The Inner Life*, Fénélon states: 'Free and intelligent creatures are his as much as those which are otherwise. He refers every unintelligent thing totally and absolutely to Himself, and He desires that his intelligent creatures should voluntarily make the same disposition of themselves' (ch. 3).

to appreciate human beings more completely for what they are. For example, human life is subject to moral categories in a way that animals are not. We do not normally hold animals to account, despite records which show that in the Middle Ages human beings, for example, tried a pig for a purported 'crime' (murder) and of which the pig was then found guilty and duly punished by hanging. (If this sounds strange and medieval, I knew a farmer in the late twentieth century who *hanged* his two dogs for savaging and killing some of his sheep. This was not a case of putting the animals down but of executing them.) Normally, animals such as dogs, which savage humans or harm some human interest, for example, a flock of sheep, are simply but 'humanely' put down today rather than tried in a court. We do not judge animals morally; however, in contrast to them, human beings *are* subject to moral evaluation.

In addition to the moral category that is applied exclusively to human beings, one may need yet other additional categories, one of which may be the 'spiritual'. Human beings have a capacity for the infinite or the Eternal, or, to express it in more religious terms, they are the objects of gratuitous love offered by the Eternal. And people may become conscious of this love and respond to it.

Within twentieth-century Christian theology the possibility of the 'spiritual' was explored by reference to the *imago Dei* (the image of God). This concept was distinctly ambiguous. Reinhold Niebuhr (Niebuhr, 1941) suggested that this *imago Dei* in human beings only existed in a distorted form. A fundamental tension is created between what human beings actually are and what they ought to be. If human beings do possess an *imago Dei,* they do so only problematically. Emil Brunner also echoed this ambiguity (Brunner, 1947) and tried to explain this with the academic distinction between form and matter,[10] and to claim that the *form* of the *imago Dei* exists in human beings but not its *substance* (matter). However, this claim does not really make sense, since a 'matterless form' or 'formless substance' are meaningless in practice and could have no actual application. Karl Barth, on the other hand, claimed more consistently that the *imago Dei* was utterly destroyed. The upshot of this theological claim is that human beings are not *naturally* different from animals. The difference that happens to exist is created by the Divine itself, by its otherworldliness, rather than by some natural attribute of human beings. With the *imago Dei* destroyed, Barth could only conclude that any reflection that is *exclusively* about human nature (i.e. without any reflection on the impact of the Eternal on human life) cannot be theologically significant.

The basic problem with these particular theological discussions is that theologians are sometimes misled by their own terminology. They treat the *imago Dei*, as they once mishandled the concept of the soul, as if a soul was something

---

[10] A distinction which goes back to the ancient Greeks, who had what is called a 'hylomorphic' universe – one made up of form and matter.

substantial, even tangible and weighable[11] – it is a 'reification'[12] which is best put to one side. If the biblical imagery of an image or likeness to the Divine is to be taken seriously, it must refer to a possibility or capacity for a relationship to the Eternal. To unpack this possibility within the Christian tradition is to explore, *inter alia*, a) concepts of covenant, human freedom, responsibility and duty, b) concepts of finitude, death and eternal life, and c) concepts of guilt and forgiveness.

To understand human beings as the sciences do is to examine human beings as part of the causal nexus. However, to the extent to which they are a part of this nexus, human beings are not considered to be free – not even if we introduce the idea of the accidental into the narrative, since accidental events are not freely chosen ones. This is in part the implication of what St Augustine meant when he insisted that simply doing what we want is not freedom, since we are driven or caused to do what we do by our needs and wants. We are in effect enslaved to our physical nature, to which we in the twenty-first century could add, and also enslaved to our psychological and social natures.

The eternal quality in human beings, i.e. that quality of not solely being a spatio-temporal reality, is the real source of freedom. As such, it may appear to be elusive and unrealisable. Perhaps it can be approached through another story, that is, the story of the prodigal son, which can be read as a parable of the human soul. Human beings have the inheritance of the physical world, which is enjoyed to the full. Once filled, it fails to satisfy. In the face of this, the prodigal son 'comes to himself', at which point he begins his journey back to where the Father has been looking out for him all the while. 'To come to oneself' is what Kierkegaard calls a reduplication; it is a form of self-awareness that by way of the recognition of another self or selves ultimately leads to an awareness of being before the God (the abyss of the Eternal) in which all things become possible. Theologically, it is faith in this reality, the faith of a self in relation to the God, which sets us free.

From this position Kierkegaard raised the possibility of an eternal happiness, i.e. a fulfilment that comes from one's relation to the Eternal and a happiness, which is not dependent on how life goes in the world. For him this was always a personal and individual matter, but looked at in this way, it seems one-sided or incorrect. If a relation with the Eternal and its associated happiness is what liberates human beings to enjoy freedom and be at home in the world, it must also be an at home *with others*. The outstanding question is whether humans can be free only as lonely individuals before the Eternal or whether it is always with others and with the world. There must be, so to speak, an ecology of liberation. It is in this thought that we must come to grips with 1) the concept of the church, the people of God (or in Muslim terms, the Ummah, and in Jewish terms, the people of Israel) and 2) a deeper understanding of the natural world.

---

[11] Some people have actually tried to weigh the body immediately prior to death and immediately after death to ascertain the weight of the soul and to prove its existence!!

[12] I.e., as if the abstract is a thing.

An important question is whether this eternal happiness is a possibility for *all* human beings or only for a few. Vis-à-vis the Eternal, is there some advantage in being rich? Intelligent? Tall? Old? Male? White? Western? Educated? Attractive? Privileged? If there is no advantage in any of these, so that in the religious life with its intrinsic freedom one might equally well be poor, simple-minded, short, young, female, hermaphrodite, green, non-Western, uneducated, repulsive and under-privileged, what would this say about understanding human beings under the religious category? This is no longer familiar territory since we are both prone and used to judging all people in the world's way, i.e. in precisely those terms which distinguish us over against others, in which some people are higher and better than others. In opposition to this worldly or secular understanding, there is a fundamental equality within a religious understanding of human beings that one cannot find elsewhere (see Kierkegaard, 1938, entry 1089). How can we, or should we, take this equality for granted?

Chapter 6
Living Well

Socrates: 'I learned it [the healing charm] when I was away on an expedition with the army from one of Zalmoxis' Thracian doctors, the ones who are said to be able to give men immortality ... He said all things, both good and bad, in the body and in the whole man, originated in the soul and spread from there, just as they did from the head to the eyes. One ought then to treat the soul first and foremost, if the head and the rest of the body were to be well. He said the soul was treated with certain charms, my dear Charmides, and that these charms were beautiful words. As a result of such words self-control came into being in souls'. (Plato, 1987)

What are we?

Speculation about what human beings *are* can obscure the fact that human beings can also be defined by what they *do*. In other words, we can begin to understand human beings not by looking at them as objects with a somewhat peculiar nature, different from other animals, but by inspecting their activity.

The focus on activity immediately brings us back to a fundamental issue raised earlier, i.e. should we seek to understand human beings as part of some mechanistic causal nexus or as 'free' agents (or both)? These two ways of thinking about human behaviour and action are deemed by many to be incompatible;[1] either that, or we are confused and not sure how they are related.[2] In trying to be

---

[1] It is this very incompatibility which is viewed by S. Weil as the energy of life. Thus, she observes: 'The essential contradiction in human life is that man, with a straining after good constituting his entire being, is at the same time subject in his entire being, both in mind and in flesh, to a blind force, to a necessity completely indifferent to good.'

From the quite different perspective of gaining a better view of science and which genuinely has a bearing on the good for human beings, M. Midgley complains that some views of science (perhaps including the one held by Weil here) have 'distorted and divided our imaginations by seeming to cut science off from the rest of thought, leaving us with two disconnected cultures – all simplicity being on the scientific side and all complexity on the humanistic one' (1992, p. 36). In decrying the divide, she effectively admits its prevalence in our society.

[2] Note how K. Popper connects them: 'But is it not possible to control the human factor by *science* – the opposite of whim? No doubt, biology and psychology can solve or will soon be able to solve, the "problem of transforming man". Yet those who attempt to do this are bound to destroy the objectivity of science, and so science itself, since these are both based upon free competition of thought; that is, upon freedom' (Popper, 1961, p. 158f.).

consistent, we are often inclined to refer to the one and to ignore the other.[3] So, there are some who see human beings as wholly determined causally speaking, for example, by their genes and environment (such as Dawkins). There are others who see human beings as quintessentially free spirits, temporarily, if somewhat inconveniently, imprisoned in a body.

The truth is we cannot, in fact, avoid seeing human beings both 1) as part of the predictable world order of cause and effect and, at the same time, 2) we must acknowledge the character of our life as something that hinges on deliberation and free,[4] purposive action. The latter aspect raises, *inter alia*, questions of responsibility and with it the possibilities of praise and blame, of reward and punishment, and of hope and grace. If we did try to ignore these features of our life and contend that everything is reducible to a deterministic account, as some philosophers with a zealous logic have attempted to do, then our whole world would have to change. Education, the legal system, the entertainment industry, the creative arts, perhaps even the world of business with its system of incentives and 'compensation packages' – *all* would have to change. Alternatively, we would begin to evaluate all these human activities differently. The reason is that every one of these activities, in some respect, hinges on an axiomatic recognition that human beings are 'self-conscious agents', 'deliberative', 'responsible', 'accountable' and 'free'. Without the acknowledgement of freedom, education becomes conditioning, the legal system a charade, the creative arts no longer creative but some inevitable or accidental production and, in the world of business, ideas of motivation and confidence would be replaced by more behaviouristic versions of a stimulus and response mechanism. Economic theories which eliminate concepts of trust and confidence will look very different from those which recognise these concepts as integral to understanding the functioning of economic life.

If human beings are fundamentally free to live as they choose to do, what is the next most important question?

Once the freedom of human beings is granted, then the urgent question that follows ineluctably is: what is it to live well? What, through our choosing, have we become? Can we become? From this process of becoming, the past and the future become important considerations. The past can come to exist for us as something

---

[3] Aquinas, 1989, Part 1, 75, 1: 'We turn now to man, a creature who is neither pure spirit nor pure body, but has a nature compounded of both. The theologian considers man's nature primarily from the point of view of his soul.'

[4] Existentialism maintained that with respect to human beings 'existence precedes essence' (Sartre, 1958), that is to say, *that* a person is comes before *what* he or she is. This is supposed to mean that whereas with animals their nature (the what) is a given and determines what they do, human beings can choose what it is they want to do and hence choose their nature. However, even existentialists acknowledged the 'facticities' of life, those things which limit what we can do.

to be undone, a guilt from which we must be freed; on the other hand, with an eye to the future, what through our choosing are we becoming? The future beckons, but can we rely on human beings to choose well? Scientific endeavours may augur a healthier, longer, better life, but they may at the same time augur an Orwellian nightmare.

What is it to live well?

One basic answer is to say that to live well is to live in a decided but orderly way. The well-ordered life[5] is one that forms character constituted by certain desirable qualities (virtues) or is governed by certain recognisable principles and rules.

Does everyone agree that the good life is the well-ordered life?

There are some who disagree – for instance, anarchists. They resist the notion of ordering life with rules. They claim that we are never more alive and free than when we live spontaneously and, as it were, live without rules. Another way of expressing the anarchist position is to hold that we show our humanity most in an indifference to rules. However, in a genuinely rebellious existence, the determined breaking of rules implicitly acknowledges the existence of these self-same rules and their intrinsic claim to regulate action and behaviour. We take it that it is part of the meaning of freedom that we possess the power to determine (where we do have a choice) whether or not we shall conform to those rules which are perceived to direct or to bind us in some way.

But perhaps we are being misled by the word 'spontaneous'. To live spontaneously does not necessarily mean that we live chaotically.[6] Spontaneity indicates that human actions are self-generated and not coerced behaviour. Spontaneity locates the source of action in a living self rather than in the demands of others or of an Other. In brief, an anarchist interest in spontaneity does not seem to require the elimination of rules as such; rebellion against rules implicitly acknowledges the power of these self-same rules to occasion the reaction. It appears they dislike the *nature* of the rules and how the rules govern them. They do so largely, but not exclusively, on the grounds that it is others (or an Other) who

---

[5] 'This is what I want to say. That by which humans are ranked above the animals, whatever it is, be it more correctly called "mind" or "spirit" or both – we find both terms in Scripture – if it dominates and commands the rest of what a human consists in, then that human being is completely in order' (Augustine, 2010, p. 15). Fénélon in *The Inner Life* stated: 'There are blessings, however, of a purer and higher order than these; a well-ordered life is better than life; virtue is of a higher price than health; uprightness of heart and the love of God are as far above temporal goods as the heavens are above the earth' (ch. 2).

[6] Augustine's exhortation 'Love God and do as you please' does not mean the anomic or lawless life. To do as one pleases is to be governed by what it means to love God. It paradoxically affirms a freedom yet 'binds' it by its location within the sphere of love.

issue the rules. In the dispute with anarchists, the critical issues are mainly *whose* rules are they and *which* rules, not rules or no rules.

Apart from the desire to safeguard spontaneity, another reason that anarchists may have for their rejection of rules is that rules only work where there is uniformity. They may protest that every human being and life is, or should be, unique. Anarchists may indeed have a serious point when they impress on us the uniqueness of a) every person and b) every situation. This individuality and singularity may limit the application of rules (Fletcher, 1966). Rules implicitly trade on the existence of likenesses and similarities between human beings and the different situations of their lives, so that the rules can be said to apply to them. In contrast, to emphasise differences is to undermine the *relevance* of the rule(s).

It may be possible to meet the anarchic objection based on the uniqueness of every individual by admitting that there will always be differences. But one might counter this with the fact that not all differences are *significant* (we insist, for example, that all are equally bound by the laws of society whether we are rich or poor – wealth, for example, is not a significant difference before the law). Whether or not differences are significant may not be decidable in any final or objective way, but within society there are processes of coming to an acceptable agreement. In the more important situations, disputes are settled in courts of law. Even then, some may wish to challenge the judgment. A religious person in such a case might appeal to a 'higher court' before an omniscient judge from whom nothing is hidden and who administers an eternal law and applies the rules knowing all the relevant details.

The possibility of divine judgment has raised some interesting speculations. Can one appeal against a 'divine' judgment? Is a 'divine' judge bound by rules or can he decide arbitrarily what is good? The theological response has been that the God, unlike a human judge, is not bound by rules but by His or Her nature,[7] namely Goodness itself. It is possible that human beings in the image of God are religiously speaking not ultimately judged for conforming, or failing to conform, to rules, but are judged on what we *are* and on our *relationship* to the Eternal (and unequivocally) Good.

---

[7] Consider here Plato's discussion in the *Euthyphro*, in which he poses the dilemma: is the God good because He conforms to the moral law or is something good because God wills it? The latter hints that goodness could be arbitrary, in that God might have willed otherwise and chosen an evil. However, God only freely wills what is in accordance with his nature, which is Goodness itself, and since God is omnipotent, He or She will always will the good. This resolution is important if the end result is not to believe that there is something more ultimate than God viz. the moral law which constrains the Divine. In Plato's dialogue the issue ends in *aporia*, i.e. it is unresolved.

If there are rules, whose rules rule?

Since the Enlightenment, the critical issue has often been the ownership of the rules. Are we ruled by the self,[8] i.e. are we autonomous,[9] or are the rules of life constructed and imposed by others, i.e. heteronomous? If it is the latter, we are deemed by many thinkers to occupy the position of children or, worse, that of slaves, and in their view, by accepting the rules of others, we are forced either into being less than human or not yet being fully human (in a state of immaturity). True humanity, it is said, lies in the exercise of our freedom and hence being *self*-ruled, 'coming of age' and being 'mature'. Such a view led to a powerful objection to belief in God; God is perceived as the Other who imposes the rules of life on us and thus reduces us to the status of children. To be fully human is to reject God. To grow up is to become an atheist!

To avoid the conclusion of atheism, Paul Tillich (1886–1965) proposed that we were not faced with a choice between autonomy and heteronomy but with a third possibility, viz. theonomy (Tillich, 1953, vol. 1, pp. 92ff.). Autonomy for him was never just the 'freedom of the individual to be a law unto himself' (ibid., p. 93) but to conform to the law of reason.[10] The latter is both subjective and objective, both personal and universal. Reason is, however, constrained by the heteronomous, by something that leads reason to 'grasp and shape reality' in a particular way, something that Tillich ultimately regards as intrinsic to the very nature of reason itself as its structure and ground – it is that which gives reason its 'depth'.[11] 'Theonomy', he says, 'does not mean the acceptance of a divine law imposed on reason by the highest authority; it means autonomous reason united with its own depth.' 'God', he says, 'is the law for both the structure and the ground of reason, they are united in him, and their unity is manifest in a theonomous situation.' By this analysis of reason and by describing the 'self-ruled' individual as conforming

---

[8] Some people consider this withdrawal into the lonely self as a form 'violence'. Thus, G. Rose summarises Levinas' position: 'On the other hand, autonomy, ego, "investiture" of freedom, belong to the violence of self-reference, constituted by withdrawal from the face to face, withdrawal from radical openness to the Other, from the primordial command "Thou shalt not kill"' (Rose, 1993, p. 16).

[9] Rose writes: 'The will is autonomous or moral when it is utterly disinterested and obeys the law out of sheer reverence for it; it is heteronomous or legal when it obeys the law out of interested motives, such as fear of punishment or hope of reward, whether material or spiritual' (ibid., p. 27).

[10] Reverence for the law of reason is strictly speaking an act of autonomy but not an act of self-assertion, as in some modern conceptions where autonomy appear to be little more than unaccountable acts of self-assertion. From this modern conception, a reverence for the law is seen to be a form of heteronomy. However, reason constrains but does not coerce a person who reveres it and its rules, just as love does not destroy a person's freedom but gives a character to that freedom.

[11] There may be a connection in such thinking to the reasoning in the ontological argument that in the purity of thought there is a conformity with reality.

to reason, Tillich attempts to avoid the shallowness of individuals just acting according to whim, or as a result of whatever they happened to think best at the moment (a shallow version of autonomy), or alternatively as conforming to some alien power (a blatant form of heteronomy).

Tillich was a child of the Enlightenment, in which Reason was quite naturally both the judge and restraint on wilful existence. Despite his attempt to contain the anarchic potential of autonomy through the appeal to reason, the picture of everyone acting as he or she thinks best does capture the mood of the modern situation. Each person acting according to his or her own inner light (reason) might be a tolerable account for a modern-day 'Robinson Crusoe'. But what happens to our world when another, for example, 'Friday', enters the frame? Others might exercise their freedom to our disadvantage and readily become a threat. The existence of others sets a limit to our freedom,[12] notably, their freedom. The sheer presence of others is certainly one source of heteronomy; rules are supposedly devised to enable us to live together.

By suggesting, as Hobbes did in the seventeenth century in his book *Leviathan*, that without political organisation and law there would be 'No arts; no letters; no society; and which is worst of all, continued fear and danger of violent death; and the life of man, solitary, poor, nasty, brutish, short', it becomes clear that pure self-interest drives us to enter into an arrangement with others. Rules are adopted on the basis of an implicit contract with others. The fact that they are adopted *contractually* is supposed to mitigate the oppressive nature of the rules somewhat. If it is a *contract*, then one cannot claim that it was imposed. This is not unlike schools making an effort to encourage pupils to *own* the rules of behaviour in school. The pupils can then be said to *freely* adopt the existing school rules for their own interest. But the freedom here is very circumscribed; if anyone comes to think the terms of the agreement are unfair, it is not so easy to change or to opt out of the contract. In any case, the making of a social contract is sheer fiction or possibly a useful 'myth'; we are born into an existing society rather than establishing one afresh on the basis of a new contract with every new adult.

In the nineteenth century E. Durkheim saw that societies could regard the pre-existence and authority of many essential social rules as sufficient reason for attributing them to God. For him religious belief was a useful social fiction, but this ought not to obscure the recurring need for social change and an acknowledgement of the conventionality of the rules. The observation of the conventional nature of social rules puts the power for change into human hands, whereas one cannot alter divine law. But if social rules are conventional, who has the authority to institute change? Is it a matter of violence by means of self-assertion, an oligarchy, the power of the majority, some universal reason? Plato suggested in *The Republic* that in the ideal society philosopher-kings would rule.[13] This idea does point to

---

[12] Hence Sartre's complaint, 'Hell is other people'.

[13] Cynically, one might say that it is not surprising that a philosopher should suggest that philosophers should rule!

considerations other than the sheer possession of power as the basis for directing life. The philosopher-kings are supposed to be the only ones who could be truly *dis*interested and rule by the vision of the truth, the good and the beautiful. Generally, the only possibility for those without power in society is to be able to call upon an order higher than society either to legitimise or to challenge the practices in society. Surprisingly, the powerful, too, often seek to legitimise their rule not by an appeal to their power and capacity for violence but to another, different, higher authority.

In a democratic society it may be judged that the abstraction of 'the will of the people' could serve as the sole basis for this higher authority. But we know that democratic societies can also oppress.[14] They can act unjustly toward minorities,[15] which is especially easy if that minority happens to be a minority of one.[16] In such a case, a democratic society too must be held to account, but to whom or what? It is possible that a single individual, a poet or a prophet, for example, could present a higher vision of life than currently known, practised and accepted in such a democratic society. The ever-present possibility of a higher good opens the way to the discourse of a divine or eternal law as one possible option.

What could the divine law be? How is it recognised? What if people disagree?

One possible answer, or part of an answer, is *natural law*. In the debate about homosexuality, much is made of the fact that homosexuality may be innate, determined by genes, and that the animal world too exhibits homosexual practices. It may therefore be said to be 'according to nature'. One could test this by pressing this further with examples of other socially less defensible practices, such as incest and paedophilia. These things are done within the natural world. However, the fact that this is so will not make it morally right or wrong. The truth is that natural law is not terribly useful in differentiating what ought, or ought not, to be done. One could even say that everything that it is possible to do is according to natural law and what it is not possible to do is clearly against natural law. This demonstrates that on this basis 'natural law' cannot direct us at all in terms of how to live well. The reason is that this particular definition of natural law does not differentiate between living well and living badly; it only identifies what it is possible to do. It is of course plainly possible to live badly in the world.

It may be possible to refine the definition of natural law. Let us say: one begins by accepting that many people live badly and that the world, as we know it, hosts many evils. One, in brief, affirms that we live in a 'disordered' world. But then one can go on to assert that it is nevertheless a world in which *reason* is able to discern *an implicit order*, as, for example, scientists normally do. The claim is

---

[14] This was Plato's experience.

[15] This was the experience of Jews through the ages, culminating in the Holocaust. We cannot forget that the Nazis were first elected to power.

[16] John 11:50; 18:14.

that if we think aright we can supposedly discern an underlying or intended order, i.e. the divine law in nature. The supposition is that all right-thinking people will agree. Reason can decide ... Is that the case? There may be agreement on a limited number of basic moral platitudes, yet there may also be serious differences amongst rational people, for instance, about the moral case for abortion or birth control. One is also reminded that highly educated, intelligent people were implicated in the Holocaust. Clearly, a capacity to think and reason is not enough to agree on the good and on what the 'natural law' in this new sense might be.

Even if the human capacity to think does not suffice to determine how we can live well, it is at least necessary to reflect rationally. Our reason must be deployed in the sphere of moral and religious life if we are not to become the victims of the moment or of whim. The interesting question at this point is how does a religious view of life relate to a more general ethical (rational) enquiry? Perhaps Kant's investigations suggest part of the answer. For example, the use of reason has an important role, but his principle of universalisability is purely formal. It guides us in what it means to *reason* in the moral sphere, but it does not provide us with any specific moral content or direction. It has always been human history, with its unique circumstances and singular individuals, that has produced the *substantive* visions of the good. It is these visions, communicated through texts and practices, that have the power to inspire us to embrace ideals and to confront us with an ultimate authority, *but only as we judge them to be so*. They are not of our own making but we embrace them for ourselves. They are Other, yet accord with our reason. In this sense they are heteronomous yet belong within the sphere of *our* autonomous judgment.

The emphasis is on *our* judgment. They are never private whims but they should be universalisable and therefore they must be tested and challenged by others by means of some tough Socratic questioning. Here, democracy is a powerful means of saving us from our delusions, provided everyone is heard, especially the poor and the oppressed.[17] Experiences of exclusion can provide us with eyes to see whether the principle of universalisability is being applied. Thus, the poor and the oppressed can remind us of privileges enjoyed, privileges which have within them the power to distort what we believe to be just. We must never forget that there is a difference between what we would *like* to be the case and what *ought* to be the case, between what we would prefer to will and what the God commands.

What considerations might distort our moral judgment?

Religion has sometimes been criticised for distorting moral life by introducing considerations of reward and punishment, which are perceived to be external to the moral life itself. Thus, it may be thought that religious people are only committed to doing good because they fear the punishment of hell or seek the

---

[17] Essential to any Judeo-Christian confession is the demand to remember that once we were enslaved; mythically, the God brought us up out of Egypt.

reward of heaven. The truly moral life, it is claimed, is the life that values the good for its own sake.

This is not the full picture. Augustine, for example, wrote:

> In vain, however, does anyone think himself to have gained the victory over sin, if, through nothing but fear of punishment, he refrains from sin; because, although the outward action to which an evil desire prompts him is not performed, the evil desire itself within the man is an enemy unsubdued. And who is found innocent in God's sight who is willing to do the sin which is forbidden if you only remove the punishment which is feared? ... He, then, is an enemy to righteousness who refrains from sin only through fear of punishment; but he will become the friend of righteousness if through love of it he sin not, for then he will be really afraid to sin. For the man who only fears the flames of hell is afraid not of sinning, but of being burned; but the man who hates sin as much as he hates hell is afraid to sin. This is the 'fear of the Lord,' which 'is pure, enduring forever.' For the fear of punishment has torment, and is not in love; and love, when it is perfect, casts it out.[18]

---

[18] Augustine's letter to Anastasius, 412–413 AD (Schaff, 1979, p. 496). For similar sentiments, see *Theologia Germanica* (Blamires, 2003, ch. 10), where the late medieval author from Frankfurt sees the essence of religious life to be wholly absorbed by the Eternal Good, which involves a decentring from the self to the point where one could not even claim the desire for the Good as one's own. The consequent state of disinterestedness renders one indifferent to reward and punishment. As he describes such people he states: 'Moreover, these men are in a state of such freedom, that they have lost the fear of punishment, or hell, and the hope of reward, or heaven; nay they live in pure submission and obedience to the Eternal Good, in love freely given and intensely felt ... For a true lover loves God, or the Eternal Good, alike in having and in not having, in sweetness and in bitterness, in joy and sorrow; for he seeks alone the glory of God and of that which is God's, and he seeks it neither in spiritual nor natural things, and therefore he stands alike unshaken in all things, at all seasons' (pp. 130f.). See also ch. 38, pp. 180f., where love excludes considerations of reward and becomes indifferent to the so-called problem of evil. 'But a true lover is offended neither by toil nor time nor suffering. Therefore it is written: "To serve God and to live in Him, is easy to him who does it." Truly it is so, to him who does it out of love. But it is hard and wearisome to him who does it for reward. It is the same with all virtue and good works, and likewise with order, law, obligation, and the like. But God rejoices more over one true lover than over a thousand hirelings or mercenaries.' Meister Eckhart states the same sentiments when he states: 'The just man does not seek for anything with his works, for those who seek something with their works are servants and hirelings, or those who work for a Why or a Wherefore' (1963, p. 49). There are good religious grounds for thinking that virtue is its own reward.

Nothing expresses more clearly in a religious context the internal relationship between virtue and its consequences. Virtue is its own reward,[19] loss of virtue its own punishment.

So what could living well mean for the religious person?

In submitting to the moral law, or to the demand of the God, we are not left unchanged. Firstly, from one perspective we are no longer wholly the master of our own life, in that we conform to an eternal law that is not of our own making.[20] From another perspective it is precisely a case of full mastery of the self[21] when, through obedience to divine law, we realise our ideal self. Secondly, insofar as we do choose and practice to live according to our vision, we may begin to habituate the appropriate forms of life. Habits are essentially dispositions to act; together they constitute our character. The ideal end-product is to become a *magnanimous* self, literally 'large-souled', large in the sense of embodying all the key virtues and eliminating the narrowing, key vices.

What are the key virtues?

Fundamentally, as Thomas Aquinas states (1989, Part 2, 56, 3): 'Virtues are dispositions to act well.' There are many virtues, but he sees that virtues are also interdependent and interrelated, that they constitute the web of one's character. In this web he identifies four key virtues (or cardinal virtues) on which the others hinge. He also distinguishes between *moral* virtues and *theological* virtues. The moral virtues are those that dispose us to act well in relation to naturally attainable goals and grounded in reason. He states: '*Prudence* perfects reason itself and is the source of goodness in the other moral virtues; *justice* perfecting the will, is preferred to *courage*, perfecting our capacity for aggressive emotion, and courage

---

[19] This is sometimes expressed in terms of 'delight'; thus, Augustine states that 'hence we agree that someone is happy when he takes delight in his own good will, and on account of it he attributes little worth to anything else that is called good but can be lost even when the will to retain it remains'. In other words, a good will can never be denied its own intrinsic satisfaction compared to those goods which are extrinsic to it and ultimately not under its control. Extrinsic goods, such as riches, honours, pleasures and physical beauty, are ultimately insecure. We can lose them despite our will to have them.

[20] Despite this feature of the moral law, Aquinas recognised the importance of 'autonomy'. He notes (1989, Part 2, 57, 5): 'Living well is not only doing good things but doing them well, choosing them in a right way and not simply acting on impulse or emotion … Doing something good on another's advice rather than one's own judgment is not yet perfect activity of one's own reasoning and desiring. One does the good but not altogether well, as living well requires.'

[21] A purity of heart is that which is motivated *solely* by the good will, i.e. 'a will by which we seek to live rightly and honourably, and to attain the highest wisdom' (Augustine, 2010, p. 21).

is preferred to *moderation*, perfecting our affective powers.' In short, he sees human beings as thinking, willing, emotional and feeling persons; each aspect has its place in the virtuous life.[22] But they should be ordered in a hierarchical way in which human reason predominates. Each aspect of the person generates or demands its own particular virtue (strength): reason – prudence or wisdom; the will – justice; the emotions – courage; and the affections – moderation.

Much of what Aquinas has to say about the moral virtues is derived from Aristotle's reflection on ethics. The Christian contribution is seen by him to complement this general ethical thinking and also to transform it, that is to say, the cardinal virtues are transformed or perfected through their interconnection with the theological virtues. Essentially the religious life has a more ultimate, or 'supernatural', goal than does the moral life. And in this context the virtues, which are related to that ultimate goal, can only be instilled by the Divine; in other words, these virtues rely on the divine initiative, on grace. The key theological virtue he identifies is love – in this Aquinas concurs with Augustine, who said that true virtue is to love *proportionately*, thus: 'Virtue is the love with which that which ought to be loved is loved.'[23] However, love cannot exist without faith and hope, which relate one to the God; on the other hand, faith and hope would not be virtues but for the presence of love.

A clear picture emerges in the thought of Aquinas of the ideal Christian person, notably one who acts in a principled way and who seeks to embody various virtues, which mostly hinge on prudence, justice, courage and temperance but which are transformed by the theological virtues of Love, Faith and Hope. Considerations occasioned by the theological virtues suggest that there is a vision of life which goes beyond the alternative posed by the anarchist and the moralist. The anarchist looked for spontaneity and the freedom of the self from the constraints set by others, while the moralist looked to duty and rationally endorsed rules. But are these the only alternatives? The anarchist appears too self-absorbed to be truly attractive. The moralist's obsession with the rules will strike many as lacking warmth and as too insensitive to the idiosyncrasies of human life. Moreover, both may ultimately be grounded in a form of violence or at least in a form of self-assertion.

By placing love at the apex of human virtues there is a transformation of the virtues determined by reason alone. Love is a passion driven not by self-interest but by the well-being of the other. The other may well be a class or group of people, but more normally it is directed towards an individual or particular being, cherishing the other for all his or her individuality and idiosyncrasies. In the Christian tradition this kind of love is made possible or initiated in the first instance by the self-giving, gratuitous love of the Eternal. Unless one has the confidence that one is loved in the heart of one's own being, it is difficult to love the other

---

[22] Just imagine a person who thinks clearly about others but who feels nothing for them! Is such a person genuinely human and genuinely virtuous?

[23] Augustine's letter to St Jerome, 415 AD (Schaff, 1979, p. 537).

human being purely for his or her own sake. Love incorporates spontaneity for the sake of the other; love does not behave chaotically but neither is it rule-bound. It transcends rules to serve the well-being of the other.

Chapter 7
Sin

How do we achieve the important goal which, according to the religious life, is to live well?

It may be that the fully good life is to have learned to love (the right 'object')[1] deeply. But the process of *learning to live well* also requires the cultivation of a degree of self-consciousness that comes through self-examination[2] and, through this, to know oneself in the context of the world, acquiring understanding and recognising shortcomings and failings, developing one's sensitivities or feelings and being committed to living in an ordered and purposeful way.

If a guiding interest within this overall agenda of living well is the cultivation of a relation to the Eternal (the One: Good, True, Beautiful, Love), what rules (if any) should we follow and what kind of character should we strive to acquire? And how does one achieve[3] that ultimate state of affairs in which we are in fact related to the Eternal?

A reflection on following set rules led us earlier to consider the notion of 'natural law', its appeal and its weaknesses. It is clear that we need a deeper appreciation of rules and how they come to be recognised by us as authoritative and binding. In addition, the reflection on character led to a consideration of the virtues (strengths) that need to be nurtured and habituated. Virtues are in effect the cultivation of specified dispositions to act that may bring about the qualitative relationships to others, to oneself and the Eternal[4] that collectively were thought to be at the core of

---

[1] In the Judeo-Christian tradition this is the summary of the Torah: to love the Eternal, to love neighbour, to love self.

[2] The tradition of reflective self-examination is a key part of nearly every religious tradition; classic expressions are to be found in Augustine's *Confessions* (1991) or Tolstoy's *A Confession* (Tolstoy, 1987).

[3] One asks this with the reservation and knowledge that it may not be all under our control. For example, a loving relationship with another depends on the love freely offered by the other. It cannot be coerced. The relationship to God may similarly not be under human control. The best we offer is attentiveness, or a 'waiting on God' (Weil, 1959).

[4] We may need reminding that sin is not just the opposite of virtue but relates to the character of our relationship to the Eternal; virtue is a derivative quality from this relationship. S. Kierkegaard wrote, for example: 'But too often it has been overlooked that the opposite of sin is not *virtue*, not by any manner of means. This is in part a pagan view

living well. At this point it is also clear that we need to reflect deeply on the nature of human freedom and human will, since we do not seem to realise our goal fully in this life. And ultimately we shall need to reflect on 'grace', in other words, that which facilitates the art of living.

What is perceived to be the main obstacle to living well?

A dose of reality normally forces us to admit that we do not live the ideal life with any steadfast confidence, either individually or collectively;[5] an element of disorder appears to confront us at every point. In particular, from a religious point of view, one loses sight of the Eternal and with that loss there are dislocations of priorities and ambitions, confusions about ends and means, misperceptions about what is intrinsically valuable and what is only contingently valuable or that we love disproportionately.[6] With such dislocations and confusions we may lose our sense of gratitude and live instead with resentment or in the grip of other vices.

What is the nature of the disorder that catapults us wholly into the temporal, that prioritises the momentary and ephemeral. And to what is this disorder to be attributed (what is its source)? What is to be done about it? In short, what stands in the way of living well?[7]

What can be done about a disorder depends on its nature, on how deep and extensive it is. One can be either *optimistic* or *pessimistic* about the situation.

One might think that all it takes is a bit more attention, knowledge and self-discipline to bring about a meaningful, ordered life and character. Thinking and believing a relatively easy cure exists (for what is easier than giving a little attention to whatever it is that is so vital to our life?) is the optimism of many; on the other hand, thinking and believing that in reality there is little we can do – 'the poor will always be with us', there will always be 'wars and rumours of war', one can never really know the good, etc. – is the pessimistic option embraced by

---

which is not content with a merely human measure, and properly does not know what *sin* is, that all sin is before God. No, *the opposite of sin is faith*, as is affirmed in Romans 14:23, "Whatsoever is not of faith is sin". And for the whole of Christianity it is one of the most decisive definitions that opposite of sin is not virtue but faith' (Kierkegaard, 1980, p. 82). On the other hand, one might also add that there can be no faith without virtue.

[5] Contra Feuerbach, human ideals and perfections are not somehow realised in the species – for example, human beings are not collectively 'omniscient' simply by pooling our individual finite knowledge.

[6] Thus, for Augustine, sin is the failure to love proportionately: see Chapter 6.

[7] 'Religion is rooted in the human response to evil' (Byrne, 1998, p. 92).

others. If optimism seems facile and too easy,[8] pessimism is debilitating (Rhees, 1997, p. 279) ('what can I do?' syndrome).

Apart from seeing this as a religious problem (i.e. as something to do with the human relation to the Eternal), what other analyses are available to us in the secular sphere?

There are not many people who happily believe that this is the best of all possible worlds. If there are any, they must be the true pessimists, given the evil and suffering with which we are continually confronted. The tension between the world as it might be, or ought to be, and the world as it is leads nearly everyone to hope for something better and to consider what might be wrong with the world and what is to be done about it.

Obviously there is a logical connection between the diagnosis of the problem and the prescription that would heal or overcome it. Perhaps we should hesitate at this point, for possibly in formulating the issue in just this way is to make a challengeable supposition. The implicit assumption in the question is that the problem is due to *one* single cause. It is, of course, possible that the cause of our suffering is multi-factorial; we are not troubled by one problem but by a combination of many problems. In such a case we might reasonably suppose that there is not just *one* prescription or, if there is only one, then that it is a prescription that must address all of the problems individually. Perhaps in a complex world we should adopt a strategy of isolating the problems one by one, for then we might be able to resolve the disorder piecemeal.

There have indeed been many different diagnoses of the human condition, some of which may be complementary, whilst others are clearly incompatible with one another. Some of the most notable analyses contending for attention in the modern world have been provided by Marx (*Das Kapital*), Nietzsche (*The Genealogy of Morals*), Freud (*Civilization and its Discontents*) and socio-biologists of various kinds. One interesting example is K. Lorenz (Lorenz, 1966), who suggests that the essential human problem is an uncontrolled aggression. He notes that most animals have an inbuilt mechanism to control intra-special aggression (aggression against their own kind):[9] dogs and other animals have a submission gesture that normally 'turns off' the aggression of the stronger; animals seldom fight to the death! Unfortunately, the history of human evolution[10] in Lorenz's judgment has

---

[8] Look at the classic *Candide* by Voltaire, in which he parodies this easy optimism through the character of Dr Pangloss, who persists in confessing that this is the best of all possible worlds whilst undergoing just about every conceivable evil.

[9] But note C. Taylor's comment: 'The roots of respect for life and integrity do seem to go as deep as this, and to be connected perhaps with the almost universal tendency among other animals to stop short of killing conspecifics' (Taylor, 1989, p. 5). This suggests that human beings are not totally debilitated as regards other people.

[10] In the eyes of some, such as J. J. Rousseau, it is human culture which is the culprit.

greatly weakened this mechanism in human beings, so from time to time amongst human beings we see this intra-special aggression of which the extreme example is genocide, the outbreak of mass slaughter of human beings by human beings. In this context the prescription he recommends is that we build up the weakened control mechanisms in a rational way, for example, through the institution of the United Nations.[11] One can see that Lorenz has a point.[12] But we may not see this account as the only or final solution, simply because his diagnosis of the problem does not appear to be comprehensive enough. Is physical aggression the only or most fundamental problem in human life? What about psychological aggression? One might even suggest that indifference towards others, ignoring others, is equally problematical. The problems that confront us are surely more than physical aggression and are not solely reducible to it.

Another analysis is provided and discussed by Nietzsche in *The Birth of Tragedy*. He notes that the myth of Prometheus, like the Genesis myth, attempts to identify the fundamental problem of human existence. Prometheus stole fire from the gods and as a consequence he was tied to the rock and daily a vulture came to eat part of his liver, which (as it happens) also grew back daily. In essence the story hints that there is perpetual suffering that is a consequence of the human aspiration to knowledge and technology. For Nietzsche the solution is not to give up on human aspirations but to accept our suffering and to endure it willingly, because in this lies human glory.

One could continue with other accounts giving further and more detailed analyses of human disorders. The religious position is *not* that they are not relevant but that they never go deep enough by failing to see the disorders in connection with the relation to the Eternal. To the religious mind, this is perceived to be more fundamental.

What precisely is the Christian analysis of disorder in human life and in our world?

The Christian analysis of human and worldly disorder attempts to recognise both its manifest plural nature and at the same time seeks to root this diversity of problems in a common source. The latter can be briefly stated as *human alienation from the Eternal* or, to put it in more traditional terms, 'sin'. We simply cannot live well without a recognition of, and an acknowledgement of, our dependence on the Eternal in life. That is the underlying condition which is the source of human despair. In contrast, the many different human actions which follow from this single underlying condition and the associated forms of alienated life with its manifold related problems are simply (if somewhat confusingly) called 'sins'; the latter are, for example, the general and individual moral failures one encounters everywhere.

---

[11] Before the last Iraq war, many protested at the weakening of the United Nations in part because of the increased risk of further wars.

[12] Particularly in a world in which the military plays a dominant role, possibly threatening the whole of the human race with nuclear annihilation.

Particular sins, which happen to be expressed on specific occasions and in specific settings, are products of despair. This Christian position invites some important observations: firstly, it is fundamentally a *human* problem; secondly, it is a feature that characterises *all* of us in every age, both collectively (i.e. its universality and hence the reference to original sin) and individually; thirdly, it is nevertheless not intrinsic to human nature as such, and hence it is curable.

Let us consider the implication of these features. The observation that the problem is fundamentally *human* is grounds for optimism. It had been suggested by Augustine's Manichean opponents, for example, that the world is governed by two warring principles, Good and Evil. From this viewpoint, the disorder is attributable to an unresolved conflict between two supernatural principles in which human beings are effectively caught up. There is little to be done but endure the consequences, so it is an essentially pessimistic doctrine. Similarly, when it is suggested that the disorder[13] is attributable to an original chaos,[14] to a primordial matter that is resistant to the creative energies of a Demiurge[15] or attributed simply to being physical and to our finitude,[16] in each and every case there is little to be done but to suffer and endure. In short, the problem admits no human resolution.

On the other hand, Augustine faced another opponent, Pelagius, who believed that the resolution of human disorder was very much in human hands. With Augustine, Pelagius held that the disorder was neither alien (supernatural) nor an intrinsic part of human nature,[17] and hence human beings could potentially undo the evil themselves and attain the highest good. For him it was all a matter of *will*, about having sufficient self-discipline and determination. It is an optimistic creed shared by most modern-day liberals. The liberal view holds that with good paradigms, education, sufficient knowledge and technology, such problems as human beings encounter in life can be resolved. All we need to do is to apply a) our minds, b) human resources and c) sufficient will-power, and the disorder will be brought under control. So, for example: are there parents and carers who abuse their children? Then we need more effective social services to supervise such parents and carers. Does it appear that human beings are about to run out of sufficient energy? Then with further research we can develop nuclear power. Does it appear that human beings will run out of sufficient food to feed everyone? Then through genetic modification of plants and animals we can increase production.

It is only when we recognise that these 'solutions' harbour within them yet more challenging problems that our confidence is shaken (bureaucracies can dehumanise and undermine human responsibility, nuclear power can be used in destructive bombs and genetic modifications of plants may do incalculable environmental

---

[13] It is not difficult to think of modern counterparts to these ancient views.
[14] Genesis 1:2.
[15] Something that fashions the world – see Plato.
[16] See Gnostic teaching.
[17] One must distinguish between 'created man' who was declared to be good and 'fallen man' at this point.

damage – or so it is supposed). The application of mind or ingenuity, of the will, of human sympathies may indeed all be necessary, but on their own they do not appear to suffice. The optimistic belief in a steady, evolutionary progress has been shattered, once and for all, by sundry events of the twentieth century. The traditional Christian conclusion has been that the solution of our disordered existence is paradoxically neither entirely beyond the reach of humans nor entirely within their control. Human effort is necessary but not sufficient.

So, if everyone is part and parcel of the dire situation in which human beings find themselves, who is really responsible?

This is known as the paradox of the universality of sin and responsibility for sin in Christian theology.

Augustine's basic position was that creation is fundamentally good and that human beings are fundamentally good. This basic affirmation is why, despite evidence to the contrary in Scripture,[18] he insisted that the world was created *ex nihilo* (from nothing) and being derived only from God, there can be nothing but good in creation. Metaphysically, evil was seen by him to be a *privatio boni* (an absence of good). But his optimism in this regard is tempered when he also attempted to recognise the intractability of the problem facing us and thus to recognise the 'gravity of sin' in the human condition. There is simply no easy resolution for the challenge posed by evil and human sin. In part, this is due to a human solidarity in sin; we are all collectively involved. In part, the intractability is due to a) human habit and b) to the fact that it is not possible to undo the past, to turn the clock back on those occasions when the consequences of our actions become all too evident. Moreover, evil and our fundamental orientation towards the temporal has c) a logic and d) a dynamic of its own. Overall, our temporal orientation renders us anxious and leads us into an inordinate desire for security.

Augustine finds an authoritative basis for his view in Scripture, for example, when he insists on human solidarity in sin. Paul stated in Romans 3:23: 'For all have sinned and come short of the glory of God.' This cannot be an empirical statement. Paul did not check the credentials of everyone and discovered that every person he happened to encounter was weighed and found wanting,[19] nor is it a social scientific generalisation based on a significant sample. It is a *dogmatic statement*, or at least a working principle. It is taken to be a warranted assumption given the evident ubiquity (the omnipresence) of evil and the far-reaching nature of human problems. Augustine found further support for it in the story of the fall in Genesis, where Adam, as the representative man, implicates us all. As his descendants, Adam transmitted his alienation from the Eternal onto us and, according to Augustine, does so through the process of procreation. Of course,

---

[18] Genesis 1:2.
[19] Daniel 5:27.

a modern perspective, forged by historical biblical criticism, cannot accept this account at its face value as history (it may not even have been so for Augustine either). At best, its explanatory power is grounded in its *mythological* nature. Thus, we are left with the question of what could the narrative mean for us?

The central claim is that human beings are inextricably interdependent. We are not isolated monads. We are what we are by virtue of the society and culture to which we belong. Through each of our actions we confirm our collective condition and consolidate it for the future. Our ancestors have made us what we are and our descendents show us what we were. This means that as human beings there is a collective responsibility for the condition in which we live. It also means that if the situation is to be turned round, a single individual benefiting himself or herself alone[20] cannot do it. One might try to make a fresh start by living as a hermit, or as a select, isolated community (such as the Amish or the Hutterites in North America), but this only serves to focus attention on the underlying problem. The basic human failure is a failure to wait upon the Other. For Augustine, this was a failure of a proper love.

The failure is at its root a failure to look beyond the horizons of our spatio-temporal world, a failure to attend to what beckons from beyond the self, a lack of openness. This is manifested narratively as disobedience, choosing what is lower in preference to what is higher. There is an implicit hierarchy in our loves. For Augustine, all human attempts to engage in creative love inevitably, sooner or later, end in being self-serving or self-interested. This is reckoned to be the case whether we think of the individual person or of collective groups of human beings.[21] Only through a more radical love, grounded ultimately in a love of the other-worldly, the Eternal, does the self avoid this inward curving in upon itself (*curvatus a se* was Augustine's classic definition of sin), this self-enclosing existence. Some modern theologians echo Augustine (for example, Pannenberg) by stressing the basic attribute of 'openness' as being definitive of a flourishing human life, but it must be a radical openness. The 'unlimited openness [of human beings] to the world results only from his destiny beyond the world ... What the environment is

---

[20] This is an important observation for those evangelicals who believe that salvation is essentially an option for those individuals who convert. This is being denied here. There is no salvation unless it is salvation for *all*.

[21] 'It is not success that makes good genes. It is good genes that make success, and nothing an individual does during its lifetime has any effect whatever upon its genes' (Dawkins, 1995, p. 3). Here Dawkins offers a deterministic creed. He also makes clear that survival is his overriding value. However, he ought to acknowledge that nothing whatsoever will survive in the end – all will fail. His position is in that sense an essentially pessimistic creed. It is also pessimistic in another sense, namely, an individual can do little about his or her genes. Dawkins' standards appear to be quantitative; success biologically is to survive as long as possible and perhaps in as many forms as possible. But might life not be valued qualitatively rather than quantitatively? The singular and unique life in all its brevity might be valued above others. If so, the reference to the 'good' gene is entirely irrelevant.

for animals, God is for man. God is the goal in which alone his striving can find rest and his destiny fulfilled' (Pannenberg, 1972, pp. 12–13).

So where does responsibility lie for the human condition?

The Augustinian Christian position is fundamentally problematical. A twofold problem emerges from its account: firstly, whence is evil?; and, secondly, how can we be responsible for this solidarity in sin? We did not initiate it. And if this solidarity in sin has us in its grip, how can we be blamed if we cannot avoid it – if, in other words, we are not free to do otherwise? Augustine was quite clear that responsibility for the human condition lay with human beings. He located it in the conative faculty, i.e. in the human will. In contrast to Augustine, Plato saw it as a cognitive issue; thus, through the mouthpiece of Socrates, he thought that no man would do evil *knowingly*. Evil ultimately harms the soul, the essential human self, and who, he asks, is so foolish as to deliberately set out to harm himself? So, he concluded, human beings commit evils because they do not fully understand or know what they are doing. For Plato, ignorance was *the* problem.

Augustine, however, tells a story from his youth in his *Confessions* (1991, Bk. 2, IV, 9) to contradict Plato's position (whom he normally follows). In the story Augustine recalls how he set out to steal some pears from an orchard. He admits that he knew it was wrong but that he did it anyway. He did not even do it out of need; he hardly tasted them and most of the pears were thrown to the pigs. He observed that he enjoyed stealing and the more so because *he knew* it was wrong! He told this autobiographical story primarily to illustrate the point that it was not *knowledge* but a *perverse will* that was the real source of human sin.

Suppose Augustine's account is accepted. What makes us responsible if we cannot help but sin? We know that we cannot be blamed if we shoot someone dead when another person forced our finger on the trigger. But is blame the same as guilt? Part of the answer may be that there are different degrees of responsibility. The fact remains, whether we like it or not, that in one way or another, we live from, and contribute to, the human order that is the source of injustice. It is this that leads to the sense of guilt. The fact that suffering comes through our hands, even if we did not commit the evil knowingly and willingly, does not make us, in our own eyes, any less guilty.[22] This thinking of being in solidarity with others makes us all, for example, guilty for what was done in our name in Iraq or Afghanistan. (Even if we thought that Saddam Hussein was wicked and we had a moral duty to intervene, that in some way it was the right thing to do, we still feel guilt for the suffering taking place now or that once took place at the hands of soldiers who represent us in the theatres of war.) Perhaps we are less responsible for what has happened and is happening in places like Iraq if we have actively worked and protested against war, yet so long as we are a part of this society, it is also in an

---

[22] Williams (1981) considers the position of someone who accidentally kills a child with his car. He is not blamed but nevertheless suffers from guilt.

important respect *our* action. Augustine could therefore write his book *The City of God* as a book about social solidarities. He essentially depicted a society driven by two very different forms of solidarity: one driven by love of the world (essentially a closed, self-serving form of life) and the other by a love of the Eternal (i.e. a radical openness or a cultivation of those things which are not judged on how things go). The two contrasting loves exist side-by-side, one leading to catastrophe and the other providing salvation.

On the whole, modern thinkers have rejected the idea of collective responsibility and guilt. This rejection of collective guilt seems rather surprising in view of the events of the modern period. It is precisely human beings, as part of a group, that have caused some of the worst injustices in the modern period. Thus, one thinks of nationalism, racism and tribalism, to which perhaps one should add 'religionism',[23] where in each case identification with the group (Niebuhr, 1963) is the root problem. Groups almost always act in self-interested ways to the detriment of others. It is simply not possible to disown this solidarity of the groups to which we inevitably belong; at best we can mitigate it.

And where exactly does evil come from?

To answer this first question was far more difficult for Augustine. If human beings were indeed created perfect, then from where does evil come? Relying on the Genesis story here does not help. And one cannot blame some other supernatural reality (the devil or the serpent). This kind of thinking was exposed in one medieval depiction of the fall, in which God points an accusing finger at Adam, Adam points the finger at Eve, Eve points her finger at the serpent – and in this same way we always tend to point the finger at others – but in the picture the serpent subtly points the tip of his tail towards God. The message is that the ultimate responsibility for the human situation appears to come back to God. This is a logical but theologically unsatisfactory conclusion if one wishes to maintain the holiness of the God, the creator of all and who only creates what is good.

Augustine solved his problem through the observation of a posited *hierarchy* of goods. Evil began or begins for him when human beings freely chose or choose the lesser good over the higher. Thus, the responsibility is with human beings and originates with us. This account may not convince. A simpler response is to say that it is a mistake to argue about the *origin* of evil in the face of its sheer *presence*. Rather than looking for someone or something to blame (perhaps ending by putting God in the dock),[24] we should concentrate all our energies on countering evil and acting to turn things around (Felderhof, 2004). This may be an inadequate

---

[23] A term coined by the University of Birmingham religious educationalist Professor John M. Hull.

[24] Job 1:22.

response for those who seek a logically coherent theological account because it leaves loose ends, but life is not always logically tidy.²⁵

In the Christian story, is the human condition all bad?

No, not entirely. The picture in the Christian tradition is not entirely negative when it comes to our human situation.²⁶ There is a minor tradition that speaks of '*felix culpa*' (blessed sin!). The point of this exclamation is that the ultimate condition of human beings after redemption is better than their primordial innocence; sin has been an occasion for human spiritual development.²⁷ Perhaps as children we are innocent because of our lack of knowledge. We admire children for their innocence, but we would not go back to their ignorance; ignorance may be bliss, but the bliss which is dependent on ignorance is blameworthy in adults. The wholeness that comes with full understanding is far preferable to the wholeness that comes from ignorance. If this is the case, it is possible to conceive of an analogous situation with respect to sin so that we can give thanks even for sin as that which made a higher, more complex form of life possible.

Alternatively, it may indeed be the case that sin cuts us off from God, but as the mystic S. Weil suggests, it may also be the link to God. Weil provides a couple of images to make the point. She writes:

> … this world is the closed door. It is a barrier. And at the same time it is the way through …

---

²⁵ 'What's ragged should be left ragged' (Wittgenstein, 1980, p. 45).

²⁶ This is the case, despite the Calvinistic tradition which speaks of the 'total depravity' of man. Calvin meant that there is nothing human beings do which is not in some way affected by human sin. Thus, he writes: '18. We must now see what he [human beings] may be, in respect both of soul and of body. The understanding of the soul in divine things, that is, in the knowledge and true worship of God, is blinder than a mole; good works it can neither contrive nor perform. In human affairs, as in the liberal and mechanical arts, it is exceedingly blind and variable. Now the will as regards lower and human affairs, it is uncertain, wandering, and not wholly at its own disposal.

19. The body follows the depraved appetites of the soul, is liable to many infirmities, and at length to death' (Calvin, 1899, vol. 2, p. 679). Or see Book 2, ch. 3, section 1, where, *inter alia*, he writes: 'You see that he [St Paul] places unlawful and depraved desires not in the sensual part merely, but in the mind itself, and therefore requires that it should be renewed. Indeed, he had a little before drawn a picture of human nature, which shows that there is no part in which it is not perverted and corrupted.'

²⁷ Nietzsche also suggests in *The Birth of Tragedy* (1993, pp. 62ff.) that mankind develops positively through its act of hubris. This is supposedly depicted in the Promethean myth, which shows that mankind's glory is to be found in suffering: 'Man's highest good must be bought with a crime and paid for by the flood of grief and suffering which the offended divinities visit upon the human race in its noble ambition' (pp. 63f.).

> Two prisoners whose cells adjoin communicate with each other by knocking on the wall. The wall is the thing which separates them but it is also their means of communication. It is the same with us and God. Every separation is a link. (Weil, 1972, p. 132)

Through the very sin that is an alienation or separation from God, we also find ourselves in connection with the Divine. Thus, those who have absolutely no sense of sin may also find themselves without a sense for the Divine.

Chapter 8
Forgiveness

If we aim to live well and we actually and inevitably live a disordered life (as exhibited in our moral failures, spiritually shallow life or our lack of moral ambition), what are we to do to put it right?

The answer is to be found primarily in what is reckoned to be the precise diagnosis of the disorder. Various possibilities vied for our attention; not all of these were mutually exclusive, but the Christian theological analysis of the disorder located the diversity of human problems in an underlying alienation or estrangement from the eternal. On this basis the evident solution is a recovery of the sense of the eternal and our reconciliation with it. But the issue is: how is this reunion to be brought about? Could it hinge on either 1) developing our character with its relationship to the eternal or 2) depend on a renewed obedience to divine law? In short, the questions of who we are and how we must live persist.

1) What can we do about our character? How are the virtues in our character to be developed and our vices to be overcome? 2) What can we do about the breaking of the divine or moral law that we have committed? How is a renewed conformity to divine or moral law to be brought about?

The first set of questions relate to moral life in terms of who we are and how we construct the self that we are, or hope, to become. The second set thinks of moral life as a life ordered by principles and rules. Let us consider the issues generated by these two different conceptions in turn.

1. Supposing Aquinas is right, virtues are those strengths of character that reflect the diverse aspects of human nature: a) reason, b) will, c) emotions and d) affections. A particular virtue may primarily be a feature of one aspect of our nature, for example, wisdom is usually attributed to reason and justice to the will, but of course all virtues belong to the person as a whole so that wisdom must also have affective dimensions and require the exercise of the will even as it gives primacy to reason. This rather complicates matters. If the issue at this point is what we must do about the relationship to the Eternal if we do not have those strengths of character, it will not be enough to address one aspect alone; instead, we may have to address all four together.

    It is possible that with respect to reason, we have not been endowed with great intellectual gifts or have been enfeebled with age. In such a case the power to change our disordered life may well be beyond our reach (and out of the reach of the majority). One might then suppose it is available only to the select few who, circumscribed within strict limits, have trained their intellect and put it to good use. But even these privileged intellectuals with their well-honed intellects may not have a very great advantage over the rest of us. A human capacity for 'rationalisation' demonstrates that the mind (reason) can serve two very different masters: good and evil. This defect of reason, together with the evident social and moral failures of many gauche intellectuals, will soon convince us that possessing and developing intellectual acuity alone can only be a very small part of the solution. History has produced too many intellectuals who turned out to be moral monsters for us to rely on reason alone for a restoration of the relationship to the eternal good.

Turning to the second aspect, namely, the will, it is also possible that we suffer from a 'weakness of will'. In such a case we may well understand what needs to be done, but we have not the *will* to bring the necessary change about.[1] We tend to pray with Augustine to 'save us from our sin but not yet'. Trying to change ourselves when we do not have the *will* is like trying to pull ourselves up by our own bootstraps; it is simply self-defeating. Alcoholics who do not have a *will* to change cannot change.

Similarly, if we do not have the emotions to move us or the affections, the sympathy and empathy to feel deeply about what needs to be done in our personal and collective life, then we cannot change; cold and hard-hearted, we are rooted to ground, to the point where we are unable to move. We are, as Augustine expressed it, 'enslaved to the self', unable to liberate ourselves from our own condition.

The plethora of self-help books provides testimony to the human desire for change and also to its fruitlessness in the moral sphere.

2. The second set of questions relates to what we do and to what directs us to act in a moral way, i.e. to an appreciation of the moral law.

Instead of relying on the transformation of character, we may look to obedience to the moral law to direct us into that new life which beckons. To do so is to come up against the problem with which the Apostle Paul wrestled in the early part of Romans 7. So long as we live in perfect obedience to the Law we are fine, but the moment we fall foul of the Law, *as will inevitably happen*, the 'juridical' conception of human life turns on us. The moral law, as one author put it, cannot forgive. It can only condemn and exact punishment;[2] to do anything else with the 'law-breaker' would be

---

[1] Romans 7:15: 'For that which I do I allow not: for what I would, that do I not; but which I hate, that do I.'

[2] We need not become gruesome at this point. The ultimate punishment for sin is its own condition, namely, the alienation or estrangement from the eternal. The ultimate

regarded as unjust. What follows from moral failure is aptly described by D. M. Baillie (Baillie, 1961, pp. 161f.). 'For the fact is', he states, 'that if we are serious-minded and morally earnest we shall quite inevitably brood over our moral failures unless we have some deeper secret of dealing with them. I am not maintaining that we *ought* to brood over them, but simply that we shall.' On this point I believe that Baillie is somewhat optimistic. He presumes that people are normally morally serious, whereas I believe that we can grow morally dull and obtuse so that we can no longer recognise the state of moral degradation in which we may live. Most Nazis were neither brooding nor suffering from some purported malaise – they were simply caught up in a stupor of immorality. However, Baillie also notes that one response to this condition of moral failure is to adopt a defence mechanism, which suppresses it with a disillusioned cynicism, pretending it does not matter after all. From this indifference issues what Baillie describes as the 'perennial *malaise*', 'which surely underlies the superficial complacency of the modern mind' (ibid., p. 162).

So what is the religious solution?

The brief answer is: forgiveness.

The 'deeper secret' to which Baillie referred above is, of course, the possibility of forgiveness. Certainly, the concept of forgiveness and what it denotes are central to Christian life. This is evidenced in the creed where Christians confess: 'I believe in … the forgiveness of sins.' And all Christians regularly recite the Lord's Prayer: 'Forgive us our debts [trespasses], as we forgive our debtors [trespassers].'[3] So, as a concept and as a practice, forgiveness is not something that can be passed over lightly within the Christian faith.

What are some of the main critiques of the whole idea of 'forgiveness'?

There have been two basic negative reactions to the Christian analysis of the human condition that happens to see forgiveness at the heart of any programme to correct the disordered life of human beings. The first rejects forgiveness on the grounds that it is fundamentally unjust and immoral. The other rejects the whole idea of forgiveness on the grounds that it is undemocratic[4] and gets in the way of more constructive ways of dealing with problems in human relationships. Let us examine these criticisms more closely.

---

punishment for an immoral life is that we are unable to appreciate what constitutes our good.

[3] Matthew 6:9 or often 'Forgive us our trespasses as we forgive those who trespass against us'.

[4] Supposedly by putting people on different socio-ethical levels – wrongdoers are made subordinate to the wronged – negating the fundamental equality in democracy.

Is forgiveness unjust and undemocratic?

It is proposed here briefly to state and then to consider the objections, testing them in order to gain a better view of what forgiveness means. The first view held that forgiveness is essentially immoral and the basic reason offered for this view was that all forgiveness entails a fundamental injustice. To explain this, we need to note that the exercise of justice demands giving everyone their due and safeguarding the common good. Violations of justice require the imposition of a fit punishment, as in the case where a crime has been committed. Bearing punishment is the means by which the offender is able to expiate the crime and put right the disordered relationship within himself or herself, with others and with the very source of justice. In the context of justice, to forgive without imposing punishment is effectively to suspend the order of justice and to let the 'criminal' off. Such actions of leniency appear to condone crimes and treat offences as if they do not matter and ultimately as if justice does not really matter.

This is what upsets the victims of crime, or their relatives, when they perceive that a criminal is not dealt with in a manner that befits his or her misdeed. A criminal may be found guilty; forgiveness intervenes and the criminal is let off, possibly with a warning not to commit the crime again. In such a situation, forgiveness, it appears, does not properly reflect the seriousness of the misdeed or the reality of justice. If any judge were to listen to the evidence, were to find the defendant guilty and were then to say 'I forgive you your crime, go and live a better life', the victim would have good reason to feel aggrieved. He or she relies on the institutions of justice to act on his or her behalf, and in such a situation he or she may rightly sense a betrayal of trust. The judge's role was to impose an appropriate punishment. In short, in this imagined context, to forgive is an act of injustice; the judge had no *right* to forgive.

Fyodor Dostoyevsky raises precisely the point of the 'right' to forgive in his book *The Brothers Karamazov*. In the narrative the atheist Ivan Karamazov recounts stories of incredible wickedness. One of these repeats an account of a little boy who is torn apart by a pack of hounds at the command of a local nobleman, which was done before the very eyes of the boy's mother and her neighbours. All this happened because the boy had thrown a stone and accidentally hurt a paw of the nobleman's favourite hound. At this point in Dostoyevsky's narrative, Ivan objects to the Christian 'myth' which offers forgiveness and purports to put things right at the end of time, i.e. with the totality of human existence in mind, in the presence of the Eternal. In particular, he objects to the promise of forgiveness made by those who were not themselves the victims of the offence. Thus, in the novel Ivan takes the view that neither the mother nor even God has the *right* to forgive. Conceivably, he says, the mother might forgive the nobleman for the pain he had caused *her* by his action, but she had no right to forgive him for the suffering and terror endured by the little boy as the dogs were set on him. There is no room for forgiveness here, but only for proper justice with a punishment matching the crime. According to Ivan, the offence of causing suffering to innocents cannot be forgiven by God and to suppose that He might forgive is to suppose that He acts unjustly. The expected conclusion from this vivid example is that whatever the misdeed, forgiveness constitutes a form of injustice and hence is immoral.

Indeed, there is a serious issue here. Theologians sometimes speak of the *gravity* of sin and by this wish to acknowledge and assert that the 'gravity' of any immoral act demands not forgiveness but punishment. In this context, one wonders, for example, whether a father has genuinely appreciated the *gravity* of a wrong in a case where terrorists have killed his innocent daughter and he responds by stating that he forgives the wrongdoers. Here forgiveness – it is said by others – is simply inappropriate.

If forgiveness is morally inappropriate, is it not also socially inappropriate, for example, by preventing the formation of better and more constructive social relationships?

One can see here the elements of a criticism that comes from quite a different direction. Apart from the question of justice, it simply questions whether forgiveness is ever a desirable, or even a reasonable, attitude to adopt in the formation of good social relationships.

To illustrate this point, we might turn to a paper offered by Professor Patricia White (2002). She notes that forgiveness, possibly under the influence of Christianity, is frequently commended in official school documents and taught in school as a suitable attitude for pupils to adopt to one another, but as a philosopher of education she argues that the invocation of forgiveness is not appropriate in school and should give way to what she calls a 'more generous spirited attitude'. She claims that, compared to forgiveness, there are alternative attitudes that one could more reasonably and appropriately adopt and encourage.[5] She would much prefer it that when a wrong has been committed, one should take a more forward-looking view and adopt a 'no problem' attitude as the means of 'limiting conflict and disharmony in the school and promoting a co-operative ethos' (2002, p. 66). We should teach people to take a more 'relaxed view' and to 'negotiate' a better relationship. On the one hand, this means encouraging a 'willingness to apologise and make amends (if possible) combined, on the other, with a generous acceptance of people who have caused one hurt' (ibid., p. 64). She does concede that on occasion and in exceptional circumstances, it will not be possible to be reconciled, for a variety of reasons, in which case she says it is best to go one's separate ways.

White's objections to forgiveness are, in part, rooted in what she regards as the 'strict view of forgiveness'. Her definition of forgiveness includes four constituent elements: a) repentance on the part of the perpetrator; b) a return to the original

---

[5] Revenge, attributing it to one's karma, shrugging it off and ignoring the wrongdoer, the perpetrator and victim looking forward and moving on are some examples that she suggests (2002, p. 58).

condition before the wrong; c) a declaration of forgiveness; and finally d) adjusting one's feelings and reactions towards the perpetrator.

Should we accept these critiques of forgiveness?

There are, of course, a number of evident difficulties built into this (and other) descriptions or conceptions of forgiveness in these critiques. For example, we do not have to accept White's 'strict' definition of forgiveness as if this truly characterises forgiveness as understood in the Christian tradition.[6] After all, her account of forgiveness begs a number of questions.

Firstly, the control White imagines that people exercise over their emotions is not wholly human; clearly, most people cannot adjust their emotions at will. More importantly, we do not need to accept that an adjustment of one's emotions is a *sine qua non*[7] of forgiveness. Her demand that one should exercise such emotional self-control builds into the concept of forgiveness a degree of unreasonableness from the very start. Secondly, it is not obvious that repentance is in every case a prerequisite for forgiveness, as she suggests. Conceivably a victim might forgive without any repentance, or change, on the part of the perpetrator. Christ prayed on the cross: 'forgive them because they know not what they do'. This was not a response to repentance. Thirdly, it is not obvious that repentance of the perpetrator puts the victim under an obligation to forgive, as White claims at one point.[8] Her account of forgiveness is far too mechanical. She makes it appear as if one can earn forgiveness by repenting, or demand forgiveness by repenting; Kierkegaard, in contrast, insists that one cannot earn or pay for forgiveness. There is nothing automatic in the relationship between repentance and forgiveness, so that if there is repentance, then forgiveness *must* follow morally or otherwise. The relationship at issue is always one between free beings. Fourthly, it is not obvious that forgiveness necessarily restores the original condition prior to the wrong done, as White claims. It may simply initiate a new, and possibly more constructive, relationship; it does not simply take one back to the original situation. An example might be the forgiveness offered to an unfaithful husband by a loving wife – despite the forgiveness, the relationship can never again be one of an innocent trusting. Forgiveness is neither an act of simply forgetting nor an act of ignoring an intervening wrong done. Fifthly, against the position that sees forgiveness as essentially a form of injustice by remitting the punishment due, it is not evident that forgiveness always means that there is no punishment or that

---

[6] For a detailed critique of White's position from a Christian point of view, see L. Philip Barnes (2002, pp. 529–44).

[7] That is, a stipulation *without which* there would be no forgiveness.

[8] White writes: 'On the strict view this victim should be urged to express forgiveness, produce the appropriate behaviour and strive to bring her feelings into line and forgive her attacker. But can it be argued that she has a moral duty to do so?' (2002, pp. 60f.). But who says that the person offering forgiveness is under a moral duty to do so?

the remission of punishment is the core meaning of forgiveness. Certainly, bearing punishment expiates guilt and wipes the slate clean as far as the perpetrator is concerned, but this is quite independent of any forgiveness. The expiation of guilt is not sufficient to bring about a new and more constructive relationship with the victim and it is a new relationship at which forgiveness aims. Finally, forgiveness is never inevitable, nor is it always even a possibility – Scripture itself speaks of the unforgivable sin (Mark 3:29). In short, White's account of forgiveness is deeply flawed and partial.

Do White's supposedly constructive suggestions for a different approach in life make better sense?

Professor White's recommendation of a 'no problem' attitude is, of course, subject to the very same moral objections that were raised by her against the notion of forgiveness. If forgiveness appears unjust, then surely the 'no problem' attitude is even more so. (This presumes that the misdeed is a genuine moral wrong and not simply an infraction of some trivial social etiquette, which might be the case with very young people.) A 'no problem' attitude ignores the moral offence and what has happened, and introduces an element of pretence. In the real social world where one has been emotionally upset and morally maltreated, there *is* a problem that cannot be ignored. It is a deceit to pretend otherwise. A moral injustice must be confronted and dealt with.

Perhaps Professor White's 'no problem' approach may work in school, where misdemeanours are usually of a trivial nature and where an overly refined sense of justice sometimes found in children can set up a vicious cycle of tit-for-tat. What this indicates to me is that we should not be discouraging children in their sense of fairness and justice but instead developing it still further and possibly teaching them that justice is not the only consideration in life.

If there is a meaning to forgiveness, it is the recognition that justice is vital but that human life goes beyond what can be encapsulated in the rules that govern human behaviour. Justice is not yet love and love is the higher relationship. It is true that reconciling justice and mercy has always been the key theological difficulty. The tension is never resolved and it should be noted that forgiveness does not come without cost. The victim in an act of forgiveness frequently internalises the hurt done to him or her so that it does not impinge on the relationship to the other. In human life it is the voluntary suffering of the innocent victim that breaks the vicious cycle of deteriorating relationships.

There is nothing in the Christian account of forgiveness which warrants the accusation of what White calls 'moral imperialism'. Firstly, those who have not committed any moral offence whatsoever are never envisaged as genuine objects of forgiveness, as she supposes. Sometimes there are situations in life where people sanctimoniously offer forgiveness when it is precisely they who are at fault.[9] These are not genuine cases of forgiveness; they are examples of moral blindness.

Of course, the human acts which occasioned the purported forgiveness may be subject to the kind of re-descriptions offered by Professor White. The actions may consequently come to be seen as requiring something other than forgiveness – a joke perhaps to break the ice after a social gaffe. Evidently, it is not always clear in every situation that an immorality has occurred that would require forgiveness. Re-descriptions provide a means of testing or of assessing this. A hurt committed unwittingly, for example, may be a case in point. Something done in ignorance, such as accidentally knocking over a toddler whom one did not notice at one's feet, may not be regarded as morally blameworthy. This is not to admit that all wrongs committed unwittingly are therefore without blame. There are times when one must say that one should have known or should have known better. Moral obtuseness is not a basis for the construction of a wholesome society.

In addition, there is nothing in the usual Christian account which warrants placing people on different socio-ethical levels (sinners and the saved) or of putting some people beyond the pale,[10] as White appears to claim. By putting the matter in this way she misrepresents Christian thinking. Firstly, in the Christian narrative *all* have sinned so they are *all* on the same level and, secondly, none are beyond the pale (Christ died for *all*). Further, could a perpetrator of evil who actively seeks forgiveness[11] really be taking part in a form of self-indulgence, as White proposes? To substantiate the point that it might be, White uses Chekov's story of *The Death of an Official*. However, her illustration is simply dishonest. In using this example of a distorted social relationship (moreover, one in which nothing immoral[12] was actually perpetrated), she does not provide us with a genuine case of something to be put right morally; the example cannot therefore function as a suitable description of what forgiveness can be.

One might agree with White: of course, one should respond in a more relaxed way when perceived wrongs are trivial or trite. It would be a mistake to resort to the discourse of forgiveness simply when there was a minor breach of social

---

[9] I am thinking of an English clergyman who sanctimoniously 'forgave' the Irish over a national radio network. This struck me as overly presumptuous.

[10] Nor can it be a proper complaint (White, 2002, p. 63) that forgiveness is a part of a wider Christian narrative, except that White works with the assumption that it would be wrong in school to implicitly convey a Christian view. The need to convey a wider Christian view (if one is to make life intelligible to the young in school) is one of the consequences of living in a society that owes many of its key concepts to the Christian tradition.

[11] An example of a serious effort to put things right is to be found in the life of Wittgenstein, who systematically went to visit the families of pupils he had taught in school to apologise for physically maltreating them. This is not self-indulgence but an example of moral courage and moral seriousness.

[12] On White's own grounds, one cannot be blamed for what one could not help but do – in this case, to sneeze.

etiquette. Forgiveness comes into play only when there are moral wrongs and a genuine situation of religious alienation. White's main objection ultimately comes down to the fact that sometimes people see the wrongs committed against them in a distorted way. The fault of others is perceived as disproportionately large; their own innocence in a broken moral relationship is presumptuously treated as obvious. Christian faith has always warned people against these two possibilities.

To sum up, one can agree that there are distortions in the concept and practice of forgiveness but that the distortions do not in themselves invalidate it. Forgiveness is effectively an invitation to a form of life that goes beyond mere justice. A life bound by the considerations of justice alone has the power either to cast us into despair or into a state of mind described as an 'easy conscience', a condition where we believe that moral failure does not really matter.[13] The introduction of forgiveness into our relationships at various levels is actually the source of moral perseverance. It recognises that moral failure and alienation do matter and yet that a new beginning may always be made.

Where should we locate the concept of forgiveness?

Forgiveness ultimately is a function of inwardness that operates at different levels. At level 1, the disorder one encounters within oneself needs to be addressed by

---

[13] What S. Kierkegaard describes as 'light-hearted': 'The light-hearted would allow all to be forgotten – he believes in vain. The mournful heart would allow nothing to be forgotten – he believes in vain. But he who believes, believes that all is forgotten, only in this wise, that he is bearing a light burden – for is he not bearing the memory that he has been forgiven? The light-hearted would let even that memory be forgotten – all is forgotten and forgiven! But Faith says: all is forgotten; remember that it has been forgiven. One may forget indeed in many ways. One may forget, because one gets something else to think about. One may forget thoughtlessly and frivolously. One may consider that all has been forgotten because one has oneself forgotten – but the eternal righteousness can forget and only in one way, through forgiveness. And so the believer himself must not forget, but on the contrary must constantly remind himself, that all has been forgiven him ... do not forget that it has been forgiven. It has not been forgotten simply, but it has been forgotten in forgiveness. Every time thou dost remember the forgiveness, then it is forgotten, but when thou dost forget the forgiveness, then it is not forgotten, for then forgiveness has been forfeited' (1955, p. 45).

Thus, there is another sense in which he reckons the burden of forgiveness is light: 'But one who takes away the consciousness of sin and gives instead a consciousness of pardon – he takes away indeed the heavy burden and gives the light one in its place.

But how! A burden, and we may call it light? Yea. If any man will not understand that forgiveness is truly a burden to be borne, albeit a light one, then he is taking forgiveness in vain. Forgiveness is not to be earned, it is not as heavy as that; but neither is it to be taken in vain, for neither is it so light. Forgiveness is not to be paid for, it is not as costly as that – for it cannot be paid for; but neither is it to be taken as if it were nothing, it is too costly for that' (1955, p. 44).

a willingness to love oneself, and therefore to be willing to be forgiving with oneself.[14] At level 2, the disorder with one's neighbours may require penitence, but it will also require forgiveness to initiate a renewed relationship. At level 3, the deepest and most basic level, because the disorder within oneself and with others is ultimately also an offence against what is holy and against an eternal justice, it requires an eternal love and forgiveness in order to repeatedly renew our relationship to the Eternal in our lives. The Christian gospel is that the God forgives so that we too can forgive; we forgive so that we may inhabit the realm of deepening relationships and learn to live with others and ourselves in conditions of moral failure.

---

[14] An awareness of the gravity of human failures prevents this willingness to accept forgiveness from turning into an easy conscience, which was criticised earlier.

Chapter 9
Church

Do we need others and institutions to live well? Do we need the church?

Our aspiration to live well required a means for dealing with the disorder in our lives and in our world. The Christian analysis roots the disorder which we encounter nearly everywhere as ultimately due to our estrangement from a deep otherness. 'Forgiveness' is what is supposed to reconcile us to whatever is eternal and, as a consequence, also to ourselves and with one another. Certain conceptual issues were raised about forgiveness. We saw that we cannot abrogate justice but must seek to raise our various relationships to one another, onto a higher plane, namely to that of love, which has the power to transform juridical categories, deepening them and giving them a different character. We can now ask about the 'spirit of the law' and not just the 'letter of the law'. The spirit of the law refers one to the end (purpose) or point of the law, which is to be found in its capacity to support the life of love in the form of true communion between people.

Since human beings are curved in upon the self, the source of regeneration must come from elsewhere, from outside us. According to John's Gospel, we love the Eternal because 'God *first* loved us', i.e. the Eternal always presents and relates itself to us as an initial given. It is the faithfulness and constancy of the God's love which ultimately ensures that we cannot be separated from the Eternal. This constancy of divine love in the face of our disorder, we experience as forgiveness. This foundational forgiveness issuing from the eternal God enables us in turn to love and respond in kind, i.e. to begin to love and forgive the self and others for the failures in which we have become enmeshed. It also enables us to appreciate the natural world as something of value in its own right, having been created good by its eternal source. In brief, this eternal love and forgiveness draws us out of ourselves and enables us:

a. to recognise a common humanity and a common human dignity (i.e. perhaps even because of, and not despite, a social solidarity in 'sin');
b. to treasure a given beauty that we may contemplate;
c. to aspire to the good that exists as a given end for us; or
d. to thirst for a knowledge that beckons from beyond the self, (i.e. it is not just a socially constructed reality but, strictly speaking, 'objective').

This interdependence of love of the Eternal, self-love, the love of others and the love of the (natural) world constitutes a kind of ecology that leads us to consider that collective and communal life we find in the 'church'.

Ideally, the church as a social reality is the community of love; it is supposedly a fellowship *constituted and created* by divine love. As such, there are some basic criteria by which it can be judged. It should be seen to *facilitate* and *mediate* the love that derives from the Eternal and promotes a proper love of self, love of others and love of the natural world. The operative word was 'ideally'. On this basis and with this role, the church is able to confess in the creed that it believes in its own role and status in the world, namely (traditionally expressed), as 'the holy, catholic church and communion of saints'. In my view the so-called 'marks' (unity, holiness, catholicity and apostolicity) of the church ultimately derive from, and should testify to, the *unity* of the Eternal, and to the Eternal's *holiness* and *ubiquity* (catholicity) within the world. *Apostolicity* is in this context a mark of authenticity and continuity that reflects the unchanging character of the Eternal which sends and commissions testimony to its love. Any particular social organisation can only claim these marks of the church if it is faithful to its mission.

What is the constitution of the church? Does it have any authority and, if so, where does this authority come from? Can there be an authority today which is not rooted in the 'will of the people'?

The credal confession above raises many issues, particularly in an age of individualism. In this, our modern Western culture, other people, all organisations and institutions are instinctively regarded with suspicion. Sometimes they are even treated as if in their very existence and by their very nature they were already in some significant sense oppressive. Whether the 'church' is in fact oppressive can only be properly resolved by examining the role of the church and the nature of its basis. In doing so it becomes evident that it often claims an 'authority' for itself (which is not based in 'the will of the people') – in modern times this claimed authority is seldom welcomed. An authority outside the self is something against which any autonomous adult naturally rebels. However, even supposing the church to have 'authority', one should still ask what is the *scope* of this authority?

With respect to the church and its claimed 'authority', one can broadly observe *three* distinctive theological positions that might be adopted. Firstly, some regard the church as a divinely constituted society with a divinely commissioned function. Secondly, others regard the church as a deeply human institution that should be treated as such, i.e. admired or deprecated, depending on its character and functioning. Thirdly, a mediating position will see the church as founded in a mixture of these two constitutional sources. If the latter is the case, we could have difficulties in defining the limits of the 'church', distinguishing its divine qualities and separating them from its very fallible human incarnations. These three theologically distinctive possibilities need to be examined more closely.

Why do some people think the church is divinely constituted?

Some theologians take, or have taken, what is called a 'high' view. The clergy in particular are readily tempted to endorse the claim that the church is fundamentally a *divine society*, instituted by Jesus Christ himself.

Thus, as K. Barth rather grandly said, 'the church is Jesus Christ', and as H. Kung wrote in his impressive book on the church:

> The church did not come about of itself. God called it into being as the *Ecclesia*, the body of those who answered the call, and this he did in the world, from among mankind. God himself convoked the Church in the call that issued through Jesus, the Christ.[1]

From these two quotes one can see how theologians establish a link between the Divine and the social institution one encounters in the world.

Some of these august claims are related historically to what Jesus reputedly said and did. Jesus, it is said, called 12 disciples. This is taken to be a symbolic act, signifying the renewal of Israel, a defined society. Jesus sent his disciples out on a mission; he instituted the Eucharist and bade his disciples to do it in memory of him. He said: 'Go, Teach, Baptise.'[2] All of this, it is claimed, indicates an institution called into being by a divine command due to the fact that Jesus himself initiated and commissioned it.

Scripture too backs the perception of a divine constitution: in Matthew 16:17–19, after Peter's recognition of Jesus as the Christ, Jesus is quoted as saying:

> Blessed art thou, Simon bar Jona: for flesh and blood hath not revealed it unto thee, but my Father which is in heaven. And I say also unto thee, that thou art Peter,[3] and upon this rock I will build my church; and the gates of hell shall not prevail against it. And I will give unto thee the keys of the kingdom of heaven: and whatsoever thou shalt bind on earth shall be bound in heaven: and whatsoever thou shalt loose on earth shall be loosed in heaven.[4]

This seems to be an unequivocal endorsement of the church.

Of course, one can be suspicious about this text. This vision of a divinely constituted body with divine authority is something in which the professional clergy quite naturally have a stake or an interest. It appears to give *them* authority and power in the world. An outcome of this is that the clergy will dominate and decide what it means to live well. Some critics think that this power is exercised at the expense of the freedom of the laity, the ordinary people. But perhaps the

---

[1] Kung, 1976, p. x.
[2] Matthew 28:19–20.
[3] Meaning 'rock'.
[4] Or Deuteronomy 7:6ff.

laity also benefit from the arrangement; they can pass responsibility for the key character of their life to others[5] (passing responsibility to others is something many are all too ready to do) whilst at the same time taking advantage of any consolation it offers.

What are the problems with this lofty view of the church as a divinely constituted body?

Given its supposed divine origin, there is one very obvious objection to these claims for the church: namely, one might reasonably expect perfection, but this is not what one finds. Although Peter seems to be given a founding role in the church according to the text cited above,[6] it is always worth remembering that Peter was also one of the first disciples to abandon and deny Jesus at the first sign of opposition, before dawn and before the cock crowed thrice. Any claims to a divine constitution on the part of the church must reckon with a history of betrayal[7] that begins with Peter himself and that continues right up to the present time. In the original vision the church may have been marked by the defining qualities mentioned earlier, but any *actual* social organisations that bear the name show all too clearly that the church is neither *one* nor *holy* nor *catholic*.

One response to this problem, and a corollary of the view that the church is a divinely constituted society, is to insist that the church should be reformed in order to be itself; indeed, that it should be continuously and continually reformed.[8] On the basis of this reforming agenda, the church is urged again and again to return to its originating vision. In this view, the nature of the early church becomes historically decisive when making any judgments about what the church should be like.[9] Thus, it is assumed that the church today should seek to conform to its first embodiment. In many ecclesiologies (teachings about the church), the Scriptures are scoured to determine what was done in the early church: how was it organised? Did women have a role? Did they baptise infants? Was the church ruled by elders

---

[5] Exodus 20:18–21. See what the grand inquisitor says in Dostoyevsky's *The Brothers Karamazov* (1958) or see Nietzsche, who said: 'If you wish to strive for peace of soul and pleasure then believe; if you wish to be a devotee of truth, then inquire.'

[6] It should be remembered that the Scriptures are the product of the church.

[7] Or Deuteronomy 10:13ff. When we examine the history of the church, we see examples of persecution, inquisition, self-aggrandisement, materialism, exploitation, anti-Semitism and paedophilia, to name but some of the self-evident failings. The presence of violence in its own history makes it difficult for the church to criticise others for their violence or moral failures, or to offer them moral and spiritual leadership.

[8] A motto of the reformed churches is 'always reforming'.

[9] 'I have tried to allow the original Christian message to dictate the themes, perspectives and balance of the book, so that the original Church may light the way once more for the Church today' (Kung, 1976, p. xiii).

(*presbuteroi*) or was it ruled by bishops (*episkopoi*)? And if by bishops, did Peter and Rome have primacy?

Historical and biblical research is supposed to provide the evidence, but of course this research into the early church is never decisive – historical research seldom is. However, one suspects that even if it were, it might not suffice to change current practice[10] in the church. Too much is at stake. This judgment points to yet another consequence of the view that the church is divinely constituted: namely, the possibility of a deep conservatism. It is a logical conclusion. After all, if it is divinely instituted, then who are we to change it? What was done in the past must continue to be done in the present.

What are the advantages of just straightforwardly thinking of the church as humanly constituted?

It would be more modest and would avoid some of the less congenial consequences of the assumption of a divine constitution (backward-looking, conservative, unrecognisable) if we believe the church to be an essentially human institution. We can then see it as the product of social and political forces at work in the world and evaluate it on that basis. If genetically we are social creatures, then it makes sense to think that our religious interest should be collectively expressed in the form of social organisations. It is society that provides the language and the concepts with which to articulate and to think about religious life. Without them, one would be dumb and intellectually incoherent, so it can be concluded that as individuals we are utterly dependent on this social contribution.

As a *human* institution one could, for example, be more honest and admit that the church needs to be politically astute: 'Behold, I send you forth as sheep in the midst of wolves: be ye therefore as wise as serpents, and as harmless as doves.'[11] The problem then is that as a human institution we can also see that the church has been neither as wise nor as harmless as it was counselled to be. This failure of the church to match its ideal is easily attributed to the failings of human beings generally. As a social group, a self-interested quest for power dominates (Niebuhr, 1963). If an observer lives under the expectation of a church manifesting an eternal perfection, derived from its divine origin, he or she will be all the more easily appalled and disillusioned at the paedophilia and sundry other vices of priests and laity alike that he or she will encounter within it. By removing the expectation of perfection, observers will be less cynical and the church's leadership will, more realistically, begin to devise the safeguards deemed essential in a modern civil society against all the predictable human vices.

Stripped of its divine illusions, the church is free to respond much more flexibly to diverse human needs and circumstances. If the modern media demands TV

---

[10] Thus, the clear evidence of female leadership in the early church seems not to have moved many churches very much on the admission of women into the priesthood.

[11] Matthew 10:16.

personalities, for example, then the requisite requirements could be major criteria in the appointment of its bishops. If on the grounds of justice a secular society demands the equal treatment of women, then clearly the church should comply if it is not to fall into moral and social disrepute. The church no longer needs to be bound by its historical precedents, even if one takes these precedents seriously as valuable experience – they will be helpful, but not in any way prescriptive. In the current jargon, the church is free to 'modernise' because nothing is sacrosanct.

Stripped of its divine illusions, we can reject the arguments from history that stand in the way of reform because we are no longer bound by past practice (and not just because the evidence on many key matters is held to be indifferent or historically ambiguous). The church will be free to embody the lessons of modern management. The early church can no longer pre-empt or dictate the structural requirements of a modern organisation seeking to meet modern needs.

In any case, there probably never was *one* fixed structure in the earliest phases of Christianity. As far as the organisation of the church is concerned, it is likely that church structures only gradually evolved and were formalised to meet the needs of a growing body of people. At its inception church structures probably reflected the structure of the Jewish synagogue which, after the destruction of the Temple in 70 AD, meant there was no priesthood (the separation from Judaism came later).

Finally, to support the case for a human constitution, any remaining reservations about a divine constitution for the church could be dispelled by challenging the claim that Jesus actually instituted the church in the first place. Jesus, it is sometimes said, did not institute any religious organisation because he expected an imminent end to the world, so that there was no need for organisation, just as Paul later advised people not to marry for much the same reason! Jesus' message was fundamentally eschatological (to do with the end times or end of the world). His ethic was an interim ethic and whilst it had social implications, it was not directed at creating or changing any particular social realities as such. Jesus, on this view, was not a social reformer, nor did he try to overthrow Roman rule. On the contrary, it is argued that his ethic was highly individualistic, i.e. it demands a personal response and decision-making and it is this that occupies the centre stage of his thinking. The last thing on Jesus' mind (it is claimed) was the creation of a social institution!

Is there nothing special about the church?

Many of the preceding arguments reinforce the view that the church is essentially a human society established to meet the growing needs of human beings in a particular time and place. However, those who wish to defend the view of the church as a *divine* society are not entirely without a retort. They could say that it may indeed be the case that Jesus expected the end of history and preached 'the coming of the kingdom of God', and, if so, the very idea of 'kingdom' clearly has *some* social dimension. Further, in Scripture there was also the promise of the 'gift of the spirit' and, as H. R. Mackintosh once stated, 'The spirit is always figured ... as the possession of the believing society', i.e. of a church. Moreover, the Acts of the Apostles (the story of a community) in the New Testament naturally follows the gospels (strictly speaking it goes with the Gospel of Luke as one story). Biblically, the story of the church is a logical sequence in the story of Jesus – both concern the actions or the influence of the God in the world.

Moreover, the 'church' may also be part of the prequel, for the actions of the Eternal and *the community of the faithful* may be said to precede the historical Jesus. If in the Middle Ages some people could ask Socrates to pray for them, it was because they assumed he was in the presence of the Divine; in the evangelical religious jargon of today, he was one of the many 'saved' who lived long before the birth of Christ.

What is the real issue in the debate about the nature of the church?

At this juncture it may be important to make a distinction between fellowship or *sociality*, on the one hand, and *organisation*, on the other, as Emil Brunner does in his book *The Misunderstanding of the Church*.[12] It would seem that the church is essentially about sociality rather than organisation. Organisations are more or less fit for purpose. Communism, fascism, and liberal democracy are all regarded to be forms of *social organisation*, but they are not all equally congenial or conducive to a flourishing human fellowship or sociality. Authoritarianism, almost by definition, divides human beings from one another. If the church is truly about sociality, it must mould its organisational character accordingly. The church's authority is solely the authority of its capacity to nurture love.

It should be pointed out that any fellowship or sociality would be difficult to create and sustain without some form of social organisation and institutionalisation. If this is recognised, the question is focused on the criteria which ought to be applied in the development of any social institution. One might ask: 1) is the institution truly prescribed by virtue of some divine calling?; 2) do its members take due cognisance of human nature?; 3) are certain identifiable features necessary or merely desirable and useful?; and 4) might certain other features not only be *un*necessary but also be useless, or worse, harmful to promoting and sustaining human sociality? With these questions, one might be able to direct the theological discussions about what is the best form of church government, whether, for example, women should be ordained as well as men, or whether the church should be entirely made up of lay people and rid itself of professionals, whether there should be balancing power structures and clearly written rules specifying appropriate behaviour and so on.

---

[12] A similar distinction may be implicit in Calvin's distinction between the visible and the invisible church. In a similar vein, S. L. Frank, (1946, p. 246) says: 'I prefer therefore to speak of the "mystical" and "empirically real" church.'

The tension between the ideal and its actual social reality led John Calvin to speak of a *visible* and *invisible* church. The invisible church is an eternal reality that is not spatially and temporally limited. Thus, to quote him, the invisible church is:

> the church as it really is before God – the church into which none are admitted but those who by the gift of adoption are sons of God, and by sanctification of the Spirit true members of Christ. In this case it not only comprehends the saints who dwell on the earth, but all the elect who have existed from the beginning of the world.[13]

The visible church, by contrast, consists of those who profess faith and conform to all the rites:

> In this church there is a very large mixture of hypocrites. Who have nothing of Christ but the name and the outward appearance.

However, for Calvin, it is not a question of trying to belong to one whilst avoiding the other; on the contrary, the invisible church is a matter of faith, while the visible church is that to which we as social beings are bound to belong. He writes:

> Hence, as it is necessary to believe the invisible church, which is manifest to the eye of God only, so we are also enjoined to regard this [visible, fallen] Church which is so called with reference to man, and to cultivate its communion.[14]

In his position there is no escaping to an other-worldly reality but a call to accept the church 'warts and all'.

Is it possible to see anything of a divine constitution in the church?

The introduction of any claim to a divine constitution must rest on whether it fulfils the divine command to 'love the Lord, thy God, with all thy heart and with all thy soul and with all thy mind'[15] and 'thy neighbour as thyself'.[16] That is the final test. The issue becomes how to translate this paradoxical command to love into the practicalities of everyday life. Does the institution convey this in word and deed? Even if one is tempted to say the church normally fails the test, perhaps the institution still proclaims and achieves its purpose simply by striving to love. It should also be recognised that whatever institutions are created, no matter how good they are, they will always be capable of being subverted by a thoroughgoing human double-mindedness, which has the power to transmute the most august

---

[13] Calvin, 1899, Bk. IV, ch. 1, p. 7.
[14] Ibid.
[15] Matthew 22:37; Deutoronomy. 6:5, 10:12, 30:6.
[16] Matthew 22:39; Leviticus 19:18.

aspirations into dross. At the same time, if the Eternal is to be known at all, it must be encountered in the this-worldly realm and thus perhaps also in this-worldly institutions, remembering that in traditional Christian thinking it was this world and sinful people that the God redeems – redeems, not abandons!

The (invisible) church is to be found amongst all those (no matter where in the world or in what historical period) who in response to divine love aspire to the Eternal and who share this aspiration with others through teaching and a collective, holy life.[17] Nevertheless, it has been claimed that outside the church there is no salvation. Certainly, theologians would agree that outside the love of the Eternal there can be no true wholeness, but to claim there is no salvation outside of one's own responsive group or historically bound organisation (visible church) is a gross delusion. An example of this delusion is found in W. Hermann (the teacher of Barth), who once claimed that:

> God cannot disclose Himself to all men without distinction; He holds indeed the guidance of every life in His hand, but He can open His inner Self only to such as are in the Church, i.e. the fellowship of believers.[18]

This in my judgment goes too far and is at variance with all the theological claims about the omnipotence of God. An affirmation of 'omnipotence' will not allow us to go on to specify what the God can and cannot do. No one and no secular or worldly institution can control the spirit of the Eternal as Hermann envisaged in the quote above. If we think and truly believe that we are empowered by the Eternal, then we can hope to see this reflected in the love we bring to the world. The Eternal itself knows no boundaries, calls *all* to be faithful and, if this is true, the first reasonable response to those who belong to different religious groups, institutions or traditions from one's own is not to seek to change or to convert them (on the assumption that they know nothing) but to learn from them how they too love the Eternal and what this love might teach us. (These observations will have consequences for any missionary or 'jihadi' endeavours.) We will recognise members of the communities of faith and their institutions by the fruit of love and those outside the church by their hate. Unfortunately, too many have a stake in both camps.

The theological position forces us to think 1) about the relationship between the communities of the faithful and 2) about the nature of the ecumenical drive. It

---

[17] Copleston writes about Sebastian Franck (1499–1542): 'He was hostile not only to Catholicism but also to official Protestantism. God is eternal goodness and love which are present to all men, and the true Church, he thought, is the spiritual company of all those who allow God to operate within them. Men like Socrates and Seneca belonged to the "Church". Redemption is not an historical event, and doctrines like those of the Fall and the redemption by Christ on Calvary are no more than figures or symbols of eternal truths' (Copleston, 1963, p. 79).

[18] Hermann, 1971, p. 190.

also forces us in the Christian tradition to consider 3) the relationship of Christian churches to other faiths and, indeed, to the secular society in which we live. The God is ubiquitous and thus may in principle be found everywhere. The God is eternal and thus may be encountered at any point in time, from its very beginning up to its very end. These theological judgments lead variously to the inclusivism of the anonymous Christian, Muslim, Jew, etc.[19] or to the acknowledgement of a plural relationship to the Eternal.

---

[19] That is to say, where we recognise in others the identity we hope to share. 'Neither the sacrament of baptism in the sense of an empirical act performed in accordance with definite rules, nor the confession of faith in the sense of a clearly expressed rational admission of its truths, necessarily marks a "Christian" as a member of the mystical Church of Christ; the only thing that does is the unceasing participation – invisible to all but God – of the human soul in the truth and reality of Christ. Even the empirical ecclesiastical rules admit in principle that men who do not come under any formal definitions of Church membership may nevertheless belong to the Church' (Frank, 1946, pp. 249f.). This mid-twentieth-century expression of inclusivism should not be interpreted to be an act of condescension towards others, but simply as a theological statement that we may encounter a genuine relationship to the Eternal in the religions of others.

Chapter 10
Relating to Different Faiths

Are churches voluntary organisations, constituted by a contract between individuals,[1] or do they have a different basis? How does this affect the relationship with those outside the church?

An awareness that religious life is essentially a social activity has led us to consider the nature and character of the church and its constitutional basis. We saw that as a social organisation the church understands itself as somehow established by a divine commission, with authority over individuals. There are reasons to question this ecclesial judgment about itself because it is so clearly a very human institution, given its evident failings. In its supposed dependence on the Eternal, its essential marks are unity, holiness and catholicity, but the organisations we actually know are neither one, nor holy, nor catholic. To resolve this tension between the ideal and the reality, we saw that John Calvin had proposed that the church is both invisible and visible, a distinction between the Eternal and the outward reality.

Now think in terms of a Venn diagram. The first conclusion might be to suppose that circle a (the visible church) is larger than circle b (the invisible church). After all, 'not every one that saith unto me, Lord, Lord, shall enter the kingdom of heaven; but he that doeth the will of my Father which is in heaven'.[2] There are plenty who *profess* but who do not *live* the life of faith! Alternatively, there are plenty who may live the religious life in the form of some outward practice but who lack the necessary inwardness that is constitutive of it. Any practice with a clear disjunction between the inner and the outer is deemed by many to be mere show and hypocrisy.

However, we can also imagine a different scenario. One can envisage ambiguous situations where people might be thought both to belong to the invisible church and yet to not visibly belong in the full sense of the word. In addition, it is possible to imagine people who from time to time move between the two categories of belonging so that they belong at one time but not at another. The reason for the ambiguity is that our motives are mixed and we do not always know why we do the things we do. As such, people may sometimes be faithful and act with integrity, while at other times not doing so, or may sometimes believe and live from faith whilst at the same time wrestling with unbelief.

---

[1] The position that the authoritative basis of society is generally rooted in an implicit contract has been widely held since Hobbes' *Leviathan*.

[2] Matthew 7:21.

Much of Calvin's thinking was based on a more religiously uniform society. His theology was clearly thinking *within* the Christian tradition. But how would a global perspective or a more multi-faith society affect this thinking about a 'visible' and 'invisible' church? It is, of course, possible to conceptualise a different Venn diagram from the one above, namely, one in which the invisible church is a much larger category than the visible church, i.e. where circle a (the members of the visible church) is much smaller than circle b (the invisible church) or where the number of those who belong to the invisible church is much larger than the number of those who happen to belong to the social institution with which we are familiar. After all, according to the Scriptures, there are the many righteous who do what is required of them but who do not know that they do so 'unto Christ'.[3] In addition, there are those who have the law of God written in their hearts[4] and those who worship the unknown god[5] (of this selfsame God, St Paul says, 'him declare I unto you'), to name but three groups mentioned in Scripture whom Christians are duty-bound to acknowledge as people of faith, i.e. those people who are in a relationship to the Eternal. Christ himself recognised in the Roman centurion a faith which he had not found in the whole of Israel! In brief, the Eternal is to be found everywhere,[6] at all times and in all places, and there are many witnesses throughout history and throughout the whole world who testify to it. The visible (institutional) church with its 'invisible' members on this scenario is but a small part of a very much larger constituency, namely, that of all those who love the Eternal or who are lovers of the God. This constituency is to be found in 1) those members of other faiths, 2) those people who lived before the advent of the church (how else could one speak of Abraham as the father of faith?), 3) those people who profess belief in God in our culture but who do not associate with the 'visible', institutional church or with some other religious institution and 4) those who confess no religious faith at all but who nevertheless clearly live responsibly before the Eternal.

How do these distinctions between the visible and invisible church or community of faith help in understanding inter-faith relations?

These two patterns just outlined (in which 1) the 'people of faith' comprise a smaller constituency than those engaged in 'organised' religion and 2) the people of faith comprise a much larger constituency) can guide and help us to draw up a number of important affirmations and conclusions that should have a bearing on any discussion we may have and on the judgments we may make. The principles are as follows:

---

[3] Matthew 25:34ff.
[4] Jeremiah 31:33.
[5] Acts 17:23.
[6] Jonah 1 and 2; Psalms 139:7–8.

1. In general, social traditions and practices are a *necessary* condition for any articulate knowledge about the Eternal. Life, language and concepts are ultimately social in nature and consequently there is a 'sociology' of knowledge. If all this is true, faith is *not*, firstly, the private experience of an individual, which then becomes foundational for communal religious life; instead, it is the other way round. The life of the human community defines the character of the religious life of the individual. It is the human community's religious life which provides the criteria by which to judge any particular practices, actions and experiences of the individual. Of course, it is vital to remember here that the human community should not be confused with any one more narrowly defined social organisation. Human society is larger than the church.
2. *Knowing about* the Eternal is not a *sufficient* condition for *living from*, and *for*, the Eternal (or what in traditional terms might be called 'salvation'). Knowledge is not the same as salvation. On the other hand, it is equally conceivable (given the concept of the 'grace' of God) that we might be saved without having *any* knowledge – nothing can separate us from the love of God – an insight which leads to 'universal' salvation. All this puts the possession of 'knowledge' in its proper perspective! Knowledge is to be treasured but it does not of itself transform life.
3. *Knowing about* the Eternal is not confined to any one religious or social tradition. This follows theologically from affirmations about the ubiquity of God and the consequent affirmation in theology of a general revelation (see Jonah 1 and 2; Psalms 139:7–8). A relationship to the God is possible anywhere and at any time; that is what ubiquity means. The omnipotence of the God means that the God's relationship to human beings may be formed in divergent and unexpected ways.
4. Seeing how people live ('By their fruits, ye shall know them') may be a *necessary* condition for knowing whether other people live *from*, and *for*, the Eternal, but it is not a *sufficient* condition. The latter would require access to the state of their inwardness. Since we do not have such deep access, we cannot judge the status of others before the God.
5. *Conforming* to some particular religious practice or belonging to some particular religious organisation may be neither a *sufficient* (given the demand for inwardness) nor even a *necessary* condition for living *from*, and *for*, the Eternal (given the possibility of knowing the Eternal outside the confines of any particular tradition). This rules out 'exclusivism' (see below) and follows from points 1–4 above. More modesty and less confidence is called for when judging who precisely belongs to 'the so-called saved' and who does not. We can be 'saved' whether or not we belong to the church, the ummah, the people of Israel, etc.
6. *Knowing* about the Eternal is not a *necessary* condition for living *from*, and *for*, the Eternal. We can live from, and for, the Eternal without recognising that we are doing so and living in response to the Divine (see, for example,

Matthew 25:34ff.). In brief, we can clearly live well or be deeply moral without knowingly being religious. We can live enthralled by the God without knowing that it is the God whom we love.

7. Different religious and social traditions and practices may yield different conceptions (beliefs) of the Eternal or the Divine. Our different human histories and different experiences may teach us to know the self-same countenance of the Eternal differently.
8. Different religious and social traditions may agree on some conceptions and disagree on others. (It is a nonsense to speak of worshipping different 'gods'; we do not worship our conceptions.)
9. If religious and social traditions disagree in some respect, it is possible that one (religion A) is right and the other (religion B) is wrong *or* that they are both wrong. If one religion A is right in some respects, it does not follow that it is right in every respect or in other respects, or that religion B is wrong in every respect. The different religions can agree on some things and each one of them can be right in some respects, and wrong in others.
10. Where religious traditions do disagree, it may happen that we do not *know*, or know for certain, which is right or wrong, given the transcendence of the Eternal.
11. The judgments we do make about which is right or wrong in the case of a religious belief is normally based and assessed on two very different types of sources: a) the *unique* cultural traditions and history that each has; and b) the *shared* experience of human life. The latter provides a good basis for dialogue, while the former often leads to differences and different evaluations. However, the differences should not constitute an insuperable barrier to mutual understanding, given human imagination and empathy, and a shared humanity.

How can these affirmations help sort out relationships between faiths?

One problem between faiths is the way in which one religious faith may believe that it, and it alone, has 'saving knowledge' and hence that the adherents of another religious tradition are in an important respect deemed to be damned or cut off from the Eternal. However, there is an important observation that one can make from the list of affirmations above and which could affect how we think about the evident plurality of faiths in the world, notably the observation of a difference between 'knowledge' and 'salvation'. Theologians are apt to overlook the difference or assimilate the one into the other. In addition, there are forms of religious life in which this assimilation occurs, i.e. where to know is to be saved and vice versa. Thus, one finds within Christianity that there are some who hold that to affirm certain beliefs is to be saved, or to be saved means the same as affirming certain beliefs. No doubt, by 'affirm' they mean 'held with sufficient conviction so as to trust them as demonstrated in action'. But there is the rub. There is a difference between what we *know* and what we *do*; we know, but do not always do. And there are other times when we act rightly without being very clear about what we are supposed to know. The difference in question, i.e. between knowing and living, can have a significant impact on what are taken to be the most basic attitudes (dispositions to act) toward other faiths, dispositions which are said to follow from certain religious affirmations.

What are these most basic dispositions towards faiths other than one's own?

Various people have classified prevailing attitudes to other religious traditions as:

1. exclusivist (we only are right; all others are wrong because they differ from us);
2. inclusivist (we are right; others may be right too because in practice, if not in their confession, they think somewhat like us; they may be anonymous Christians, anonymous Muslims or Sikhs by sharing the same conception of the good, etc.);
3. pluralist (everyone is right in their own way, even when they appear to differ).

For the sake of clarity, the important question to ask in being confronted with this choice of labels should be: exclusivist, inclusivist or pluralist in what respect? Are the dispositions based on judgments about *knowledge* or about *salvation*?

In the sphere of *knowledge*, anyone who makes a claim of any kind is logically committed to being an exclusivist. If I say '"p" is true', then I am simultaneously committed to the view that all those who say '"not-p" is true' are wrong for the reason that, logically, p = not, not p. In effect, I exclude all the not-p'ers from the group of people who I think are right. This is a straightforward epistemological point and does not mean that one must be an exclusivist with respect to *salvation* because the latter does not depend on knowledge (see statement 6 above), nor does my knowledge guarantee my own salvation (see statement 2 above). In other words, when I think others are wrong, I am not making any judgments about their relationship to the Eternal, nor am I claiming a privileged state vis-à-vis the Divine for myself.

Are we bound to be 'exclusivists' the moment we make knowledge claims in religious life?

Strictly speaking, in the sphere of knowledge we do not have to be exclusivists about the most important things. Logically, with knowledge claims, it is also possible to be an inclusivist. If I make the claim that colour enhances the world, I am not disagreeing with someone who says that the colour green enhances the world, but I include his or her affirmation within my own. Similarly, in the sphere of knowledge it is easy to be a pluralist. If I make the claim that colour enhances the world, I can allow others to claim that music enhances the world even if I personally know and care little about music. And what, pipes up a third, about perfumes? Whether we are exclusivists, inclusivists or pluralists epistemologically depends very much on the nature of the claims that are made. It will vary. Perhaps one should be careful about reducing everything to a broad set of classifications. More importantly, none of these epistemological positions have any implications about what we think is the status of others, soteriologically speaking. Whilst considering different knowledge claims, it is worth remembering that it is not *knowledge* but *salvation* (realising 'eternal' life, living well), which is of most interest to the average person.

Usually the use of the terms 'exclusivism', 'inclusivism' and 'pluralism' in a religious context are intended to refer to those making soteriological claims. Traditionally the church has echoed St Cyprian, *Extra ecclesiam nulla salus*, that outside the church there is no salvation, thus apparently damning all who do not agree with it (the church). One has to belong, it is assumed, to have any chance of having a *saving* relationship to the Eternal (i.e. truly to live well). The affirmations above may clarify to what extent this is be true. We are dependent on others for our language, meaningful actions and existence, and thus must look to others and possibly to a social institution, such as the church, to facilitate our religious understanding. But our discussion of the church raised questions as to what constitutes its boundaries and the degree to which it supports or subverts our religious life, and the degree to which it 'saves'. It is also clear that one can make few, if any, assumptions about the saving relationship others may have to the Eternal; it is simply beyond our ken.[7] All that any religious tradition can do is to witness to what it has learned or has come to understand, and to live by that.

What then is the Christian contribution to any inter-religious discussion?

Firstly, what it can do is to contribute to the discussion in the public square its own analysis of the disorder in human life, the disorder that is seen to inhibit human

---

[7] Note, for example, the position of Dante (1265–1321) (Reynolds, 2006, pp. 363ff.). Reynolds makes two points very clear. Firstly, Dante challenged the capacity of human beings to know and hence to judge the ways of God. Secondly, he included King David, Emperor Trajan and a Trojan, Rhipeus (representative non-Christians, before and after Christ, amongst the elect) who testify to the glory of God. By way of explanation, Dante says:

'And mortals, keep your judgment straitly checked,
for here we see God face to face, and still
we know not all the roll of His elect.'

From Dante's Christian perspective, we shall never know or have reason to exclude non-Christians from salvation and we will not even know it in the life to come; on the other hand, he was equally clear that some Christian rulers were definitely excluded!

flourishing and preventing people from living well. Secondly, it can only witness to what it believes is the *solution* to this disorder.

The first item of the testimony points out that human love has gone awry and has become self-serving so that human beings are turned in on themselves, a condition from which they cannot readily extricate themselves. The second, and explicitly salvific, contribution is to indicate that only the presence of divine love or eternal love can forgive the consequences of human self-aggrandisement and restore us to our proper love. Human beings can only come to themselves through the presence of the radically other.

There is no indication that the second contribution, the idea of a dependence on divine love, is uniquely Christian. In the first instance, the contribution may simply be an *idea* or a *hope* for the possibility of such a divine love. It is an idea that anyone might play with and cultivate. An active engagement with the idea and reality of love may in fact be encountered in diverse places in human history. There may be no way to explain why people came to the idea (or the hope) other than by referring them to the experience that acknowledges the sheer presence of divine love as something ubiquitously present throughout the world and throughout time. However, there can also be a loss of confidence in such an idea, a hopelessness or despair can creep into human life following suffering and anxiety caused by our mortality. As human beings, we are all too aware that we are prone to rationalisations and wish-fulfilment. We may come to think the life of love is all a utopian dream. At other times, human beings are simply too self-absorbed to acknowledge the love of the Other. It is at this point that the Christian revelation comes to bear on the situation.

The fragility of the sense of being loved is countered in the gospel, which announces that divine love is shown in one of the deepest points of offence and rejection. In suffering, the love perseveres to the bitter end, and it is a love that is vindicated rather than defeated. It is the sheer particularity, its spatio-temporal dimension, which is critical. If eternal love is encountered at *this* point, it provides the irrefragable basis for *all* human hopes and dreams of divine love both before and after, both here and there. It is no longer an idea but a present reality. There is in the Christian revelation a gospel that which serves to provide confidence in the love of the Eternal wherever and whenever it is found. It proclaims that if eternal love is encountered at *this* point, then, as St. Paul wrote (Romans 8:38–9): 'I am persuaded, that neither death, nor life, nor angels, nor principalities, nor powers, not things present, nor things to come, nor height, nor depth, nor any other creature, shall be able to separate us from the love of God, which is in Christ Jesus our Lord.' In short we shall always and everywhere be the objects of divine love, which is demonstrated and guaranteed by a perception of the presence of divine love in the suffering, death and vindication of Jesus.

In this position there is no justification for boasting or claiming a privileged position soteriologically speaking – the attitude that is found, for example, in the position that 'we are saved, but you are not'. It is not what the God has done for Christians but what was done for everyone, which, if it is true, gives everyone, everywhere cause to celebrate and to live from their own religious traditions with renewed confidence and hope. The capacity for the life of love no longer arises from hopes and dreams cultivated in our religious traditions, whether Christian or non-Christian. We live from the grace of God's love; Christians are merely grateful to know this with confidence, a confidence nurtured by focusing their eyes clearly on re-living and re-experiencing that lonely figure, suffering, dying and vindicated.

There is no need here to deprecate other religious traditions. Nor should we fear for the futures and prospects of their adherents; on the contrary, we know that the Eternal is what will always be present, no matter what happens. We must look to see from where confidence in this knowledge is attained in other traditions and bolster it with the Christian's own confidence, so that, together, Christian and non-Christian may flourish in the life of love and learn to love more deeply.

Religious faith has, in the end, a curious structure which it is as well to remember. Firstly, human beings relate to the Eternal as individuals. It is as an individual that our love is tested. Do we have the capacity to be gracious? Is it wide enough to embrace those members of the human race rejected by others? Are we sufficiently alert not to confuse self-indulgence and wooliness with true love? Is our love deep enough not to wither and fade away with every new fashion and wind of opposition? Do our habits and cultural traditions stand up to close moral scrutiny?

Secondly, it is important to be reminded that the relationship we have as individuals to the Eternal is always mediated by the social. This social dimension determines our thoughts and directs our practices. It is also particularising and universalising. Its universalising elements come from our shared humanity, reason, logic and mathematics from which spring the disinterested, and often interpersonal, qualities and activities, such as the sciences. Other features of social life, such as language, music and art, may be more individuating, but even here much of this is recognisable and shared. It may take effort to understand the languages of others, their art, and their music; sometimes we might conclude that the 'music' is a cacophony or the art repulsive – but with more effort we can grow together and share our interests,[8] influencing each other to good effect.

There are other individuating dimensions to human social life: its cultures, histories and scriptures. These individuating features should not be deprecated as was sometimes done in the Age of Reason, when such matters were labelled as 'positivistic' and not truly amenable to reason. But these individuating features make each one of us distinctive and, indeed, valuable. They contribute to each person's peculiar identity. In the end no one wants human clones or humanity to be a mere uniformity. A world without the diversity of faiths would be spiritually

---

[8] According to Sharpe (Sharpe, 1999, p. 100ff.) Hannah Arendt was suspicious of a political and social life based on love. She preferred friendship. Love appeared to remove a necessary distance between people but surely this is the wrong conception of love. Love creates a bond between people whilst acknowledging real and continuing differences.

impoverished. Everyone should therefore be encouraged to treasure their histories and traditions, no doubt subjecting them to the universal scrutiny of reason, to moral and aesthetic evaluation; this requires listening to the contribution of others. Humanity's universal qualities exist only in individuals and each human being must take responsibility for his or her own life; in doing so, collective traditions are renewed and take on new directions.

PART II
Clarifying to What Christians are Committed

Chapter 11
Believing in the Spirit

Why do we need to speak more directly about the God in our story about human beings with their religious life and what would be the implication of doing so?

So far the purpose of our theological attention has largely been to point out a characteristic human interest (in eternity), to draw attention to what human beings do (worship, pray and engage in sacramental ritual) and to what they think of themselves as religious beings through a 'theological anthropology'. Now our theological discussion must turn more specifically to 'the God'. Of course, none of the other topics would have made much sense without the supposition of *this* focus on the God in these human activities or in the expression of love referred to earlier in the discussion of worship. With a modicum of self-awareness, one cannot help but ask oneself whether these religious interests and activities are not in some way perverse or a form of self-deception. Certainly much of the atheistic criticism of the nineteenth and twentieth centuries is rooted in the fundamental supposition that religion is the consequence of some psychological or social pathology, i.e. a diseased form of human thinking and existence, largely because they do not think it makes much sense to speak about the God except as a form of human projection, fabrication or illusion.

Christians, of course, are the first to admit and agree that people generally do suffer from some form of diseased thinking and existence (and they include themselves among the sufferers), so there is little disagreement on that point, except that Christians will not agree that atheists may safely assume that they are not fellow sufferers. Contrary to atheists, Christians also insist that the religious attention to 'the God' is rooted in the apprehension that a right relationship to the God is the source of life, health and happiness. Thus, the disagreement between atheism and theism is precisely on this point, i.e. on the role of 'the God', either as the source of salvation or as a sign of pathology in human life. Confronted with this dispute, the theological problem is that this disagreement between believer and unbeliever is not amenable to an easy resolution. The primary reason for the impasse is that there are no agreed criteria that could be used to resolve the differences except possibly this: does religious life in which unconditional giving and creativity is taken as the ultimate reality lead to liberation or to enslavement?

Does the difference between the atheist and the believer consist only in this: of one seeing the God as a source of pathology and the other as a source of healing?

No, not entirely. Some commentators try to depict the difference between the 'believer' and 'unbeliever' in another way, notably as one in which they both share the essentials of life but where the believer takes on board an additional optional extra(s). Religion on this view becomes a 'bolt-on' extra set of beliefs that might well be jettisoned if it did not suit the person. In addition, it is then supposed that at the core of religious life there lies a fundamental decision, a decision in which one chooses to accept these optional beliefs as true or otherwise.

However, there is something fundamentally odd about this picture of the state of play concerning religious life, particularly in the supposition that the beliefs one holds are a matter of decision. It is true that one sometimes *decides* to trust a person or to undertake certain actions, but beliefs are different. Beliefs seem to be more like something at which one arrives, as it were, unwittingly. Often one is not sure what one believes until another person points it out, the belief(s) being implicit up till then in how one lives and in what one does. The upshot of these remarks is that religious *beliefs* are often misconstrued; they are in fact not so much a selected 'bolt-on' extra than directions which permeate our life and appear to give this life its characteristic form. It is a practice that comes first, and from this life with its varying imperatives, goals and motivations, we rightly or wrongly deduce some beliefs or attribute beliefs.

The main way to resolve the differences between the believer and unbeliever is to attend to the character of their life. From this one may discern the real differences between them and whether their respective lives are liberating and flourishing or not. There will, of course, be a dispute over what defines freedom and flourishing. A believer might, for example, prefer martyrdom to a life of betrayal; he or she dies for what he or she lives for. An unbeliever would have little reason to follow this example, though he or she may die because he or she no longer has cause to live.

The believer's life importantly differs from the unbeliever's in that it is a form of life in which a sense and recognition of 'the Eternal' and 'transcendent' plays a defining role. To a believer, the God opens possibilities of creativity, making whole what is broken and providing a consoling freedom. The alternative is perceived to be to live in a mood of despair, because the reality of mortality creates anxiety in the struggle for survival. One might note that if the source of unbelief is the causal explanations of a scientific world view, then a mechanistic world picture does not offer much scope for freedom.

Is the believer's life characteristically different from the unbeliever's life?

There is no simple answer to this question, for it will depend on the nature of the religious life and on the nature of the unbeliever's life. Each presents itself in different guises. In thinking about examples of the distinctively religious 'forms of life', there is something that is strikingly different about Christian life in comparison to its 'close relations', Judaism and Islam. The latter are clearly well-ordered forms of life, that is to say, they are closely governed by the guidance and rules to be found in their primary (the Torah and the Qur'an) and secondary (Mishnah and Hadith) scriptures. The rules which govern their lives are developed from these sources. Human well-being is cultivated through this structured living. The rules will determine how their respective lives differ. Put simply: are you or are you not governed by these rules? Christianity in comparison looks distinctly 'lawless' – anomic. But, of course, there are *some* rules and laws that guide Christian living and the faithful community, such as those found in canon law. Nevertheless, the rules here have a different status, as they have been given a subordinate role. If one asked 'subordinate to what?', one could only answer that it is subordinate to the creative freedom and mystery of the God. But what does that mean?

In practice, Christian interpretation of what Christians are required to do seems to swing between a strict rigorism (Kirk, 1932) on the one hand and an utter lawlessness on the other. So, in its extreme, the expression of Christianity varies from the rule-bound life of the monastics to an unrestrained secular life.

One can already see some of the problems in the New Testament. Matthew's Gospel is explicit; he quotes Jesus as saying: 'Think not that I am come to destroy the law, or the prophets; I am not come to destroy, but to fulfil. For verily I say unto you, till heaven and earth pass, one jot[1] or tittle[2] shall in no wise pass from the law, till all be fulfilled. Whosoever therefore shall break one of these least commandments, and shall teach men so, he shall be called the least in the kingdom of heaven: but whosoever shall do and teach them, the same shall be called great in the kingdom of heaven' (5:17–19). Thus it is that Matthew sets out to show how what Christ requires is *more than* law. As such, he provides such sayings: 'Ye have heard that it hath been said, an eye for an eye, and a tooth for a tooth: But I say unto you that ye resist not evil: but whosoever shall smite thee on thy right cheek, turn to him the other also. And if any man will sue thee at the law, and take away thy coat, let him have thy cloak also. And whosoever shall compel thee to go a mile, go with him twain' (Matthew 5:38–41).

In contrast to Matthew's exhortations to do more than what the law requires, we have Mark's depiction of Jesus as condoning law-breaking by his disciples, which he justifies, for example, with the statement 'The Sabbath was made for man, and not man for the Sabbath' (Mark 2:27 – this was said on an occasion when they appeared to onlookers to be breaking the prohibition of working on the Sabbath). In general, Mark's Gospel accepts that Jesus challenged the religious authorities rather than conformed to them and their rules.

The ambiguous status of rules in Christianity is also evident from one of the very early controversies in the church. This centred on whether Gentiles in

---

[1] The smallest Hebrew letter.
[2] A small part of a Hebrew script that distinguishes the letter 'k' from the letter 'b'.

joining the Christian community had to conform to such legal requirements as circumcision, which existed in Judaism. Here Paul, as a Jew, conformed to the law but insisted (against James and Peter) that Gentiles did not need to conform. Although he wavered from time to time, Peter finally went along with Paul. In the end, Pauline Christianity, i.e. the supposedly anomic Christianity, prevailed so that Augustine could say much later: 'Love God and *do as you please.*'

Of course, the strict ambiguity between the rule-formed life and the lawless life is not removed, for what does the qualification to 'love God' mean? One can sum up: for Christianity, a) adherence to laws or b) the abrogation of laws is subordinate to the condition provided by, or set by, the nature of the relationship to the Eternal or to 'the God'. On the face of it, it presents us with an alternative either of compelling a strict adherence to law or of inviting a radical freedom.

So what is the difference created by a relationship to the God?

The question is: how is a person to understand the notion 'the God'? Here again Christianity does not provide a straightforward answer.

Judaism and Islam are very clear. God is 'One'. As such, all the complexities of life are transformed by a singular condition, a prevailing unity that binds the diversity in the world. One must serve this unity and live responsibly before the God, i.e. one is answerable to this unity. There is a deep seriousness in this position. Life is to be judged by what one does and not by what happens to one!

In contrast to this recognition of unity as ultimate in Islam and Judaism, in the Christian calendar, the teaching part of the year begins with *Trinity Sunday.*

So is Christianity not a monotheistic religion?

Whatever the Trinity means, it should be stated from the outset that Christianity is, and remains, first and foremost a monotheistic religion. At no point should the doctrine of the Trinity be used to undermine the assertion that the God is 'One'. Nevertheless, Christian theologians have discerned a degree of multiplicity associated with this unity. This may not make much *logical* sense, so it is all the more surprising that for so long Christian theologians have held on to the doctrine of the Trinity with such tenacity. It should be acknowledged that this persistent affirmation of the Trinity did not happen without protest. There was always a Unitarian stream within the Christian tradition and during the nineteenth century many liberal theologians had all but dropped the doctrine of the Trinity, only for it to return with a vengeance in the twentieth century due to the somewhat strident insistence on it by K. Barth and all those influenced by him. It is difficult to read Christian theology today and not come across someone who insists on the primacy and crucial role of the 'triune' nature of God.

The persistence of the doctrine of the Trinity within Protestantism becomes all the more surprising when it is noted that it is not particularly biblical either, in that it is not specifically mentioned there, although of course Trinitarian theologians claim to infer it from Scripture, for example, from the final commission given in Matthew 28:19. The problem is that this is probably a late text. Moreover, it is not at all clear that the text means or implies the doctrine of the Trinity. The persistence of the doctrine in the face of an apparent illogicality and the lack of a biblical warrant should at least stimulate us to examine this issue more closely.

So what, if anything, is at stake in the affirmation of the Trinity?

A clue to what may be at stake is in a basic distinction that is often made in 'Trinitarian' discussions between what is called the 'economic Trinity' and the 'essential Trinity'. The former effectively refers to what 'the God' does, and this is elaborated specifically in relation to human beings, to their life and their world. The Trinitarian conception suggests that this divine activity, whatever it is, cannot be readily defined through reference to an overriding singularity only, but requires one to mark some important differences. We must remember that our capacity to know and to speak of the God at all may only be made possible by reference to the immediacy of what the God does for us. This varies. Briefly, the *economic* Trinity is therefore the God as It is *for us*. The *essential* Trinity is the God as It is *in and for Itself*.

For our purposes we can largely ignore speculation about the essential Trinity as it largely arises out of what is sometimes called 'ontological' speculation, i.e. metaphysical speculation about the nature of ultimate reality. Since, apart from how this ultimate reality exists *for us*, it must be entirely beyond our ken, we must therefore be wholly silent about it. Theologians who persist in speaking about the essential Trinity in my judgment simply overreach themselves. To use an illustration, they want a guarantee that the insurance policies mean what they say by referring the policies to something else. However, in my view there is no way of ascertaining the meaning except through a close examination of the text of the policy; there is not a policy behind the policy to which one can refer for an assurance of what the policy offers. To conclude: if there is any point in speaking about an *essential* Trinity at all, it is done, firstly, to espouse religious and theological modesty, namely that there is more to the God than we could possibly know, understand, express or experience and, secondly, it is rooted in a confidence that the varying ways in which the God shows Itself to us is how the God really is. But neither of these two points authorise one to speculate substantially about how God is in Its essence.

In brief, the economic Trinity arises from the distinctive character of the God's *actions* towards us, while the essential Trinity (if that concept makes sense) belongs to the mystery of the God and what is effectively ineffable. One may think of the essential Trinity as *the implication* derived from theological terms which have greater immediacy and application. For example, if 'God is Love' for us, and yet in an important sense is also 'self-sufficient' and not dependent on 'our world', one can then say with Augustine that God in Itself is Lover, Beloved and the Relationship of Love, all in One. Love requires an object and the God's independence ensures that it is not us and our world, therefore it must be that the God is an object to Itself and the relationship between subject and object must also be intrinsic to the being of the God.

So what does the God 'do' in relation to human beings and our world that warrants describing the God as triune?

The traditional terms used to describe divine activity are: Creator, Redeemer, Sanctifier or, liturgically, as Father, Son (Logos) and Holy Spirit (Wisdom). H. E. W. Turner in his article on the 'Doctrine of the Trinity' in A. Richardson's *A Dictionary of Christian Theology* claims that:

> ... the structure of the NT is basically triadic and it is verified in the three aspects of the Christian experience of God: dominion, communion, and possession. These are, in turn, closely linked with the decisive moments of revelation: God over us, God with us, and God in us. All these together exhaust the spiritual possibilities of knowing God. (p. 345)

Perhaps all of this should be treated with a pinch of theological salt, in that the chosen language presumes a certain psychological satisfaction with a tradition of threefold repetition (listen closely to political speeches). After all, in addition to those three prepositions (over, with and in), one could always use other prepositions to articulate the relationship between human beings and the God, such as the God *under* us as the foundation of our life. What is clear is that the Christian tradition has found that the relationship of the God to human beings is best organised in a threefold manner.

What I wish to discuss briefly is the *third* way in which the God is said to impact on human life, viz. the God in us.

How and why do we want to think of the God acting in us?

There are three major festivals in the Christian year: Christmas, Easter and Pentecost (Whitsunday). Easter is associated in the New Testament with the Jewish Passover, which remembers the Exodus, a recollection of the activity of the Divine in securing a delivery from slavery into freedom under the God. Pentecost, or 50 days later, in the Jewish tradition celebrates a harvest festival but it also marks the giving of the Law, another occasion for thanksgiving. If in Jewish tradition the grace (self-giving) of the God is made manifest as Torah, in Christian tradition it is manifest as *Spirit*.

In the Christian tradition Pentecost marks the end of the immediate presence of the Christ and highlights the *immanence* of the God in human life experience. The Spirit is referred to differently in Scripture. One of the descriptions is that of the breath of life (pneuma, Ruach). It is in effect the very stuff of life itself (see Romans 8:10; John 6:63; 2 Corinthians 3:6]; a fundamental test of life is that one breathes. At the same time it is depicted as what is uncontrollable: one cannot quite get a hold on it – the spirit bloweth where it listeth – and it is further described in Scripture as the truth and the comforter. The Spirit, as opposed to other enabling powers, is most importantly what unites and conciliates. Typically the story of Pentecost (Acts 2:1–13) reverses the story of the Tower of Babel where, as a result of inordinate ambition, humans were dispersed, speaking different languages and therefore becoming incomprehensible to each other, but at Pentecost the different languages are 'mastered' and understood. People have found another form of life where they are sensitive to each other and understand each other. The language of love is a universal language that commits people to each other.

Are there any other key associations with the activity of the God in us?

Typically Pentecost is also associated with a 'baptism of fire', i.e. a process of purification, and in addition the flame of fire is a mark of restless fragility. After the death of Princess Diana, some people lit a candle both to signify life with the movement of the flickering flame but also to note life's fragility as the flame can so easily be extinguished. All these characterisations are not rational descriptions, but they catch the mood of how the God as Spirit is perceived to affect Christian life, as enlivening and purifying but at the same time as somewhat fragile and elusive.

At all stages Christians are encouraged to test the spirit because the forces that empower people can be very varied (think of such terms as Zeitgeist, Weltgeist, the spirit of man and the spirit of evil). Only what unifies, enlivens, purifies and consoles in a spirit of Love is said to be from the God. Note that this empowerment is not what can be defined, bought, captured or controlled. The spirit frolics with a Dionysian recklessness and is ecstatic and enthusiastic. The rules may help in one's attempt to define its nature, but in the end these are not considered to suffice within Christian life. Rules can sometimes get in the way of the presence of love. For Christians, only love convicts a human being of his or her unconditional acceptance and thus transforms a person's life, making it holy (that is, sanctifies it). God is Spirit because the God is unbounded and always present as a life-giving power. This then is one of the personas (faces or masks) of the God.

If atheists perceive religion as pathological, then it is necessary to ask: 1) does the atheist see rightly, i.e. could he or she be mistaken?; 2) if religious life is fundamentally pathological, is it because religious persons and institutions have betrayed their faith?; or 3) does religious life truly lack the qualities that religious believers have always claimed it to have, i.e. an empowering creativity, being both liberating and consoling? Would an absorption into the realities and constraints of human nature serve us better? Is it always more fruitful to think of our world solely as causally determined or the product of accident?

Chapter 12
The Work of Christ

If the God relates to human beings and to the world through the Spirit why do Christians designate this Spirit as the Spirit of Christ? What does the Christ contribute to the picture?

Firstly, it is important to remember that when Christians speak of Jesus Christ, one should not treat Christ as a kind of surname or even as a second proper name. It is a title which gives him an identity that commits his followers to giving him a very specific role in human history. Assessing that role involves reviewing the condition in which human beings find themselves.

It was noted that to live religiously is to live *coram Dei*, before God. As we noted, atheists have claimed that religious life is a pathological form of human existence. Religious believers accept that there is a pathology that eats away at our existence, but in spite of this they also have cause to be hopeful and confident in life. Their justification for being hopeful and confident is tied to the story of Jesus Christ. So we must now turn to another persona of the God, which has a much more precise connection to humanity in the figure of Jesus Christ. The otherness of the God is qualified by the notion that Jesus Christ is fully human but also one with the God.

How is it that Christian teaching can come up with something quite so radical and unexpected as the idea that in Christ the God and human beings are one?

Just as it seemed unwise to explore who or what the God *is* without exploring who or what the God *does*, it also seems unwise to try to come to a full understanding of what it means to say that the God is one with humanity by being incarnate in Jesus Christ without first exploring what the Christ is said to *do*.

The title 'Christ' is given to Jesus of Nazareth, and in so doing he is assigned a role because he is identified according to the Scriptures with the expected one, the anointed, the holy one of the people of the God. Unlike the immanence of the Spirit, this identification with Jesus of Nazareth gives the activity of God's unification with human beings a very precise historical reference: it is located in a particular person in a very specific place and time. But the opening of John's Gospel also associates the same Christ with the 'Logos', the Divine Word. Originally in the scriptural narrative the Divine Word is: 1) that which *created* (and creates) the world, 2) that which *commands* and orders in the Torah, but now in a pivotal moment there is the perception of a further important development. With Jesus Christ, the God 3) *restores* humanity and its world to itself, overcoming mankind's self-alienation and *reconciles* this humanity and world with itself into an ultimate unity. In other words, the doctrine of the incarnation combines the particularity of the historical event with a cosmic and eternal significance by reference to a fundamental act of at-one-ment. The doctrine boldly maintained that all creation that exists or has existed in faith either anticipates as a possibility or recollects as an actuality this reconciliation of the Divine with the human. The perception of the Divine activity is that the Eternal, through the Word (the Eternal's thought-informed action), *creates* out of love, *commands* with love, and *restores and reconciles* through love, hence the conclusion that the God is Love.

In what sense does the historical moment of 'Jesus Christ' contribute to the restoration and reconciliation of the human and the Divine in the Christian narrative? What kind of account could one give of it?

Initially the Christian church tried to capture, understand and express this contribution in metaphors or what St Anselm (d. 1109) described in his book *Cur Deus Homo? (Why the God-man?)* (1989) as 'beautiful sayings' and 'pictured realisations'. The church simply pointed to the story of Jesus Christ's ministry, suffering, death and 'resurrection' that is taken to show this reconciliation. In being content to do no more than to narrate, the church was admitting that no one form of conceptualisation was up to the task.[1] Anselm's own attempt to express it seeks to rectify the elusiveness of the 'sayings', the beautiful and 'pictured realisations'[2] of the narration; they lack what he thinks of as 'reasonable solidity'. As such, he sets out to provide an account that shows 'the *necessity* which proves that God should or could descend to that which we predicate'. The twentieth-century Swedish theologian G. Aulen (1970) regrets this rational twist by Anselm and others, and tries to bring us back to what he calls the 'classic theory' with its vivid imagery and metaphor. The underlying assumption is that sometimes one can only understand through literature, poetry and myth how it is that people are redeemed and made one with the God. In the light of these metaphors, the logical rationalisations of the reality of redemption appear as puerile oversimplifications. F. W. Dillistone in *The Christian Understanding of the Atonement* (1968) takes a somewhat similar approach to fixing the meaning of Christ's activity by drawing on what he calls 'ranges of comparison', mostly of a literary nature.

---

[1] 'It is as if at the centre of the Christian faith the redemptive action of God explodes all theories and formulas. The spirit breaks and creates many forms, and no one of them can contain it' (Williams, 1968, p. 39).

[2] R. Bultmann also tries to provide some reasoned order through his existentialist philosophy. Thus, he judges all the metaphors to be 'mythological' interpretation which is nothing but 'a hotch-potch of sacrificial and juridical analogies, which have ceased to be tenable for us today. And in any case they fail to do justice to what the New Testament is trying to say' (Bultmann, 1953, pp. 35–6).

Thus, one tension in Christian theology with regard to what Christ does is between those who want to tell the 'old, old story' (gospel) elucidated by other, similar stories from the experience of human beings on the one hand and those who seek a closely reasoned account on the other. This difference among theologians is perhaps not as important as some may be inclined to think, in that the theologians are agreed that one is reconciled to the God through the *activities* of Jesus Christ and not through one's *accounts* of Christ's activities. The problem is how one arrives at the sense of what Jesus Christ is supposed to have done. We have to accept that some prefer a literary route; others turn to formal arguments, similar to those one might find in philosophy. Another possibility is that the methods should be seen as complementary.[3]

Is there another way of making sense of these various theological attempts?

Looking more closely at the accounts of what Jesus Christ is supposed to have done, one can see that they fall into two basic groups (with Aulen's dramatic theory possibly constituting a third in trying to find a way of incorporating the key elements of the other two). The two groups can be roughly called the *objective* theories and the *subjective* theories depending on where the locus of the primary impact of Christ's activity is to be found. The 'subjective' theories find this impact primarily in *individual lives* and in the way that Christ's activity changes people, i.e. in how it changes them as human beings. (Naturally, this is necessary if one is to overcome self-alienation or any other state where the individual must change.) The 'objective' theories find the impact primarily in some *state of affairs* (for example, with respect to the demands of justice) that is quite independent of how individual human beings are and live. The overall point of these classifications is to focus one's attention on *where* the essential change is made by Christ's activity.

Where things are changed also affects our conceptions of *how* things are changed. Traditionally (i.e., according to Anselm), theologians identified five competing accounts of the 'mechanics' of the Divine–human reconciliation: this reconciliation is achieved through: a) recapitulation; b) a ransom or redemption from the 'devil'; c) the manifestation of divine love; d) an inscrutable fiat (word) or act of divine will; and e) the satisfaction of divine justice. Anselm favoured the final one. On our earlier classification, a), b) and e) will all be seen to be some version of the 'objective' theory, c) will be seen to qualify as a 'subjective' theory, whereas d) cannot be classified at all, but this is solely because it essentially refuses to say how or why the reconciliation is effected, except to say that the God willed it. Its inscrutability prevents any further comment. (It is said that when the nineteenth-century atheist H. Heine was asked to repent of his sin on

---

[3] Abelard, Grotius, H. R. Macintosh, R. W. Dale, F. W. Dillistone, R. C. Moberly, H. Rashdall, L. Hodgson et al. have all made interesting contributions to theories of the atonement. More recently Christological discussions have not focussed so clearly on atonement as on other concerns.

his deathbed, he refused and replied: 'God will forgive that is his business!' If one took this response seriously, he was a believer par excellence because he trusted that all would be well!) Anselm refused to accept option d) not only because it fails to demonstrate its rationality but also because the sheer arbitrariness of it seemed to offend against God's justice, that is, in his view the God is bound to act reasonably. Justice must not only be done but must be seen to be done, i.e. it must be understood that the action taken is in fact just.

The *recapitulation* theory in account a) was effectively inspired by St Paul with his description of Jesus as the second Adam. The thinking behind this is that the alienation of human beings from the God was effected by the action of a representative figure (Adam) who acted on behalf of us all and can now only be undone by effectively reversing the action through another representative figure (the second Adam, i.e. Christ) who also acted on behalf of us all.

For the modern person there are two basic issues with this recapitulation theory: firstly, Adam is clearly a mythic figure and can a mythic figure be said to act for us in any meaningful sense? Secondly, how can this representative figure act on our behalf and implicate us all? The answer depends on the extent to which we can think of a human solidarity represented in one individual, i.e. of humanity as a collective reality that is also collectively responsible in terms of being embodied in one individual. One potential example might be as follows: it is possible to see that somehow we all belong to a nation. The British nation is represented by the prime minister and his or her action implicates us all, no matter how much one might protest against, for example, a declaration of war. For this declaration of war, we are collectively responsible and guilty. So far, so good – but could another 'representative' *undo* the actions of, for example, a Mr Blair? A successor might reverse national policy or try to compensate victims, but can he or she undo what has been done? Perhaps he or she could only do so through a collective national act of atonement. It is more difficult to think of the act of a single individual being sufficient in this context.

The talk of 'ransom or redemption from the devil' in account b) may also strike the modern person as altogether too mythical to be obviously credible. Can we still believe in Satan? An alternative to this personification of evil might be to try and demythologise the theory by emphasising that evil when it exists is a kind of reality with power over us, from which one cannot simply escape through an act of will. It has a logic and a claim (or hold) on us that does not permit us simply to turn over a new leaf or to let bygones be bygones. But if this is the case, how does any action of Jesus Christ break this power?

We (together with most liberal theology) might turn to c) and say that Christ does it through his example by inspiring us to act differently and more nobly. There is no doubt that Jesus and, indeed, other heroic and impressive figures have inspired others to act and to live differently from how we might otherwise have lived. Christians are constantly invited to imitate Christ just as Muslims might be encouraged to live by following the example of Mohammed. Somehow, no matter how impressive the figure may be, this account of the human state of affairs on its own will not do for the Christian theologian – more is required to be said. This is, firstly, because the theologian (and the believer) can never be sure that he or she has an accurate historical view of Jesus. Do we have an accurate picture to imitate? Do we know enough? Another question that arises is could not a literary figure or a mythical saint, i.e. an imaginary being, serve the same purpose just as well? Alternatively, might not more recent heroic figures such as Gandhi and Martin Luther King serve our purposes in life better? They at least were closer to the world we now know.

Anselm himself sought to answer these problems with his 'satisfaction' theory in his book *Cur Deus Homo?* The outline of his argument goes somewhat as follows:

- Human beings have sinned, i.e. dishonoured God through disobedience.
- God upholds His honour justly.
- God's honour is upheld through the punishment of the one who causes offence.
- Not to punish is to forgive unjustly and fails to re-establish God's honour.
- The one who has caused offence must, in addition to perfect obedience in the present and future, either repay the honour of which he robbed God or must suffer punishment (eternal death).
- Human beings cannot repay because they already owe all that they are and have to God.
- Thus, human beings must pay but cannot; on the other hand, God can repay but need not.
- If human beings are to be saved and not be punished, what is required is a God-man, one who both can (as God) and ought (as man) to repay and re-establish God's honour.
- The God-man can only repay with what is not already owed.
- As man, he already owes the perfect obedience that could warrant eternal life.
- So what can be offered?
- What the perfect man does not owe is death.
- Being perfect, the free offering of his death for others is of infinite worth or merit.
- This infinite merit is available to all human beings, and all human beings may avail themselves of it.

By this means the moral order is maintained, God's honour is upheld and human beings are restored in their relationship to the Eternal. The possibility of living a fulfilled life that depends on a relationship to the Eternal is once again open to every individual. Thus, for that end and by these means we can see how Anselm attempted to show the 'logic' or necessity of a God-man.

But does the 'logic' work? Anselm's account generates a number of issues that appears to challenge the 'logic':

1. Whence comes the compulsion of the law that appears to bind even the God to exact punishment?
2. There is the problem of a distinct discontinuity in divine operation: the God *both* commands *and* obeys; punishes *and* bears the punishment. Does the God suffer from a form of divine schizophrenia?
3. There is obfuscation on the precise relationship between merit and justice.
4. The concept of justice implied in a situation where the innocent (Jesus) suffers for the guilty (us) is distinctly questionable (most people would consider a situation where the innocent suffer due to the actions of the guilty to be unjust).
5. One might reasonably conclude that none of the theories of the atonement may suffice. They all trade on some very basic perceptions: a) a perception that human beings have a problematic, fractured relationship to the Eternal; b) a perception that human beings do not have the capacity to correct this condition; c) a perception that human beings are dependent on the activity of the Eternal and are not in control of forming this relationship; and d) a perception that this activity and reconciliation of the Eternal with humanity is demonstrated and realised in at least one individual. It is a historical event known as 'Jesus Christ' (it is not a mere idea) and it is an event which is depicted as one in which the whole of humanity (from the beginning of time and everywhere) might share or participate. As a consequence, in this event the God is now known differently, notably as redeemer, even though it is the same God, the One who creates, commands and inspires.

To understand all this, we may have to rely on stories, as Dillistone and some other modern commentators have suggested, rather than on some algebraic logic.

Chapter 13
The Person of Christ

What is it that drives our interest in the figure of Jesus of Nazareth?

The basic response to this question is that human beings have an interest in the Eternal and engage in religious practices that express and cultivate that particular interest in a form of life. Christians have found that Jesus mediates and sustains this interest in the Eternal in a significant way, hence our turning towards this figure.

Of course we might have turned elsewhere. We might simply have begun with human nature to explore the reasons why people have this interest in the Eternal, but unfortunately 'who' or 'what we are' is largely in a state of confusion, so self-examination is not a very reliable guide. Therefore, we cannot simply rely on a process of self-examination to come to any definite conclusions about what the interest in the Eternal amounts to or what the Eternal signifies.

The main reason that human beings have an interest in the Eternal is due to the inescapable *presence* of the Eternal, which claims human attention just as much as 'physicality' (of the physical world) does. Alternatively, it claims attention just as the 'aesthetic' and the 'moral' constrain human beings to acknowledge the realities of moral and aesthetic life and force us to speak about them. For the Christian community of faith, the presence of the Eternal has shown itself as a life-giving spirit since Pentecost. It was also a spirit that was associated with 'Jesus Christ', i.e. Scripture speaks of the 'spirit of Christ'. To understand 'who Jesus Christ is' meant that we had to look at what he did or does. What is clear to Christians is that whatever 'Jesus Christ' did (or, more accurately, what the God did in Christ), it both changes them and appears to change the human situation vis-à-vis the Eternal. As such, Christianity is a religion of redemption and theologians in turn have constructed various atonement theories to articulate the sense of what 'Jesus Christ' did and does that was examined earlier (this is a part of soteriology, the reflection on the subject of salvation).

So what can one say about Jesus Christ that brings the Eternal into sharper focus?

In responding to this question, we are turning to the subject of Christology proper, i.e. the reflection on the person of Jesus Christ. When looking at what Jesus Christ did or does, we are in fact also trying to ascertain who Jesus Christ is. However, according to D. Bonhoeffer, this is putting things the wrong way around. The work, he says, is always capable of various interpretations; thus, he states: 'I have access to the work of Christ only if I know the person who does this work. It is essential to know the person if the work is also to be known' (Bonhoeffer, 1966, pp. 37ff.). He relies here on an encounter theology, where it is reasonable to know a person without reducing it to what we might know *about* a person, for example, historical information on what a person has done. He does not want our religious life and faith to be dependent on historical research!

Perhaps it is not so important to decide whether who Christ is or what he does should be considered first, so long as we see that the 'doing' and 'being' of a person are interdependent and interrelated. This could be seen from St Anselm's account of what Christ does. It was part of Anselm's endeavour to show, on the basis of what Christ does, who he is, namely, the God-man. We may conclude that in reality, who Christ is and what he does are inseparable in any serious Christian account.

Within Christology there has always been the danger of focusing exclusively on 'who Christ is' without thinking through what this means *for us*, i.e. without thinking about what he does. The separation of who Christ is from what he does has led some to adopt an exclusively historical approach, with a study of Jesus of Nazareth. This concentration on the history of Jesus can be theologically simplistic by ignoring the continuing role of the Christ in the lives of the disciples after Jesus' death, a role that persists to the present day. In actual fact, the motivation of many of those who pursued the original quest for the historical Jesus in the nineteenth century was not theologically neutral as regards what Jesus Christ does. Their motivation was often to counter and challenge the traditional Christian doctrines that mainly sought to account for Jesus' continuing place in Christian life, i.e. why Jesus happened to be an object of faith.

There were nevertheless some who did seek to reinvigorate Christian life with a picture of Jesus that better fitted the canons of modern historiography. The problem that they encountered was that on that narrow basis alone they could never ascribe to Jesus anything other than the status of a more or less impressive human being. In other words, they could not arrive at anything that looked like the traditional teaching of the church of Jesus as the God incarnate or, in Anselm's terms, as a God-man.

From the historical studies, Jesus emerged as a moral teacher and exemplar, a wandering preacher and healer, a heroic revolutionary figure and, for a few, a deluded man. When at the climax of the Gospel of Mark (8:27), Jesus asks 'Whom do men say that I am?', various answers were forthcoming. But one is bound to say that with the confession of faith by Peter that 'Thou art the Christ', we are dealing with much more than a historical judgment. Matthew, for example, makes that clear in a parallel passage where Jesus responds to Peter's confession: 'Blessed art thou, Simon Bar-Jona: for flesh and blood hath not revealed it unto thee, but my Father which is in heaven' (Matthew 16:17), i.e. it is not a human judgment but is divinely inspired. To summarise: firstly, what Jesus Christ does and who he is are intimately connected; secondly, historical research may be essential in the efforts to discover who he is, but historical research alone will not suffice in helping us to understand who he is without first locating him and his activity religiously, and this is not just a historical issue.

How can we go about finding out who Jesus Christ really is?

We can see from the earlier discussion that the question about who Jesus is, and consequently the key Christological issue, raises the subject matter of its *methodology* – how does one go about finding a reasonable answer? Despite my reservations about relying exclusively on historical research, there are some modern theologians who think that this is precisely the method one should adopt. One must start with history. W. Pannenberg in *Jesus: God and Man* (1968, pp. 33f.) tries to force the issue by suggesting that there are essentially only two methods and two types of theological accounts to choose from: there are what he calls 1) the 'Christology from above' and 2) the 'Christology from below'. He defines them as follows: 'For Christology that begins "from above", from the divinity of Jesus, the concept of the incarnation stands in the centre. A Christology "from below", rising from the historical man Jesus to the recognition of his divinity, is concerned first of all with Jesus' message and fate and arrives only at the end at the concept of the incarnation.' Pannenberg has opted for this latter Christological approach – the Christology from below – but not without first tinkering with what he considers to be appropriate historiography. He has to do this in the light of our earlier observation that on its own historiography does not, and cannot, lead to affirmations of faith.

So how does Pannenberg revise the understanding of historiography which would lead him to affirmations of faith?

Pannenberg's attempt to redefine historiography is most starkly evident in his treatment of the resurrection. He states: 'As long as historiography does not begin dogmatically with a narrow concept of reality according to which "dead men do not rise", it is not clear why historiography should not in principle be able to speak about Jesus' resurrection as the explanation that is best established of such events as the disciples' experiences of the appearances and the discovery of the empty tomb' (1968, p. 109). The trouble is that this 'narrow concept of reality' is precisely what determines our normal historical imagination and reconstructions. Our historical imagination depends on the world with which we are familiar, and in this world, as he puts it, 'dead men do not rise'. Pannenberg is driven to adopt an implausible historiography in which it is conceivable that dead men do rise because, without it, he could come to no religiously significant conclusions.

Pannenberg sees some basic problems with 'Christology from above', which he ascribes to K. Barth. His complaint is that: 1) Barth's approach presupposes the answer rather than finding reasons for the answer; 2) the approach loses sight of the singularity or particularity of Jesus; and 3) in viewing the matter, it presupposes the standpoint of divinity rather than our finite perspective in the world. We might be tempted to agree with him that Barth's approach with a 'Christology from above' is mistaken, but Pannenberg is the first to admit (1968, p. 33) that the ancient church had already espoused this approach in the second century, and indeed there are already echoes of it in the New Testament itself (i.e., Philippians 2:5ff.; Romans 8:3; Galatians 4:4), Despite Pannenberg's protest, I think that any and every Christology is bound to introduce religious categories from the start. This immediately presumes that the normal categories of secular disciplines and discourses will not suffice as a basis for an object of faith. This is sometimes known as 'theological non-naturalism', i.e. secular disciplines cannot suffice for religious and theological conclusions. One finds a parallel situation in the field of ethics where it is supposed that one cannot derive an 'ought' from an 'is', that is, statements of value from statements of fact alone. It confirms our judgment that the category of the Eternal is *sui generis*.

Did the early church have any fixed ideas about Jesus Christ?

What Pannenberg does demonstrate successfully is that Christian thinking about 'who Jesus is' was in a *state of development* from its very beginning. First, note that the disciples on the road to Emmaus (Luke 24:13–35) shortly after the crucifixion had to have the Scriptures expounded to them or 'interpreted' before they could begin to recognise Jesus for the person he was, and only then in the familiar community practice of breaking bread together. Their simple acquaintance with Jesus as a wandering teacher was not enough. From this gospel story, we see that the exegesis of Scripture and a 'religious' practice (of breaking bread together) hold the key to the developing understanding of 'Jesus Christ'.

Where, and how, can one see this development in the thinking of the early church about Jesus Christ?

A brief examination of the New Testament beginning with its earliest writings in: 1) the Pauline epistles, (which constitutes the earliest Christian documents), followed by 2) the Gospel of Mark (the earliest gospel but written after Paul's letters), 3) the roughly contemporaneous Gospels of Matthew and Luke, and finally 4) the Gospel of John (the latest gospel)[1] will show the evolutionary process of church thinking highlighted by Pannenberg.

Uncovering the meaning of the story of Jesus, so to speak, starts at the end of his life and moves backwards. Paul's reflections and Christian work began with his own conversion on the road to Damascus, which he described as an encounter with the resurrected Lord (1 Corinthians 15:8). Mark begins a little earlier, notably with Jesus' baptism and ministry of teaching and healing. Mathew and Luke begin earlier still; they try to take a perspective on the whole of his life, beginning with

---

[1] These judgments about dating appear to be the consensus amongst New Testament scholars.

his birth and supposed 'family history', locating him and his significance in the tradition. Finally, John's Gospel takes us back to the beginning of time and the creation of the universe, and thus offers a cosmological perspective. The whole Christian story becomes increasingly comprehensive and sophisticated.

What sort of things does the New Testament say about Jesus?

When we look to what the New Testament actually has to say about Jesus, we can see that it uses a number of different titles to describe Jesus: Son of Man, Messiah, Christ, Son of God and Kyrios (Lord), each of which has a range of meaning that is by no means easy to determine and which together do not provide us with any systematic account. At this stage it is almost as if the primitive church was engaged in a form of 'brainstorming' to find the right concepts to crystallise its understanding of the person and events surrounding Jesus. They were genuine attempts to locate him and his teaching within their religious horizons without coming to any fixed conclusions. The next four to five centuries were to see the church in a continuing discussion and debate which roughly divided into two phases, the first of which more or less ended in the Council of Nicea in 325 AD and the second in the Council of Chalcedon in 451 AD.

What form did the reflections of the Church Fathers take?

One of the things that was never in doubt to the disciples was that Jesus was a human being who needed to eat, drink and sleep, who grew tired, who needed his feet washed, who on occasion grew angry and who was often compassionate. With the humanity of Jesus unchallenged, the primitive church was free to speculate about where Jesus fitted into its religious universe.

The first phase of the discussions therefore focused on his 'divine' status and his precise relationship to the One God, a unity which the Church Fathers already presumed from their tradition. The second phase of the discussion focused on his humanity and how exactly this related to his supposed 'divinity'.

The range of the discussions during the first phase swung from the clear affirmation of the humanity of Jesus amongst the Ebionites without any claim to divinity on the one hand to the Gnostics on the other, who appeared to embrace a form of docetism (from *dokeo* – to appear), in which Jesus was clearly a divine being and someone who only *appeared* to be human, since strictly speaking a divine being in their view could not really be human at all. The Ebionites were Jewish Christians for whom the Torah was paramount. For them Jesus was the Messiah by virtue of his perfect obedience to the Law. Their clear monotheism prevented any kind of ascription of divinity to Jesus, and his role was more prophetic than redemptive. If Jesus' death had any meaning, it was as a demonstration of his unconditional faithfulness. The Gnostics appeared to be a largely syncretistic movement in which the material world was generally regarded as evil and as the prison for human souls, from which they had to be liberated by secret knowledge (gnosis). Their world contained many spiritual beings arranged hierarchically according to their varying degrees of spirituality, usually in inverse proportion to their materiality. Within this framework the humanity of Jesus was played down. At the same time there was little scope for seeing Jesus as the *sole* divine being, but rather, at best, as one who was, more or less, like the Divine, just as others might be.

In addition to seeing Jesus Christ as either human or divine, what other possibilities were there?

Generally, the church resisted the denigration of the material by the Gnostics, but there was a form of *Monarchianism* that went further than the Gnostics in its approximation of Jesus to the Divine. It was a position that stressed the absolute unity between Jesus Christ and the God to the point of sacrificing Jesus' distinct personality. This, in turn, invited yet another reaction that one finds in *Arianism*, which stressed the distinct personality of Jesus but to the point of sacrificing his unity with the God. Jesus Christ is a mediator, but only by virtue of being an intermediate being. Generally one finds a whole range of positions in the early church (detailed below in Appendix 1).

However, as Christianity became the established religion of the Roman Empire, the need to have a common position became imperative, as much for political reasons as for religious reasons. What was at stake was not only the unity of the church but also the unity of the state. The Council of Nicea in 325 AD was convoked by the emperor. It sought a mediating position between those of Arius and St Athanasius, between the view that supposed Jesus Christ to be '*homoi-ousios*' with God, i.e. a being like God, or '*homo-ousios*', i.e. a being of the same reality as God (note the difference of one iota, the letter 'i', physically the smallest letter in the Greek alphabet!). The question really boils down to how we can know the God at all in our world and whether we can recognise the Divine in anything human. The position of St Athanasius prevailed. The later Council of Constantinople (381 AD) reaffirmed the position of Nicea and condemned other positions that had emerged subsequently, notably those of *Sabellianism* and *Apollinarianism*, which had their own ways of stating the precise relationship between Jesus' humanity and supposed divinity.

Why did the debates and discussions not end there with the affirmations of St Athanasius?

Effectively, a second phase of the discussion began because once the divinity *and* the humanity of Jesus had been agreed, the focus turned to how these two aspects or natures related in the one person. Once again there was an attempt to define precisely in what sense a person could have two natures – a human nature and a divine nature. Again, various positions were explored (detailed below in Appendix 1), culminating in the Council of Chalcedon (451 AD), which stated that Jesus

Christ was 'homo-ousios' with the Father according to the Godhead and 'homo-ousios' with us according to manhood – two natures in one person[2] – 'without confusion, without mutation, without division, without separation'. William Temple, the former Archbishop of Canterbury, said of this famous definition that 'the formula derives part of its value from the clearness with which it refuses to explain'. Effectively, the advice was to live with the intellectual paradox.

How can one summarise these Christological debates?

It is possible to summarise the whole debate over five centuries by simply stating that through this one human life, in the totality of what Jesus said and did, and in what happened to him, the disciples, and later many others, were introduced to the Eternal. It is an acquaintanceship, which changes everything for them. The world changes; the meaning of life changes; they are changed by it, sometimes slowly but irrevocably; sometimes they are changed dramatically, as in the case of Paul. The effect on the latter was so decisive that he changed his name from Saul to Paul, reflecting a substantive change in identity. I have used the language of 'being introduced' and of 'making acquaintance' as suggesting a twofold dimension: 1) that of mediation; and 2) that of immediacy. Our knowledge of other people is mediated through what we physically see and hear, as well as the stuff of history, but we also meet them, as it were, directly. We know *them* and are not just making an inference from their physical presence. Likewise, with Jesus, we are not indifferent to the facts of history, but there is also a relationship of immediacy to the Eternal.

Why should we worry about what the decisions of the Church were so long ago?

A key theological question has always related to just how much attention we should pay to all these church council discussions and outcomes in the early centuries. Are these conciliar decisions in the first few centuries authoritative and binding on Christians today? Is one duty bound to believe what was agreed in 325 or 451 AD? The answer depends somewhat on how much we value tradition and the views of others formulated in a different time or place. On the whole, modern human beings tend to look down on men and women from earlier times, believing that we know so much more and better! Collectively this may be true in science and technology, but these are not the only matters that interest us; if this were the case, we should stop reading Shakespeare or Aristotle. In any event, one of the values of studying the history of thought and listening to voices from the past is that it saves us from the narrowness of our own world.

---

[2] There are mono-physite (one-nature) churches in the Middle East to this day, so clearly not everyone agreed. The challenge is to see the practical implications of these theological judgments.

In general, however, the Roman Catholic position is that the conciliar decisions are indeed binding because they constitute the official teachings of the church. The church's considerations override all others. It is the church that authenticates Scripture and hence has authority over what Scripture contains and how it should be interpreted. As the visible 'body' of Christ, it infallibly defines the content of faith. There may be scope for re-statements or for additions, so long as they conform with what it declared to be true in past statements.

In contrast to this, the early Protestant view was that these decisions were in no way binding, since only Scripture could play *that* role. The conciliar decisions were only relevant insofar as they clarified, expressed or conformed to the witness of Scripture. The Westminster Confession and the Thirty-Nine Articles of the Anglican Church quite baldly stated that the councils of the church 'may err and have erred'. They were human beings after all! They had their own source of infallibility in Scripture.

The more recent Protestant view is that these decisions are not binding but deserve respect as landmarks in the developing self-understanding of faith. The creed-makers themselves recognised that the Divine transcends all formulations and there is no evidence that they themselves thought they were giving the final word on the matter. The church is a *fallible* institution that lives from the expectation of a new order. Inevitably, the creeds reflect a) the intellectual atmosphere of the day with all its philosophical presuppositions, b) the nature of Scripture as it was interpreted at the time – hermeneutical theory shows that human interpretation inevitably changes with changing human interests, c) the political realities of the time and d) the insights brought to bear by other religions and by the developments in culture, such as scientific knowledge at that time. As all of these change, the theological accounts are also bound to change.

How are the theological accounts changing?

Early twentieth-century discussions about Christ are divided by John McIntyre (1966) into groups which he sees as conforming to three basic models, which he classifies and describes as a) the two-nature model, b) the psychological model and c) the revelational model. The emphasis on 'models' stresses their basic heuristic function, i.e. they explore possibilities of understanding rather than giving a final account. They do not so much picture reality as show us how we might live in the light of them. If we ask why it is necessary to choose one model rather than another, different factors come into play: 'textual/critical; historical; cultural; sociological and geographical; liturgical; and ethical'.

How can one sum up Christology?

Briefly, the Christian tradition pays attention to 'Jesus Christ' because through him the Eternal is made present. From the perspective of the presence of Jesus Christ, we can say that we are reconciled to an unchanging reality despite our past history and events, and even despite what we may yet do. Through the act of recollection, in which the past is made present, this original event of 'Jesus Christ' is made into a living reality now or, as S. Kierkegaard would have put it, we become 'contemporaneous' with it. The practice of love and self-sacrifice, which such recollections urge on us, transforms life and the world. It also constantly reminds us of the ambiguity of the world. It always tests the understanding that the temporal could be the occasion for something eternal. The Christian witness is that even extreme suffering and death, despite their 'God-forsaken' nature, have nevertheless been, and will continue to be, the bearers of love. These events test love, but love is not defeated by them and, as such, they are witnesses to a true constant in our world. Those who despair will not and cannot see this. Only the eyes of faith see resurrection.

The issue may be: do religious people see clearly? Normally we construct our world and to some extent at least do so according to our fancy. According to the modern mystic Simone Weil, we only see the world truly and experience it without delusory constructions in our suffering. The suffering and death of Christ may therefore be a final revelation.

Chapter 14
On Speaking about the God

From where do we get this habit of speaking about the God?

This may be the wrong question if we take it to be a question about human nature or about our personal or cultural history. The answers would then be only relatively interesting and may be as various as there are people or cultures. Instead the question should be taken more in terms of what makes our religious and ultimately our theological discourse meaningful and differentiates sense from nonsense.

Perhaps one ought not to rush into this topic (of the God) unthinkingly. Misconceptions abound, particularly in those efforts which set out to explain humanity's predilection for religious expression as if sociology, psychology or history could finally dispose of the issue without reference to the 'object' of religious life. Nor should we treat the topic simply as something to chat[1] about. The occasion for 'speaking' at all arises out of human existence of being 'before God' (*sub specie aeternitatis*), which introduces a note of seriousness. And if the religious interest and witness is to be taken seriously, it is important to note that the primordial response is simply silence. This should be accompanied with a patient waiting on the God, as one mystic heard it:

> I will come to you at my pleasure, when I want;
> if you are calm and quiet

---

[1] 'What is it to *chat*? It is to have repealed the passionate disjunction between being silent and speaking. Only the person who can remain essentially silent can essentially speak; only the person who can remain essentially silent can essentially act. Silence is inwardness. Talking forestalls essential speaking, and reflection's utterance weakens action by stealing a march on it. But the person who can speak essentially because he can keep silent will not have a whole world to speak of – just the one thing – and he will find time both to speak and to stay silent' (Kierkegaard, 2001, p. 87). Or as Kierkegaard wrote in *Philosophical Fragments* (1985, pp. 13f.): 'With slipshod thoughts, with higgling and haggling, maintaining a little here and conceding a little there, as if the individual might to a certain extent owe something to another, but then again to a certain extent not; with loose words that explain everything except what this "to a certain extent" means – with such makeshifts it is not possible to advance beyond Socrates, nor will one reach the concept of a Revelation, but merely remain within the sphere of idle chatter.'

If one wants to advance beyond Socrates, one has to be prepared to relate it to one's life; without this dimension discussions become chatter or, as Dostoyevsky would have it, the chatter between professors and his students in the pub, without real seriousness.

and hide your distress where you are able,
the power of love will grow in you.[2]

A secondary response may be that of Moses before the burning bush who, being enthralled with awe, took off his shoes.

Why is it important to be silent?

The silence (Weil, 2002, p. 37) arises for at least two reasons. In the first place, in dealing with any kind of given, one must begin with an alert attentiveness, and any serious attentiveness that constitutes a 'straining to hear' does not admit the distraction of talk. Secondly, the silence follows from the sheer mystery of what confronts us, a mystery that may only consequentially inspire some 'derivative' or subsequent discourse. Thus, the very first response to being before the infinite and unfathomable Eternal is that it reduces a person to a state of aphasia or speechlessness. One may conclude that the confrontation with mystery[3] induces this state of being lost for words and with it the recognition that any words and conversations that are devised will prove to be inadequate. Alternatively, perhaps one can put it more strongly than that, namely that to speak about the God or to describe the God is idolatrous.[4]

Religious aphasia is a form of inwardness and hence religious silence should be contrasted sharply with, and differentiated from, lacking the courage to speak in public. Threatened with physical violence or with loss of employment, people no longer speak their minds; however, this is not to say that they have not articulated their thoughts. As J. Pieper observed, 'under conditions of tyranny ... no one dares trust anyone else. Candid communication dries up; and there arises that special kind of unhealthy wordlessness which is not silence so much as muteness' (Pieper, 1963, p. 32). True silence is inward and something people may strive to achieve through prayer and meditation.

Religiously, when we break the silence and do resort to talking, it is because we can no longer bear the silence. Thus, St Augustine, for example, explains his doctrine of the Trinity: 'When the question is asked – what three? – human language labours under an altogether great poverty of speech. The answer, however, is given – three persons – not that it might be adequately talked about, but to avoid silence.'[5] Human beings are so made as to be driven to think and so to speak. Here, of course, Augustine is writing as a theologian, someone with a vocation to think.

---

[2] Mechthild von Magdeburg, *The Flowing Light*, cited in D. Blamires, 2003, p .9.

[3] See D. Z. Phillips, 2008, p. 12.

[4] 'For Maimonides, to think we could traffic in true literal predication of intrinsic attributes of God is in effect an expression of the idolatrous urge to contain God in an image or representation. Positive theology emerges as a kind of intellectualised idolatry' (Johnston, 2009, p. 105).

[5] *De Trinitate*, V, 10 cited in I. T. Ramsey, 1963, p. 22; See also Lash, 2008, pp. 112ff.

Perhaps he recognises a more fundamental reason for what drives people to speak before the God, namely, the religious response to life as a gift from the God. This leads people to give thanks, to express joy and to praise; thus, he writes:

> And yet, while nothing really worthy of God can be said about Him, he has accepted the homage of human voices, and has wished us to rejoice in praising Him with our words. That in fact is what is meant by calling Him God. Not, of course, that with the sound made by this one syllable any knowledge of Him is achieved; but still, all those who know the English language are moved, when this sound reaches their ears, to reflect upon some most exalted and immortal nature.[6]

Theology's indicative (descriptive) discourse, the talk *about* the God, only follows the performative (Austin, 1953, 1962, 1976) function of language in religious life, i.e. praising discourse.

Is silence with respect to God a characteristic only of being religious?

The immediate answer is no. The a-religious person is similarly conjoined to this state[7] of aphasia (speechlessness). After all, if the phrase 'before God' is empty of meaning, then there is nothing to say about it and the human condition that seeks to be defined by it. Only by re-defining the condition as essentially and exclusively human, for example, as human 'belief' or 'superstition', does it become a topic for conversation – however, it should be noted that there is a huge gulf between 1) being *before God* and 2) discussing human beliefs *about God* (the latter is done before and with human beings).

Despite Augustine's perception that religious life drives one to give voice to thanks and praise, there is ample evidence that silence is required. The religious condition of aphasia is implied, for example, in the Ten Commandments of the Judeo-Christian tradition. The Second Commandment forbids the making of an idol and worshipping it (Exodus 20:4). Perhaps it is the physical making that is the real target for this injunction, but human constructions have never been confined to the tangible, to what can be felt and handled. We are all too eager to make visual and audible images. Even the physicality that this implies is abandoned in our mental constructions as we play with concepts and ideas. 'Idol-making' is found in the very activity of human reflection that ranges over the whole of human life. Something that must never be forgotten is that the whole enterprise of theology and much of religion only gets off the ground, so to speak, by breaking one of the most fundamental religious prohibitions. By constructing a conceptual universe,

---

[6] 'Of course, Augustine says the Latin language, and talks of two syllables of the word *Deus*' (Ramsey, 1963, p. 126).

[7] 'For one who does not know God – great and glorious – silence is inevitable, while for one who knows God most high, silence is imposed' (Al-Ghazali, 1992, p. 2).

we are already well on the way to making idols. We complete that journey when we become more interested in the constructions and begin to value these above all else, so that we lose the attentiveness to the other and to the neighbour who by definition is nearest to us to mediate the sense of the other.

The Third Commandment (Exodus 20:7) seems to reinforce the second: the name of God shall not be misused. How can we not misuse the name of the God in theology? How is it possible for us to speak of the God without naming the God? And when the name of God is precisely that which is withheld, are we not in danger of misusing the name? The theophany experienced by Moses in the burning bush appears to impress on us that the God refuses to disclose its name (Exodus 3:13–14) – 'I am who I am', alternatively translated as 'I will be who I will be'. We are left solely with the identification: 'the God of your fathers'.

Potential abuse of the name is implied in another theophany, as we may gather from the response of Isaiah (6:5) who, on being confronted by an experience of the Divine, exclaimed 'woe to me, I am ruined! For I am a man of unclean lips, and I live among a people of unclean lips'. It is as if our very language is corrupted to the point where before the God we cannot speak of the God.

The prohibition on naming the God is a common practice among many Jews in the present day who, when the text names the God, can only utter the word for Lord. The vowels of the name are always omitted in the text to signal that one must not utter it.[8] It is sometimes suggested that the prohibition to name the God is rooted in the presupposition that naming and conceptualising is the source of the human attempt to master the world. Since the religious sense is that the God cannot be mastered but that It masters and subdues us, the attempt by human beings to name the God is inappropriate (Exodus 33:17–20; 20:19). Humans might name animals (Genesis 2:19) but not the Divine.

But does the God exist? And if It does, what are Its chief attributes or qualities?

God as a subject of our conversation generates a number of considerable difficulties. Perhaps even the way we pose the question about the God can mislead us. As such, the question 'who or what is God?' is sometimes associated with the question 'Does God exist?'. This latter question can wrongly[9] suggest that God is some elusive person or object. We might then mistakenly go on to ask about the *evidence* for the existence of such an elusive person or object. We would then appear to be treating the subject matter in much the same way as we might pursue the topic of the existence of the Himalayan Yeti, the Loch Ness Monster or the

---

[8] It is well known that the word 'Jehovah' in the King James version of the Bible derives from the tetragrammaton (the four consonants signifying the name of the God) plus the vowels of another word, 'adhonai', meaning Lord.

[9] See, for example, Hauerwas, 2002, p. 28. Hauerwas quotes John of Damascus: 'God does not belong to the class of existing things, not that God has not existence but that God is above all things, no, even above existence itself.'

tenth planet. Yet there is a significant difference. With these traditionally elusive objects, a world in which they exist is clearly different from a world in which they do not. This scenario is not possible to imagine in the case of God, who is not part of this world. The believer cannot think of a possible world without the God. If we were to say that it is this world which makes the denial of the existence of the God possible, then we are presuming the outcome of the argument, because this is precisely what the devout believer denies. In looking for evidence, we are looking for what would make the critical difference *in* the world. We would need to imagine two different states of affairs, but with the difference between the believer and unbeliever we are always considering the very same world. There could never be evidence that decisively makes the case one way or the other. It is the *sense* of religious belief, not the existence or non-existence of evidence which makes the difference.

That it is a mistake to think of the Divine as akin to some lost or elusive object follows mainly from one of the chief attributes normally assigned to the God, namely that the God is *Creator*. Use of this attribute effectively means that we cannot go on to specify the evidence for the God *in the universe* through which we could unambiguously recognise (or identify with any assurance) the Divine, since the term 'Creator' implies that the God is Other than the universe. With this conception there could never be any scientific necessity to speak of the God because science confines itself to causal relationships *in* the world. On the other hand, since, according to the concept of creation, the universe derives from the God, in some sense *everything* may be said to point to the Divine;[10] given this totality, nothing could be imagined in the world to disprove the Divine. To make the claim that the God is Creator is not like making a descriptive assertion in the form of 'Mrs Jones is Welsh'. To say that the God is Creator is to make what Wittgenstein called a *grammatical* statement,[11] i.e. it is a statement that indicates how the concept 'God' is to be used. To define the concept in this way is to generate certain other implications.

Firstly, to say that God is *Creator* is to introduce an important distinction that has radical consequences for the manner of our speaking about God and our subsequent methodology. The distinction is first and foremost between 'God' and 'world', reflecting the binary system of human reflection. Here the 'world' means not just the physical world but all that we are, including our culture and the environment, i.e. the spatio-temporal universe with all its 'furniture'. Our definition of the 'world' is entirely comprehensive in the sense of not excluding anything. Everything that is an object to us and that 'exists' belongs to the category of the world. This has the implication that the God does not 'exist' in any of the

---

[10] Meister Eckhart put it this way: 'The more He is in things, the more He is outside things; the more He is within, the more He is without' (1963, p. 54).

[11] See for example, '"God" and Grammar: An Introductory Invitation' (Phillips, 2008, pp. 1–17).

usual senses of existing. This is worth remembering if we are not to be misled by asking the question 'does God exist?'.

If we finally do come to use the concept and to speak of the God, it is because there is something in the quality of our life that draws us out from where we normally find ourselves. It is as if the focus of our lives lies beyond the horizons of our world so that we are drawn into thinking in a new way. (There are other examples of human interests where one is compelled to think outside a given framework of enquiries with which one may have started: for example, thinking about freedom, when one may have started with an investigation into causes; thinking about beauty, when one originally began to think about utility; and thinking about the future, when one began with the present or past.)

Normally the human self in its world is the main object of our concern, expressed in the ancient observation that 'Man is the measure of all things', so it is not at all natural to look beyond the horizons of our world. Yet the very possibility of a meaning that lies beyond the self and its world already has the profound effect of changing the focus of our interest away from the self in its world. It has the effect of a decentring of the self from the self, i.e. a condition in which the self is no longer the primary, foundational concern to the self. Now, this conceptual decentring of our life has an impact on how we subsequently value and live in our world; in brief, the self and the 'world' become penultimate, temporary and lose their finality. There is a necessity for openness and uncertainty. This is characteristic of a genuinely religious sense of life.

Secondly, to say that God is *Creator* is to introduce an asymmetrical relationship of dependence between the God and the world. The asymmetry consists in this: the world is dependent on God but, as has been maintained traditionally, God is not dependent on the world. Why this should be so is not obviously clear to the religious mind, since there are religious traditions where this is not the case (for example, in monism or pantheism, in which the God is identified with the world, which is tantamount to a deification of the universe or of nature). Some attempt will be made to show that this asymmetry derives in part from the point of making the distinction between 'God' and the 'world' in the first place.

Essentially, the asymmetry derives from the value of making a distinction between the God and the world on the one hand, together with the requirement to maintain some relationship between them on the other. If in making the distinction between the 'God' and the 'world' we arrived at a straightforward dualism, there may be little reason to speak of the God at all, for if the God were so entirely Other that there was no relation to the world, God would simply be a kind of nothingness to us, an absence that does not concern us. On the other hand, if we were *not* to make a serious distinction between the God and the world, the God would end up simply being another aspect of our world, making the dualism unnecessary. The asymmetry expresses an experience in life.

Translated into religious life, the grammar of asymmetry reflects the sense of a relationship of dependence of the world on the God, which is experienced in the world and is described as 'love' and 'grace'. Theologically, the doctrine of the creation of the world *ex nihilo* (from nothing) means the world originates solely a) in the Self-love of the God and b) in the God's determination of being for another. Religiously, the being and life so bestowed on the world and humanity is experienced as a gift, and hence is attributed to divine grace.[12]

Thirdly, from the observations that 1) the God is Creator and 2) that the relationship of dependence between the God and the world is an asymmetrical one, it also follows that the God is *free*, i.e. not bound by the world but solely bound by Its own nature. This quality of the *freedom* of the God may lead us to think of the creation of the world as God's 'fiction'.[13] The important consequence of assigning to God the fundamental attribute of creativity prevents us from constructing our realities purely out of the desire to satisfy some human need, for that would make the reality of the Divine dependent on the human. If we nevertheless persist in constructing such projections of our own nature onto some heavenly screen,[14] then they are clearly the idols that cannot liberate us from ourselves. The freedom of the God means that It cannot be manipulated, bullied or cajoled, which is the reason why prayer could not be conceived of serving any such function either.

Fourthly, the *freedom* of the God also has implications for the way in which religious people have sometimes ascribed *goodness*[15] to the God. For example, Meister Eckhart could say:

> God is neither being nor goodness. Goodness pertains to being and is not more extensive than being; for if being did not exist, neither would goodness ... God is not good, nor better, nor best of all. If anyone were to say that God was good, he would do him as great an injustice as if he called the sun black.[16]

Plato discussed the dilemma of ascribing this moral property of goodness to the God in his dialogue the *Euthyphro*. Is the good a good because the God chooses it to be so or is the God good because It conforms to some pre-existing and independent moral law? The latter option suggests that the God is not free in any absolute sense, while the former option introduces the apparent conceptual possibility that the God might have 'chosen' evil as Its good. So, by insisting on the freedom of the God, one opens up the possibility that the good is an arbitrary choice of the Divine. However, arbitrariness does not follow from freedom, as is sometimes supposed. Perfect freedom follows solely from acting according to one's nature. The God is good in no ordinary sense of the word 'good', i.e. of

---

[12] Ethically, this notion that human life is a 'gift' of God leads to the prohibition of suicide and euthanasia.

[13] The Latin word *fingo* means to make, create or shape, but it is also the root of the word 'fiction'.

[14] As maintained by L. Feuerbach in *The Essence of Christianity* (1957).

[15] For a useful discussion of the question relating to God's goodness, see Brian Davies, 'Is God a Moral Agent?', in Phillips, 2008, pp. 97ff.

[16] Eckhart, 1963, p. 12.

conforming to a moral law that transcends one's own nature. If the God is good, it is because It freely acts according to Its holy 'being'. God is not so much good as the source of the good, i.e. God is holy.

Why do we, as human beings, use the concept of 'God'?

So far we have indicated how the concept 'God' is to be used which, as we have noted, has led to certain interrelated attributes (creativity, freedom, holiness). The overriding question for many today is why should one use the concept 'God' at all? Is it redundant? Might one not use Ockham's razor (do not multiply entities beyond necessity) and end with a simpler and more reliable understanding of the world without introducing the concept of the God into the account at all? The simple answer is that for the believer, the presence of the God requires it, but traditionally there has been a twofold answer.

Rather picturesquely, Kant expressed the traditional response to what drives us to speak of the God as the 'moral law within and the starry heavens above'. Together these comprised the main reasons for resorting to the concept 'God'. Kant meant that the intelligibility of moral life required it and the sheer magnificence or impressiveness of the physical world demanded it. We can express the grounds for religious belief in the God more generally as being 1) human self-understanding as moral beings and 2) the intelligibility and aesthetic character of the world. Together and severally, they have driven people to speak of the God. Of course, these claims do not go unchallenged and the religious people themselves have reservations about any easy and presumptuous assertions that in the end would simply reveal their idols.

Should believers not be under some moral obligation[17] to prove to themselves and to others the 'existence' of God? The influential nineteenth-century theologian F. D. E. Schleiermacher considered the task to be 'entirely superfluous' (Schleiermacher, 1928, p. 136). The Danish thinker S. Kierkegaard thought it similarly pointless (Kierkegaard, 1946, pp. 161ff.; 1985). He even thought of the attempt as a kind of betrayal, the reason being that the task misrepresents the very character of religious life and the nature of theological and philosophical thinking. The latter are merely expositions of a state of being.

But is Kierkegaard simply making a virtue out of necessity? It is certainly the case that the various arguments or proofs for the 'existence' of the God that have been produced in the past have never been convincing either because they do not seem to be logically compelling or they make assumptions that need not be accepted. Despite this, not everyone has dismissed these rational exercises as entirely useless. They may not be logically compelling demonstrations, but some have taken them to be pointers to what it may *mean* to take a religious view, exercises in what St Anselm called 'Faith seeking understanding'.

---

[17] See C. K. Clifford and the ethics of belief.

What are these elaborations of taking a 'religious view'?

The main traditional so-called 'arguments' and 'proofs' may be categorised into three groups as follows: 1) the ontological argument, classically stated by St Anselm; 2) the five ways of St Thomas Aquinas, comprising three cosmological arguments (from contingency, from causation and from motion), the axiological argument and the teleological argument; and 3) the moral argument.

In brief, the ontological argument insists that if we are to know in any true sense of the word 'know', then the act of knowing must imply the existence of what is known. Of course, this does not mean that every attempted act at knowing or that every conception implies an existing reality. One's idea of a perfect island, for example, does not imply that it must exist, however good our imagination might be! Nevertheless, wherever the act of knowing was to be most complete[18] and most 'perfect', such an act of conception must imply existence or it would not be the most perfect conception. It would be possible for us to conceive of something more complete and perfect, namely a conception that includes existence. For Anselm, this notion of an absolutely complete and perfect conception is what he meant by the God and that is why in his intellectual universe the God must exist if cognition, generally, is to mean anything. All imperfect human knowledge is in some way dependent on the possibility of this ideal congruity between the most complete, perfect conception and existence.

In the case of Aquinas, the underlying assumption of his five 'ways' is that the world is completely and totally reasonable. However, a simple reflection on the explanations for what we observe about our world (such as those relating to the observations of motion, of cause and effect, and of contingent being) leads to the obvious conclusion that the explanations they yield are inevitably incomplete. They could not be completed in their own terms alone because to confine them to their own terms would lead to the different infinite regressions that by definition are never completed. Thus, in the case of motion, any thing 'y' that moves something else 'z' must itself have been moved by something 'x'. This 'x' must have been moved by something else, 'w', and so on *ad infinitum*. (A similarly structured argument can be formed for causation and contingency.) Any *complete* explanation therefore requires the introduction of a concept somewhat different from the others in the series (motion, causation and contingency; God is not just another cause, mover or contingent being). As a kind of necessity from the presumption of rationality with the implication of completion, Aquinas introduces notions that are of a different order but that are necessary to bring about completion. These notions he calls an 'unmoved mover', an 'uncaused cause' and a 'necessary being'. In turn, he was not slow to assert that these are the same as the concept of the God; they show something of the meaning of the concept 'God' in a totally rational universe.

---

[18] Anselm speaks of the 'greatest'.

In the axiological argument, Aquinas relies on the observation that a scale of values points to an absolute value in relation to which all others are relative values. And, finally, in the teleological argument, the perception of purpose in the world requires a different order of explanation from that encountered in the realm of the natural sciences. In short, the concept of an absolute and the observation of purpose also led him to the concept of God, mainly again in order to be able to arrive at the possibility of having complete explanations. Note that the theological contribution is not there to compete with the other explanations; the God is not just another value or an ordinary cause, but exists to complement them in order to achieve that element of completion demanded by his faith in the total rationality of everything.

Finally, Kant devised the moral argument for the existence of God not because, as is sometimes supposed, we cannot be moral without such a conception but in order to support the *practical* sense of striving morally when it is clear that the highest good of moral life cannot in fact be attained in this life. It may satisfy some people simply to strive to answer questions that have, and could have, no satisfactory answers in this life. Others will regard such striving to be in vain unless we can assume that, *in principle* at least, there is an answer to find. In a somewhat similar way, the striving intrinsic to moral life appears to be in vain unless we assume, and believe, the highest good is realisable *in principle* and it is this that Kant associates with religious life; in other words, religion provides the appropriate *ethos* for the ethical life[19] by believing in the possibility of realising the highest good.

---

[19] Note Pierre Bourdieu's emphasis on the importance of *ethos* when determining what is or is not rational: 'Unlike the estimation of probabilities which science constructs methodically on the basis of controlled experiments from data established according to precise rules, practical evaluation of the likelihood of the success of a given action in a given situation brings into play a whole body of wisdom, sayings, commonplaces, ethical precepts ("that's not for the likes of us") and, at a deeper level, the unconscious principles of the *ethos* which, being the product of a learning process dominated by a determinate type of objective regularities, determines "reasonable" and "unreasonable" conduct for every agent subjected to those regularities. "We are no sooner acquainted with the impossibility of satisfying any desire", says Hume in *A Treatise of Human Nature*, "than the desire itself vanishes." And Marx in the *Economic and Philosophical Manuscripts*: "If I have no money for travel, I have no *need*, i.e. no real and self-realising need to travel. If I have a vocation to study, but no money for it, I have *no* vocation to study, i.e. no *real, true* vocation"' (Bourdieu, 1977, p. 77). If in this analysis Hume and Marx are right, then with the perception that the highest good is not realisable, one would lose the desire to be good. This is the logic of practical reason even if people are seldom so reasonable and will be satisfied with lesser goods.

Why do theologians not make more of an effort to show the existence of the God?

If there is a mistake to be found in all this striving for proof and a conclusive argument for the existence of God, it is that healthily religious people do not normally seek to provide *grounds* for their belief; this activity is left to theologians who are already religiously sick. *Before the God*, one can only worship, tremble, confess and hide, but one cannot check the God's credentials, or discuss the God in the abstract. What religious people usually do is to say 'this is how we live; it requires us to acknowledge the God; for if we do not, there is little for it but to despair of finding in life any kind of meaning that is eternal, that is to say, the meaning that does not depend on how things go in life'. They would say: 'This meaning and only this meaning can satisfy and bring us happiness. Our hold on this meaning may be tenuous and may be betrayed in life, but nevertheless it is a possibility that will not let us go. If this love did finally come to mean nothing to us, then we would think that we had lost something precious, like the lost chord or our vision.'

Do these theological ways of defining religious terms solve the problems inherent in religious discourse?

The 'grammatical' move of making a distinction between the God and the world generates a number of difficulties. It immediately raises problems for how we use our 'language' relating to the God, the distinction always appearing to require us to use it in a qualified way. Normally our language is rooted in the world; its references, for example, are to things in the world. As such, when we want to use this secular, worldly language to refer to the God, its function becomes fundamentally odd. This is reflected in how theologians traditionally think they can speak about the Divine. Some of the main ways are as follows:

1. *Via negativa* (the way of negation): this effectively asserts that whatever the world may be like, the God is not like that. From this type of attempt at expressing and characterising the nature of the God, we arrive at such attributes as: immortality, immutability (unchangeable), aseity (self-sufficiency, independence), simplicity, eternity (in the sense of being a-temporal) and impassibility (incapable of suffering).
2. *Via eminentiae* (or the *via positiva*): this effectively states that whatever 'perfections' the world may have, the Divine is more so or they constitute pointers to the character of the God. Thus, such qualities as omniscience (all-knowing), omnipresence (everywhere) and omnipotence (all-powerful) are attributed to the God.
3. *The way of analogy*: Aquinas devised a theory about how language might appropriately be used about the Divine, which leads theologians to say that all language about the Divine is used *analogically*. A word can be used either *equivocally* or *univocally*, i.e. a word might either have two

very different meanings or be used with the same, or identical, meaning in different contexts. Thus, a boot can mean both an item of footwear or in Britain the back compartment of a car; here the word is said to be used equivocally. Conversely, the word 'hat' could be used to refer to very different items of clothing worn on the head and yet they could all be recognisably a hat; in such a case the word 'hat' would be used univocally in each case.

The theory of analogy was devised to show how a term could have somewhat the *same* meaning in various situations and yet incorporate a significant *difference* without being committed to the position that the word in the different contexts would mean something entirely different. As such, when one assigns the human attributes of 'fatherhood' or 'motherhood' to the God, it is thought to be done properly (i.e. there is a sameness, a consistency in meaning), but there is also a significant difference. The difference in meaning is attributable solely to the important difference thought to exist between the *Being* of God (as Creator) and the *being* of men or women (as created realities). There is in effect an *analogy* in the use of the terms when it is applied to the God and to human beings. And because of the critical role played by 'being' with the stated distinction between creator (God, as the source or power of being, is being itself) and created (those which *have* being), the theologians refer to it as the *analogia entis* (the analogy of being).

4. *Metaphor*: some theologians like to say that all theological language is metaphorical in character, attempting in this way to establish the linguistic feature of likeness and difference in God-talk.
5. *Mythological*: many theologians also think that all theological or religious discourse is best characterised as mythological because one narrates about the Divine as 'acting' in this world. Of course, this inevitably anthropomorphises the Divine in ways that are both necessary and unavoidable, but that in an important respect are also inappropriate and misleading. The stories are in that sense always both true and untrue.

One could add to this list and elaborate on the various ways of speaking, but they all indicate that discourse about the Divine must *both* be taken seriously *and* yet used with 'a pinch of salt'. Sometimes silence is best.

Chapter 15

Revelation

How do we truly come to know the God?

We saw that the God does not come within the normal orbit of existing things. In many ways it is better to say that the God does *not* exist than that It does exist because the latter claim (God exists) mostly misleads us into thinking that the God is a created thing, an entity belonging to the world, and the ensuing confusion effectively turns the God into a figment of the imagination, into idols or human constructions. Human beings are happy to engage in such speculative constructions because it makes a seemingly chaotic and uncontrollable world into something that appears, on the face of it at least, more amenable to being understood and managed. This response locates religion within the wider interest of mastering the world stimulated by insecurities brought on by the constant threat to our physical existence, for example, misfortune, illness and death. Little wonder that the idols human beings create in response to this situation are mere images of human needs and wants. However, the God who creates our universe from nothing is not quite so amenable to being called into the service of human efforts to control their environment and life.

What if human desire is truly to control life and the environment, and this is what we really want to know? What are the consequences of this?

If our desire is for control and mastery, then there may be other and better ways than to turn to scriptures and religious traditions, namely, the scientific method and technology. In fact, science brooks no opposition and quickly challenges any forms of religious superstition that seeks to provide human beings with an identical service. The struggle between these opposing perspectives is an unequal one, for it does not take long for the natural sciences to demonstrate that its method of critical experimentation endows its predictive powers with a greater assurance than any religious prophecy could ever do. The scientific account of our world, though often counter-intuitive, offers a more trustworthy narrative than the selective memory recorded in religious texts or handed down in religious traditions and institutions. However, is the source of power and mastery what we really want to know above all else or the only thing we want to know? What, for example, is this mastery for? Without a clear view of the ends of life, science driven solely by a human thirst for control, domination and mastery of the world very quickly suffers from a form of hubris that ends in it overreaching itself. Firstly, it generates expectations in the wider population and promises a security that it cannot deliver. Secondly, it itself becomes a means of human destructiveness – for example, the cures for human-induced global warming may be worse than the 'disease'. In brief, what the scientific world does not always recognise is that in its aspirations for knowledge and mastery, science has become the source for ever greater insecurities in human beings.

The achievements of science have come to be viewed by many as a poisoned chalice. Beautifully attractive, the chalice of scientific knowledge also contains increasing powers of destruction, powers to dehumanise and powers to destroy our habitat. Quite simply, in the hands of fallible human beings the mastery needed and desired always falls short, and the limited mastery that is achieved is experienced as a mixed blessing. Science cannot defeat death; on the contrary, the extent to which science has empowered humans has also enabled them to kill on an ever-increasing scale and in more cruel ways. Furthermore, in the effort to understand the general principles that inform the whole of the universe, the value of the individual and the particular easily disappears from view.[1] However, it is precisely the individual and particular that must not fall from view if our humanity and world is to flourish, hence we find in Matthew 10:29–31: 'Are not two sparrows sold for a farthing? And one of them shall not fall on the ground without your Father. But the very hairs of your head are all numbered. Fear ye not therefore, ye are of more value than many sparrows.' This is the expression of a deep-rooted concern for what is unique.

Should we always be suspicious of science or is there a spirituality from which the religious person might benefit and learn?

Of course, science need not take the destructive form which we have been indicating above. The best science attends to the detail and the particulars of every situation. The difficulty stems mostly from the representation of the scientific method as a process of *discovery* in which the scientist coerces a passive nature to manifest its secrets. The emphasis on discovery suggests that human beings are in control; it is, as it were, human imagination, reason and ability alone that determine human knowledge. Post-modern theories and the sociology of knowledge proudly declare

---

[1] A major reason for the religious suspicion of science is the unbridgeable gap that scientists frequently claim exists between their particular interest and the moral interest humans normally have. The perceived consequence is that the supposed amorality of their scientific studies often slides into immorality. Mary Midgley comments on this gap: 'Many physical scientists today do tend to see this gap as infinite. They do not deny that each scientist may have duties as a human being, or as a citizen. But they are unwilling to bring these duties into any intelligible relation with distinctively scientific duties, for fear that the latter might go under. They sometimes assert "the freedom of science" as demanding that important scientific investigations should always go forward regardless of any social considerations whatever' (1989, p. 57). As such, she shows why this separation of science and the moral is unreasonable.

that knowledge is essentially a human product. Apart from the obvious and trivial observation that it is human beings who are engaged in the search for knowledge, the declaration is a deception if it communicates the view that the character and content of knowledge is wholly within human control. It simply is not. Our knowledge grows precisely at points where we discover that our theories do not work or do not apply (Popper, 1959). This alone should induce some feelings of modesty.

In contrast to the perception of science as a human will to power, there is another view of science in which the virtue of humility is more in evidence. Science is nothing other than the development of techniques through which one disciplines the self to be attentive and to allow nature to *disclose* itself. There is a profound spirituality in this science. The impersonal and disinterested character of its knowledge has decentred the human self. It is now a matter of obedience to what nature itself is. A rigorous method is employed in which any claims are submitted to the scrutiny of others as a test of the truth; verification is the method one uses to establish the impersonal and disinterested character of what is avowed. It is also a method that must be open and display a constant willingness to be surprised. The ethos of *discovery* and the ethos of *disclosure* are very different. In one, human beings are the adventurers in search of wealth, power and fame; in the other, human beings are attentive listeners ready to be disciplined by the order of nature and to be awed by its grandeur, elegance and economy.

To some this brief reflective excursion on the nature of the natural sciences may appear to be an unwelcome digression, but it is essential if we are to comprehend the basis and nature of any theological knowledge. The similarities and dissimilarities between the sciences and theology and the reasons for them are instructive. Given the human propensity for the construction of idols within religious life, each named science (physics, chemistry, biology, psychology, etc.), with its inherent discipline and with its disinterested nature, has much to teach the religious individual whose faith happens to be essentially self-serving. We see this self-serving nature of religious faith on many occasions. When some human beings are the victims of great hardship and have to endure much suffering, it is then that they disavow belief in God. 'How could the God do this to *me*?' they cry. More often, it is not the sufferer but some onlooker who declares that such suffering makes belief in the Divine intolerable and incomprehensible. The disinterested scientist, in contrast, shows us and accepts what is necessary; the religious person can do no less. He or she too must accept what is necessary, for how could he or she be said to love the Creator who has made this world with all its inherent necessities if he or she does not? Theology must associate itself with the ethos of disclosure[2] rather than discovery, because before the Eternal only obedience and

---

[2] The expectation of disclosure can be described as attentiveness. Simone Weil writes: 'Attention consists of suspending our thought, leaving it detached, empty and ready to be penetrated by the object, it means holding in our minds, within reach of this thought, but on a lower level and not in contact with it, the diverse knowledge we have acquired which we

submission is appropriate, and it could never be a situation in which human beings vie for control.

Just as science is ready to be surprised, so too must the religious person and theologian be ready to adjust their presuppositions and conclusions, to be open and ultimately modest about the claims they make. There is risk in faith; one may be wrong. The assurance of faith, to which some believers testify, is not the certainty of being infallible but the confidence that comes from being loved. The scientist admits the limitations of his or her knowledge and is at same time utterly committed to learning more, and then confidently acts on what he or she already believes he or she knows. He or she works from the faith that the world is essentially rational. The religious person can do no less. The scientist is bound by his or her reason and empirical investigations. The religious person must equally rely on all that his or her intellect and experience have to offer. The scientist begins with the presence of what he or she takes to be the *physical* nature of his or her world, while the religious believer must no less begin with what he or she presumes to be the presence of the *Eternal* in his or her world. The accounts these individuals subsequently give detail the respective meanings of these terms.

Are science and theology essentially the same activity or are there significant differences?

Though there is much to learn from science, there are however some significant differences between the quests for knowledge about the physical world and spiritual life. It is these differences that lead theologians to speak of revelation as foundational of religious life and consequently of theology. Firstly, the otherness of the Eternal is never entirely in the form of an impersonal necessity; rather, its disclosure assumes a purposive character with direction and a specific end in view. There is what some theologians describe as a feature of *subjectivity* (in the sense of agency or freedom) about the Other.

Secondly, the disclosure is in no wise under human control but rests entirely in the 'hands' of the Eternal. Human beings learn, so to speak, by grace, a gratuitous gift.

---

are forced to make use of. Our thought should be, in relation to all particular and already formulated thoughts, as a man on a mountain who, as he looks forward, sees also below him, without actually looking at them, a great forest and plains. Above all our thought should be empty, waiting, not seeking anything, but ready to receive its naked truth the object which is to penetrate it' (Weil, 1959, p. 56). 'We do not obtain the most precious gifts by going in search of them but by waiting for them. Man cannot discover them by his own powers, and if he sets out to seek for them he will find in their place counterfeits of which he will be unable to discern the falsity' (ibid., pp. 56f). Apart from any Freudian interpretations one might put on Weil's analysis, there is a sense of the God as a 'living' God who initiates and creates what is genuinely new and *ex nihilo* (from nothing).

Thirdly, the disclosures are often, though not always, in the form of events which are wholly specific and unique; they are unrepeatable.[3] This puts them entirely beyond the sphere of human manipulation; they are strictly out of human 'hands'.

Fourthly, the Other knows human beings better than they know themselves; He 'calls each one by name', i.e. personally and individually. This suggests a deep intimacy which takes the twofold form of being both *demanding* and *commanding*. 'Demanding' is the appropriate term because the impact of the Other on human beings is such that it implicates human beings so that they recognise it as 'self-involving'. The Other, in effect, makes a claim on human beings to the point where a response is expected. 'Commanding' is the appropriate term because the claim made on human beings is directing and impresses one with moral force.

Finally, the product of such disclosures is never simply information, a theory or a set of ideas or images, but is primarily a form of life, sometimes abandoning an old way of life. Such a change of life can alter one's whole identity. Abram leaves Ur[4] of the Chaldees goes to the land of Canaan and becomes Abraham, the father of faith. Jacob leaves the land of exile, returns home and wrestles with an angel of God and becomes Israel. Simon bar Jona follows Jesus and becomes Peter, a foundation for the community of faith. Saul encounters the risen Christ, leaves Palestine and becomes Paul, apostle to Gentiles throughout the Roman Empire.

The impact of the presence of the Eternal in these five[5] distinctive characterisations ensures that theology is not simply assimilable into the scientific world. Science never takes into account purposes or final causes. Science does not purport to give moral direction or prescribe a way of life. Where science looks for cool detachment, the distinctive disclosure that stimulates our religious interest generates a passionate self-involvement, one that shapes identity without being self-serving. The shift from science to religion is a qualitative shift. It is not unlike the change of interest that takes place when one moves from considering soundwaves to one where the sense of soundwaves is considered. Suddenly there is a different debate about the nature of sound; is it meaningful, is it music, is it a cacophony or is it intentional communication?

If understanding the Eternal is different from understanding nature, are there any directions on how we should think about coming to know the God?

Having tried to distinguish the disclosures that are possible in science from those which generate religious interests, it is now necessary to define three other

---

[3] As such, revelation is associated with miracles, i.e. with events that are redolent with meaning, awesome and in important respects unique and unrepeatable.

[4] Genesis 11:31.

[5] I do not wish to imply that these five differences exhaust all the possible ways in which disclosure within the religious sphere differs from disclosure through science. The five distinctive features are designed to show why theology cannot be simply subsumed within science.

Christian theological terms: 1) natural theology; 2) general revelation; and 3) special revelation.

The term 'natural theology' refers to the rational reflection of the mind occasioned by the natural world or by the nature of the activity of human reason itself. Typical forms of natural theology are the reflections referred to earlier, namely, those of Aquinas in the five ways (proofs), Anselm's ontological proof and Kant's moral argument. These forms of reasoning call on nothing other than what is available to every man and exclude any reliance on input that is confined to an elect or select group; it is in principle open to all who have the inclination, energy and intellectual capacity to enquire. What is attractive about this form of theology is its democratic nature. It is inclusive. The question is: can it, or does it, achieve its end? The trouble is that reason is never confined to matters of logic or to mere calculation akin to the mathematical. In arguing for the total depravity of man, the sixteenth-century reformers were not saying that human beings are incapable of doing something good and worthwhile, but they were indicating that human reason is also affected by sin. Human reason is used and deployed by human beings in a sinful and self-serving way. A consequence of this is that all too frequently reason is less a tool of truth and more a tool of human self-sufficiency and self-aggrandisement; as such, it does little on its own to generate the ordered life before the God.

'General revelation' abandons any notions of human self-sufficiency and looks entirely to the activity of the Other in its process of Self-disclosure. This Self-disclosure of the Other is literally to be found everywhere in its creative and sustaining grace. The created world, simply by coming into being, constitutes a mystery and is a form of disclosure. The world's continuing existence evokes the awe of human beings if they have not already become too blasé through sheer familiarity with the cosmos, humanity and the environment. There are many religious traditions that invite human beings to attend to this Self-disclosure and practise a discipline to sharpen human 'sight' and 'hearing'. It is this same general revelation that calls all human beings to recognise the forms of life so essential for human flourishing. No one appears ignorant of the core demands of moral life. Whatever differences there may be about what constitutes the Good and the Right, there is no doubt that there is nevertheless widespread agreement about the essentials. When the moral life is shown to those who appear impervious to its claims, it does not take long for them to catch its meaning. They are, as it were, hard-wired for moral considerations. Moral commands come to us in the form of a disclosure or vision which states 'this is how it ought to be' or 'this is how one ought to live'.

For Christian theologians, general revelation has the overall effect of communicating or making human beings aware of their alienation from the Eternal and the absolute good. It may have the effect of generating guilt about moral failure or a sense of inadequacy generated by a loss of moral acuity or lack of clarity, with the result that we are no longer sure of what we ought to do. The religions that arise from general revelation often have the effect of intensifying human despair, human insecurity and helplessness, unless they become convinced of the divine grace and mercy that has the power to redeem the situation.

The use of term 'special revelation' refers precisely to that kind of divine Self-disclosure that appears to address the situation of human despair. Christians find this special revelation in the Christ-event and consequently it becomes the template against which the Christian tradition must judge (if it must judge at all) any other special revelations. The suffering and death of Christ is a moment of revelation in that the reality thus disclosed is free from all self-indulgent human constructions, and yet to find the Eternal present in that event, or as an event-in-God, is to transform everything. As an event it communicates the unconditional nature of divine love and the absoluteness of its character, in that no greater love can any man show than that he lay down his life for another. More cannot be done. The conviction of Christ's resurrection points to a vindication of his life, suffering and death; it is not in vain but reconciles the Eternal with human beings in all things, so that human beings might know and live with confidence.

Christians need not deny *special* revelations in other traditions, in other times and in other places, but they will wish to underline it with the assurance that issues from the Christ-event, in the light of which they have become convinced that absolutely nothing can separate us from the love of the God. To re-iterate what Paul wrote: 'For I am persuaded, that neither death, nor life, nor angels, nor principalities, nor powers, nor things present, nor things to come, nor height nor depth, nor any other creature, shall be able to separate us from the love of God, which is in Christ Jesus our Lord.'[6]

---

[6] Romans 8:38–9.

Chapter 16
Scripture and Tradition

What are the sources for theology? Where does it gather its material?

The simple answer is that it is the religious life that people lead, the life in which they understand themselves to be before the God. For Christianity, as for some other religious traditions, this religious life is closely bound up with the Scriptures and with the habituated life and thought (i.e. tradition) that has developed over generations. The phrase 'closely bound up with' is of course a very loose phrase which could mean any number of things. We do know that the Scriptures play a role in communicating the Divine and 'reporting' the sense of the Eternal that people have had in the past. But what kind of role do the Scriptures have or what kind of a role ought it to be? Likewise, the traditions that have emerged and developed are also thought to be means through which the Divine is communicated. Again, what is the precise role of tradition or what view should one take of it? Then there is the additional consideration that if both scriptures and tradition claim to be sources for our knowledge of the God, what is the precise relationship between them? Not least, when they do not appear to speak with one voice, which is to be preferred or given priority? It is to these questions that we now turn.

How is it that the Bible, which is but a collection of ancient texts written over centuries, has been given such a prominent role?

It has already been observed that the Bible is a focal point in worship. The text is read and re-read in the context of prayer and worship, sometimes in a prescribed cycle of readings. It is a text which is subjected to exegesis and on which comment is made in sermons. In providing this comment and exegesis, the clergy are not merely conveying their own thoughts, providing a discourse based on their own authority or on their ability to amuse or to be thought-provoking, they claim to convey the Word of the God. The assertion is made that the words are, or can become, more than human words; by being true to the words of Scripture, the utterances become the very Word of the God. The human words are transformed so that they have an authority that binds and directs those who hear them. This is supposed to be part of the meaning of existing before the God.

If this is true for the worshipping community, can it be any less the case for the religious person in private devotion or for the theologian in his study (i.e. should the text govern their thinking)? Firstly, the theologian is bound to acknowledge the communal practice in which the text plays such a central role. Secondly, if the Bible is given authority to bind and direct people in worship, can it fail to have a similar role in the study? It is only if theologians extract themselves from the practice of religious life and becomes *spectators* that they can escape the immediacy of a possible claim by the Scriptures and tradition to authority. There is always the nagging suspicion that from a religious point of view an academic escape into a neutral space is an illusion or a pretension. The affirmation of the omnipresence of the Divine suggests that no place exists to which one can withdraw and remove oneself from the divine claim, except in the minds of deluded prophets such as Jonah (Jonah has many disciples amongst contemporary theologians). The truth is that we always do our theology in the presence of the Divine.

Theologians cannot therefore escape the claim made for the authority of the Scriptures. But what they are able to do is to enquire more closely into the precise relationship between the black marks on the white paper and the meaning that supposedly exudes divine authority; this theological examination is made to ensure that the supposed authority is not confused with some human construct created to serve a human and very temporal end. People quite readily fall into the trap of devising fanciful readings because it suits them. The thorough, critical questioning of a good theological examination should avoid that particular abuse of Scripture. There are some who would like to escape the task of such critical study by simply asserting that the Bible *is* the Word of God – the 'is' here being one of straightforward identity between the Word of *God* and the meaning *they* are inclined to ascribe to it. This identity is all too convenient!

There are two issues here. The first is whether the attributed meaning is *the* meaning of the text. To avoid close scrutiny, it is often asserted by fundamentalists that their selected meaning is the *literal* meaning. Saying this, even with a loud voice, does not make it so. The second is the implausible claim of a straightforward identity between biblical text and the Word of the God. This fundamentalist claim is sometimes backed up by a theory of inspiration, as if this could give the Scriptures authority which they do not already have intrinsically.[1] However, this claimed inspiration and 'literalism' leads to all kinds of difficulties, including problems of internal coherence, of attempts to treat the Scriptures as a source of incorrigible history or of unchallengeable science, or of valuing them as the most sublime poetry. But if the text is to provide history, science or poetry, then it must meet the needs and standards of history, science and poetry. To judge the text by those standards is not to read them religiously. If the text is to be a Word of the God, then it must meet different needs and standards. In reality we are most likely to know that we have been confronted by the Word of the God when we are confronted by a sense that ignores temporal considerations. With an eternal dimension, the Scriptures will test the very meaning of our existence, i.e. not when the text suits us but when it discomfits us or, as K. Barth put it, when it puts us under judgment.

---

[1] '... the Bible and Christianity are their own sufficient evidence' (Coleridge, 1971, p. 21).

Generally, the theological questioning of the Scriptures is made possible because whatever claims are made about the text conveying the very Word of the God, one cannot claim that the latter (the Word) is simply confined to the former (the text). The Word of the God, or the self-manifestation of the Eternal, is not found in the Christian Scriptures alone. The Word of the God is free to address human beings through anything and everything that the Divine has created. The perception that the Word of the God is not exclusive to Scripture has led theologians to turn, *inter alia*, to *tradition*. It is the record in which the religiously interested have re-collected, exercised their judgment and transmitted what they have found to be compelling testimony to the Divine. This differentiation of sources (Scripture and tradition) gives the theologians a powerful tool. It enables them to triangulate, to turn the one source on the other, to compare and contrast, to test the one against the other, verifying the meanings that have been attributed to them and testing their own judgment.

This mutual testing of the Scriptures against tradition and vice versa is not as straightforward as it may sound. On closer inspection, neither the Scriptures nor tradition are simple or always self-evidently authoritative. Tradition seems to embrace sundry elements – reason, culture, history, social institutions and experience – indeed, to be of this world it must do so. The Scriptures also embrace many genres of literature written over many years in diverse places and languages which, like all languages everywhere, have no permanence or fixed meanings. The varied nature of both the Scriptures and tradition ensures that one could never take a mechanical approach to the task of attending to the Word of the Eternal. We may conclude that if tradition is to be heeded, it is not because it has some extrinsic authority assigned to it, for example, by the magisterium of the church, but because the authority has to be intrinsic to it. It must exude authority in what it is; if the tradition does not, then no amount of bludgeoning or pleading[2] will make it so. The Scriptures in their turn are also claimed to be inspired, but this claim likewise can be based solely on the fact that they are inspiring. If the Scriptures do not exude this inspiration for a person, insisting on it in an overbearing way will not make it so.

That traditions and the Scriptures are both inspiring in themselves is attested by many; the problem lies in the fact that many others do not perceive it. We may neither have the ears to hear nor the eyes to see. We can become deaf and blind to what they convey, and our culture can make us so. We can adopt a methodology so that we only see and hear the human constructions, abuses and violence which permeate the traditions and the texts. There is no easy cure except to attend honestly and patiently. Of course, the possibility exists that we may never discern an authoritative word in either the text or tradition. There is no simple way of showing where the fault lies – whether it is in us, in our methods, in the texts or in traditions. Yet another possibility is that in its freedom and for our sakes, the Eternal withdraws Itself because its presence may be more than we can bear. The

---

[2] 2 Timothy 3:16.

rich young ruler who went to Jesus to ask what he must do to be saved went away sorrowing[3] when he was told to give all that he had to the poor in order to follow Christ.

There was a period in Christian history when people had lost faith in tradition as communicated through the church to reveal the Divine; the church as an institution was perceived to be corrupt, self-interested and exploitative, and in reaction the sixteenth- and seventeenth-century reformers turned to Scripture; Scripture alone (*sola scriptura*) was their war cry. Their close reading of the text, especially of Paul's Letter to the Romans, led them to a new religious vision and inspired a renewal of faith. In brief, the new religious sense that emerged spelled out that salvation was not achieved through what human beings did for themselves or what they contributed to the developing history of the world, but on what the God did. We live, they said, by grace and by grace alone (*sola gratia*). Looking back over this history, we can see that this new religious vision subverted the church's institutional power. It not only fractured the institution, slowly and inevitably, but it also diminished the role of the church in human flourishing, as if one could do without others in one's relationship to the Eternal.

The new focus on Scripture in the Reformation led to translations of it into the vernacular – in brief, to its wider publication (helped not a little by the invention of the printing press) and distribution. Even this needed some kind of control; as such, an official translation of the Scriptures into English was commissioned at a meeting of the General Assembly of the Church of Scotland in Burntisland, Fife and was later published in 1611, authorised by King James VI of Scotland/ James I of England. The availability of the Scriptures in the vernacular was also a great spur to education, encouraging people to read and understand the text for themselves, and to make judgments on it. People began to take responsibility for their own lives in an unprecedented manner. In the Reformed tradition, they even tried increasingly to seize control of the institutional church for themselves, with the laity appointing and holding the clergy accountable for what they said and did through church courts.

If human beings must exercise their judgment, how can they be confident that they are right in their judgments?

Religion is supposed to convey a sense of assurance and confidence to people. Once we turn to the Eternal, life's anxieties are supposed to dissipate; there is nothing to fear within the orbit of the love of the God, no matter what happens to us – this is the religious sense. But this intrinsic feature of religious life led, in my view, to a serious mistake within both Protestantism and Catholicism. Instead of relying on an inner assurance, they both looked for an external basis for this religious

---

[3] Luke 18:18–30.

confidence.[4] Within Protestantism, people were inclined to think that their reliance on Scripture was warranted because the Scriptures were infallible or inerrant, without really thinking what this implied. This position effectively externalised the warrant for religious confidence and could not work. The undesirable consequence is that one could no longer read the text seriously and critically, for one was no longer in a position to challenge or question the text. Despite all the study of the Scriptures, all the exegesis that the Reformation stimulated, examinations of their actual practices led to one conclusion, namely, that only a few were prepared to be challenged by the Divine, only a few were prepared to wrestle with the 'angel of the Lord'[5] in the way that Jacob did in his attempt to return home, and from which he walked away wounded and with a changed identity.

Radical questions were asked of the Scriptures by *some* scholars, but not by many. Those who did were often cut off from the church, excommunicated or held at bay through a kind of exile in the universities, and occasionally they were not even allowed to teach there (for example, D. F. Strauss) or, if they did, they did not always teach openly what they thought (for example, H. S. Reimarus).[6]

If the vast majority of biblical scholars embrace the historicist perspective of higher biblical criticism today and reject the claims of a so-called biblical inerrancy, it is because an honest scrutiny of the Scriptures does not permit one to sustain the position of inerrancy with respect to human interests other than the interest in the Eternal, and this for a number of reasons. Firstly, it is clear that many people with great sincerity and great scholarship could, and do, come to different conclusions about the meaning of the texts. In other words, there was a fragmentation in the interpretation of the text, which in some significant instances led to institutional fragmentation.[7] What value is a supposedly inerrant text if people radically disagree about what it means or says?[8]

---

[4] It is worth considering the following question: what could persuade you to have confidence in the love which your parents may have for you? The truth is that if the love itself does not provide this confidence, no 'proof' (for example, gifts) will do so.

[5] Genesis 32:24–32.

[6] Reimarus espoused a traditional view in his university teaching, but the posthumous publication of *Fragments* (1971) revealed that he really held quite different views.

[7] The practice of infant baptism was disputed on a biblical basis. Similarly, disagreements on the basis of church government and the establishment or non-establishment of churches was disputed on scriptural grounds.

[8] See what Augustine says in his *Confessions* (1991, Bk. 12, XXV). *Inter alia*, what is critical for him is that we love the truth because it is true, which ultimately is destined to overcome differences of interpretation because truth is meant for all, i.e. it is public: 'And therefore, O Lord, are Thy judgements terrible; seeing Thy truth is neither mine nor his, nor another's; but belonging to us all, whom Thou callest publicly to partake of it, warning us terribly, not to account it private to ourselves, lest we be deprived of it. For whosoever challenges that as proper to himself, which Thou propoundest to all to enjoy, and would have that his own which belongs to all, is driven from what is common to his own; that is, from truth, to a lie. For he that speaketh a lie, speaketh it of his own.'

Secondly, how can one claim inerrancy when there are translations and significant variant readings in ancient manuscripts? Which text is to be preferred, especially when they lead to different judgments? What does one do when some translations scandalise readers or where some interpretations seem to be nothing but idiosyncratic?

Thirdly, the supposition of inerrancy was usually based on the straightforward *identity* between the text and the Word of the God,[9] but actual religious practice actively denies this supposition. If every word of the text is the Word of the God, then all passages should be treated equally seriously. In fact, not everything is read with the same frequency or interest in church or at home. And it is always the case that some passages are interpreted in the light of meanings, principles and interpretations found elsewhere both in and outside the Scriptures.[10] A critical example in the Christian tradition is the way in which the Old Testament is read through the eyes of the New Testament experience rather than being read in and for itself.[11]

Fourthly, the supposition of inerrancy, the identity of the text with the *ipsissimum verbum Dei* (the very Word of the God) fails to recognise the essential role of the readers or hearers of the text. There is no real communication without bringing *them* into the picture. The varying circumstances and experience of these recipients will always ensure that they hear and read different meanings in the text. An exclusive focus on the text as an object, ignoring the recipients, also subverts the dynamic of the living relationship that is pursued in religious life between the Divine and the human.

Given the diverse responses to the text, it is little wonder that there was a Counter-Reformation in which the church as an institution claimed for itself the right to interpret the text and to state what it meant in an authoritative way. By this device church leaders hoped to maintain the unity of the church and to set limits on the sense of the text. They took the view (and probably rightly so) that the laity on the whole was not qualified to make the essential judgments, knowing neither the history nor the original languages nor possessing the original manuscripts. The ordinary church members were simply not in a position to make refined judgments, lacking, as they did, all the skills of the professional biblical scholar.

Moreover, it was also clear to the church leaders that the religious tradition should be given priority over the text and they thought that as the 'curators' of the

---

[9] Pictures that portray angels directing or whispering in the ears of the gospel writers as if they were mere inert tools of transmission sometimes convey this straightforward identity. Of course, one might comment that if one were to communicate the idea of inspiration visually, how else would one do so?

[10] Think of the impact of evolution on our reading of Genesis or how moral considerations might affect our views of the story of Abraham's proposed sacrifice of Isaac.

[11] The Old Testament states: remember the Sabbath to keep it holy. Very few mainstream churches abide by this and instead keep the first day of the week rather than the seventh.

tradition, they could best judge the impact of tradition on the interpretation of the text. The priority of tradition over text was evident to them: firstly, in the fact that the text was initially *produced* by the community of faith; secondly, in the fact that the texts that constitute the canon were *selected* by the community of faith[12] from a much larger corpus of literature; thirdly, in the fact that it was the community of faith which *preserved* the texts. If it were not for this, we would know next to nothing about Jesus from other sources. Given these facts, it seemed only right that the community of faith should be the interpreters of the text and, in interpreting them, should draw on all its collective resources of intellect, culture, experience and will.

In reflecting on this response, one can only say that much of what is claimed by the community of faith is a proper correction to the excesses of Protestant individualism. A good counter-weight to the idiosyncratic and the bizarre interpretations and practices produced by some individuals is the 'reality check' provided by others. But in my view the Roman Catholic church goes too far in claiming infallibility for its teaching and, later at the first Vatican Council, for the pope in matters of faith and morals. In doing so it makes the same mistake as Protestantism in thinking that such a quality can be bestowed externally if it is not already evident as something intrinsic to its communication. Effectively the infallibility of the Scriptures or of an institution can only be shown through the quality of what it teaches. No external power or threat can persuade us of that quality. All Christians must also accept that whatever authority the institution or its scriptures have is purely of a moral or religious nature that must be demonstrable from what it teaches and how it lives. On this basis one can see the critical analysis of traditions, the higher criticisms of Scriptures, as the attempts by many scholars to listen more honestly, even if they can never control the authentic Word.

As such, a much better strategy for the community of faith is to pursue a policy of encouraging open and critical enquiry into its scriptures and doctrines as the best method for making what is intrinsic to it self-evident. To do otherwise and to rely on external foundations inevitably leads to excesses and immodesty. The response to such excesses is to stimulate investigation into the track record of the institution. This will show that the institution has no exclusive claim on what is true, beautiful and good; moreover, it will reveal that it is distinctly limited in its realisation of love. Its track record includes blatant grasping for political power and influence, often to the detriment of ordinary people and sometimes solely in the interest of a select group. A church that does not care for *all* by speaking up and acting on behalf of all is not worthy of its name (catholic). It must act on behalf of the spiritual interest of its own constituency but must equally act in the spiritual interest of the secular person, in the interests of the rich and poor, and even in the interests of people of faiths other than its own. It cannot do this in a

---

[12] Why exclude the *Didache* or the *Epistle of Clement*, which are older than some New Testament documents, or why exclude the *Gospel of Thomas*, which was after all attributed to an apostle?

paternalistic manner but through persuasion, dialogue and listening carefully to the contributions made by others. In doing so, it must have the courage to tell its own people when and where they are living unlovingly and have the courage to admit that the God is not without witness outside the church's own limits.

What can we be sure about in the sphere of religious faith?

In the face of the untenability of holding to the strict identity between the text and the Word of the God, some scriptural interpreters have attempted to rehabilitate the warrants for their theology by finding an authoritative basis elsewhere. Some have located the impressiveness that exudes confidence in the content of Scripture as presented in one guise or another. Thus, they have identified key *doctrines* supposedly communicated in Scripture (such as the Incarnation); others have found key *images* and *concepts* (for example, the Fatherhood of God or the Kingdom of God); others still have found it in a credal recitation of a *salvation history*. All of these are supposed to be found in Scripture as a part of its decisive content and as deserving our absolute confidence. Still others have taken a different approach and have located the authority of Scripture in its *function*, specifically in its function of disclosing the divine activity, displaying both the intentions and directions of the God's action. I am not convinced that any or even all of these together can serve as an *external* basis for taking the Scriptures seriously. This authority, as I have been claiming, must be found to be intrinsic to the text. It may be that the suggested sources of confidence can become *occasions* for an insight into the depths of life. We may recognise genuine encounters with the Eternal or see 'God's back parts',[13] i.e. where the God has disclosed itself in the past. What is required is a contemporary attentiveness that waits on the God. This attentive waiting can and must be done with others, listening to the texts and traditions recording the experiences of all people of faith.

How should we study the Scriptures and traditions whilst waiting on the God?

The people who wait are normally expectant and as such become identified as the people of faith. Although theology is, in principle, a public discourse and open to all, the Scriptures and traditions must nevertheless be read and studied whilst keeping in mind the interest that faith has. Too much contemporary biblical and theological scholarship is done solely from a perspective that deliberately and specifically omits the interest of faith in the Eternal. The objection is not that such scholarship has nothing of value to report, but rather that its scope is too narrow. The enquiry has left out the question of what it is that one must do in the presence of the Eternal. This is the question that people of faith are always bound to ask.

---

[13] Exodus 33:23.

An alternative to the practice of modern interpretation is to return to the methods of the Church Fathers,[14] who expected the biblical text to have at least one or more levels of meaning. They identified the *literal*, the *moral* and the *anagogical* as the essential ones. These levels of meaning roughly correspond to 1) any scientific, spectatorial interest one might have, 2) the self-involving interest most people have in what one *ought* to do and 3) the self-involving interest some have in finding what is of eternal significance in the text. The literal meaning aims to state what the text 'objectively' means and not just what we would like it to mean. All the devices of higher and lower biblical criticism were designed to free us from the self-indulgence and presumptuousness with which many approach the text. However, theologians have failed in their duty if they are only interested in the literal meaning. I. T. Ramsey, the former Bishop of Durham, when referring to the nineteenth-century theologian F. D. Maurice, claims that 'the "real meaning" of all theological phrases is to be found in God – that we have understood no Bible story, understood no doctrine, professed no Creed, used no prayer book in worship unless we have thereby found and known God. This seems to be Maurice's penetrating insight, his major claim, and one with immense significance for our own day' (Ramsey, 1963, pp. 7f.). The theologian must therefore reflect on the challenge to living meaningfully in full consideration of aesthetic and moral values, as well as of the dimension of eternity.

---

[14] Compare this to *Pardes* in Judaism: '*Pardes* is a mnemonic, the initials of four kinds of biblical interpretation: *Peshat* – literal; *Remez* – allegorical or philosophical; *Derash* – aggadic; and *Sod* – mystical' (Rose, 1996,pp. 83f.).

Chapter 17
Rhetoric and Hermeneutics

Words strain,
Crack and sometimes break, under the burden,
Under the tension, slip, slide, perish,
Decay with imprecision, will not stay in place,
Will not stay still.

(T. S. Elliot, 'Burnt Norton')[1]

How might we best communicate in theology? Is language the sole medium?

If theology is essentially a conversation, then it is also a form of communication. Turning to communication may be odd when so many will think that we should study the character of religious experience. The importance of the immediacy of the 'affective self-consciousness' was stressed by F. D. E. Schleiermacher nearly two centuries ago in *The Christian Faith*. However, Schleiermacher also claimed that these affections 'as soon as they have reached a certain stage and a certain definiteness ... manifest themselves outwardly by mimicry in the most direct and spontaneous way, by means of facial features and movements of voice and gesture'. Through a further process of reflective self-consciousness, they are put into speech and hence become doctrine. He writes: 'It is only when this procedure has reached such a point of cultivation as to be able to represent itself outwardly in definite speech, that it produces a real doctrine, by means of which the utterances of the religious consciousness come into circulation more surely and with a wider range than is possible through the direct expression' (Schleiermacher, 1928, p. 77). Attention to language is essential if we are to make sense of religious life.

A good theology that is self-critical cannot help but pay close attention to the elements and dynamics of communication. Marshall McLuhan once famously said 'The message is the medium, and the medium is the message', reflecting the intimate connection between *what* is said and *how* it is said, or in the world of poetry between content and form. The ideal as noted by St Augustine is that 'such things are being said that the words they are said with seem to spring spontaneously from the subject matter' (Augustine, 2002, p. 206). So far, we have concentrated a good deal on what is said and must now reflect a little on *how* it is said, i.e. its means and manner.

---

[1] Pattison, 1995, pp. 539–45.

We can, however, say things in many different ways.[2] Florists exhort us to say it with flowers! We can say things through our actions, through images, through language and language-like systems such as mathematics, logic, iconography, heraldry and musical notation. Meaning and associated understanding are, so to speak, irrevocably incarnated in these media. The way I have approached this theology was designed to convey the view that actions, rituals, making music, painting, etc. have a primary role in religious understanding and in the expression of religious meaning. Some forms of expression have a greater immediacy than others; the more reflective it becomes, the more remote it also becomes, but with the benefit of being more systematic and more 'reasonable'. On occasion, however, this very process of reflection can be the source of confusion and misunderstanding. It is not unknown for thinkers to take wrong turnings and misrepresent situations which taken in their immediacy were quite transparent. A classic case might be the doubts that some philosophers appear to have about the existence of other minds. In the immediacy of social encounter, few doubt the mental life of others. When thinkers begin to reflect on the evidence for believing in other minds, they can, and have, come to solipsistic conclusions!

How can we become more religiously educated without being misled?

As we seek to become more articulate and reasonable, we are in effect educating ourselves. This implies giving attention to the means of understanding. It is perhaps not too surprising that in the Middle Ages the basic educational curriculum[3] was divided into two parts: the *trivium* and the *quadrivium*. The *trivium* consisted of grammar, rhetoric and logic, while the *quadrivium* consisted of arithmetic, music, geometry and astronomy.

The *trivium* highlighted the significance of *language*, concepts and the conceptual connections in our understanding. To think well is to speak and write well. As Dante observed, 'language is as necessary an instrument of our thought as a horse is of a knight, and since the best horses are suited to the best knights ... the best language will be suited to the best thoughts'.[4]

---

[2] Schleiermacher identified three modes of communication: 1) the poetic, 2) the rhetorical and 3) the descriptively didactic. (Schleiermacher, 1928, p. 78).

[3] It may be interesting to note how this compares to the basic curriculum introduced in England and Wales by the government in 1988. How rigorous is the education today compared to that of the Middle Ages? English is studied in school, but do we come to grips with the basics of grammar, rhetoric and logic? Science is also studied in school, but do we see the role of mathematics in this study?

[4] *De Vulgari Eloquentia*, Bk. 2, ch. 1 (Reynolds, 2006, p. 58). Or, as the Scottish philosopher Thomas Reid wrote years later: 'Men generally find means to express distinctly what they have conceived distinctly. Horace observes, that proper words spontaneously follow distinct conceptions, "*verbaque provisam rem non invita sequunter*". But it is impossible that a man should distinctly express what he has not distinctly conceived' (Reid,

The *quadrivium* of arithmetic, music, geometry and astronomy emphasised the importance of *numbers*, measurement and proportionality in grasping the basic nature of reality in which we live. Space and time, the two most basic categories of our conceptual world according to Kant, are explored in practice through the disciplines of the *quadrivium*. Music may seem somewhat anomolous here – what after all has music to do with understanding of the physical world? – but any student of music recognises how proportionalities of time and number permeate music. From this derives the medievalist interest in the music of the spheres, for it was anticipated that the various spatial and temporal measurements of the heavenly bodies would be reflected in a form of music. Where some people have speculated as to whether the language of the Eternal might be Greek, Hebrew[5] or Arabic, others have speculated that it could be mathematics and yet others that it might be music – why else do we have cartoons depicting those who have died playing harps on the clouds?[6]

Contemporary philosophy stands, perhaps unwittingly, in the tradition of the ancients and of the mediaeval *trivium* because it also attends closely to language.[7]

1822, p. 333). The reverse might also be equally true. Once we have found the right words, we will have learned to think rightly; that is why we have poets – people who help us to find the right words.

[5] It is said that Frederick the Great ordered an experiment to resolve the matter about which language we would speak naturally if it were not for our environment and nurture. He thought that raising a couple of children in an environment where they were to hear no language spoken would resolve the dispute. The nurse assigned to look after these children was forbidden to speak to them. They grew up as idiots. There are some reports of modern counterparts of such children even if they were not brought up in this way as the result of an experiment. Children raised with animals or totally cut off from other human beings were all seriously damaged as people in a manner that was incurable.

[6] There is a Scottish saying: 'Half in fun, wholly in earnest.' Perhaps in the humour of the cartoon there is the serious theological point about the significance of music to religion. The religious divides between peoples are reflected not just in terms of their beliefs but also in their art and music, (for example, musically, in strings versus drums). There can also be a different emphasis on specific senses, such as seeing and hearing, which has consequences for their conceptualisation of the religious life and how they live; in other words, it shows the difference in emphasis given to contemplation and moral action, the *vita contemplative* and the *vita activa*.

[7] Much of Plato's philosophy was concerned with definition: for example, what is justice? What is the good? But see also Augustine's interest in language in *De Doctrina Christiana* (*On Teaching Christianity*); he did after all begin his career as a teacher of rhetoric. For another example from another period, one might look at the philosophy of Thomas Reid (1710–1796), who wrote that to understand the operations of the mind, we have to look at language: 'The language of mankind is expressive of their minds. The various operations of the understanding, will, and passions, which are common to mankind, have various forms of speech corresponding to them in all languages, which are the signs of them, and by which they are expressed: And a due attention to the signs may, in many cases, give considerable light to the thing signified by them' (Reid, 1822, p 52). In many respects,

It has been claimed that the study of language provides the key to the resolution of all our intellectual confusions. To gain that clarity, we must attend carefully to our *use* of language. This approach to intellectual issues is known as linguistic philosophy,[8] mainly because it uses this particular tool almost to the exclusion of other possibilities and considerations.

How can attention to language help?

The first observation to make about language is that linguistic communications convey meaning and understanding not in an accidental or haphazard way but in a very structured way. Without structure, the meaning of a text becomes elusive and the understanding confused. The more or less recent fashion of structuralism also arises from the notion that not just language but literature more generally has embedded structure,[9] and to analyse its meaning entails making an effort to *deconstruct* the text.

An examination of the structure of any communication shows that at its most basic, the communication involves three elements: 1) a speaker or author; 2) a hearer or reader; and 3) the medium, or vehicle, of language. This leads to three quite different disciplines. Rhetoric is 'the science of oratory or of speaking well' (eloquence and clarity); hermeneutics is the discipline through which a hearer or reader might interpret difficult texts; and grammar is 'the science of language or of words in their constructive relations'. Rhetoric and grammar are the two sciences that must be mastered by the speakers or authors if they are to become sufficiently self-conscious and accomplished communicators. The problem is what does it mean to be an accomplished communicator?

Great claims are made for rhetoric: Gorgias, a rhetorician, who is encountered in Plato's dialogue of that name, stated that by virtue of this 'science' he was able to answer any question that was put to him.[10] He went on to boast: 'I may say that no one has put a new question to me for many years.' The questions are perennial

---

Reid anticipated the modern linguistic philosophers in thinking that intellectual problems could be resolved through an attention to language in common use.

[8] Or linguistic analysis: key figures in this tradition included Wittgenstein and J. L. Austin, but even the logical positivism of, for example, A. J. Ayer was a form of linguistic philosophy. Among the theologians, a good example would be I. T. Ramsey, the former Bishop of Durham and professor of mathematics.

[9] 'The five stages of composition in classical rhetoric were *inventio* (the discovery or construction of valid arguments in support of one's case), *dispositio* (the arrangement and structuring of the arguments), *elocutio* (the verbal expression of the arguments, including the doctrine of tropes and figures), *memoria* (memorising the speech) and *pronuntiatio* (delivery) (Vickers, 1998, pp. 62–7)', in Miller, 2007.

[10] Plato, 1959, p. 448.

ones. What indeed might we not give to master those sciences that enable us to have all our questions answered so that we are never puzzled and confused?[11]

Is rhetoric the key to truth and the way to be educated in (religious) life?

There were disagreements on this point. Some might, and did, measure the accomplishment of rhetoric differently and more pragmatically. Rhetoric was not always seen as the source of truth but as the power of persuasion. They valued rhetoric as the key skill of being able to move others and by this means to acquire political skills – for political skills are nothing other than the power to move the *polis* or society consisting of many individuals and groups. But if this is all that this discipline means, rhetoric (and grammar too) soon become debased. Are these disciplines genuinely the path to truth?

The lack of truthfulness was, in fact, the main bone of contention between Socrates and the sophists in ancient Greece. The sophists in the eyes of Plato had separated the art of oratory,[12] the art of speech, from truth and from doing what is right. Separated from the truth and the good, oratory becomes demagogic, while communication skills become manipulative. They are skills to be taught or sold by unscrupulous teachers (and universities) seeking to exploit the aspiring young. The young in their turn hoped to prepare a path to political power or business success, and no doubt to exploit others for their personal benefit, or simply for the experience of power. In his final speech in Plato's dialogue of the *Gorgias*, Socrates rejects the claims of the sophists and he ends with a flourish: 'Let us then allow ourselves to be led by the truth now revealed to us, which teaches that the best way of life is to practice righteousness and virtue, whether living or dying; let us follow that way and urge others to follow it.'

The trouble is that the dispute between Socrates and the sophists was never quite as simple as the claim that one of the parties was interested in truth and the other was not. The sophists might well have taken the line that, yes, they were interested in developing the utmost powers of persuasion. Additionally they could have pointed out that nothing persuades like the truth. On the other hand, Socrates'

---

[11] In the *Phaedrus* 270B Plato writes:
'Socrates: The method of the art of healing is much the same as that of rhetoric.
Phaedrus: How so?
Socrates: In both cases you must analyse a nature, in one that of body and in the other that of the soul, if you are to proceed in a scientific manner, not merely by practice and routine, to impart health and strength to the body by prescribing medicine and diet, or by proper discourses and training to give to the soul the desired belief and virtue.'

[12] The emphasis here, as the reader may note, is on oral discourse rather than written discourse. Plato, though a prolific writer, thought that actual conversation or oral communication was much more amenable to the disclosure of the truth. Conversation enabled one to engage in the practice of mutual clarification in ways that the written text did not permit one to do. See Plato, ibid., 274Dff.

own contention (of doing what is right as something that is for the good of one's soul) might equally well be seen as amounting to little more than a sophisticated art of self-interest.

Note how Socrates himself began his last speech in the *Gorgias* in the following way: 'Give ear then, as they say, to a very fine story, which will, I suppose, seem fiction to you but is fact to me; what I am going to tell you I tell you as the truth.' He then proceeded to tell a Homeric myth about the gods and the judgment of souls. Here we have the truth dressed as fiction and elsewhere we have fictions and persuasive orations that communicate falsehoods.[13]

Rhetoric and grammar are double-edged swords. They can help the orator to conceal and deceive as well as reveal. Whether the disciplines can be trusted depends in part on whether the words which they use are intended by the speaker to reveal the truth. In themselves they are the two sciences that mediate the capacity to enable one to express one's meaning clearly; by the use of perspicuous discourse, an author has the power to *show* the truth and enable others to do what is right.

In religious discourse one must show the sphere of life where eternal love prevails and the possibility of letting this dominate one's existence. In the course of the discussion we have discovered that fictions can disclose what is true; on the other hand, much political talk demonstrates that persuasive speech can hide the truth. Whether we are deceived or gain insight from the words of others depends very much on our *interpretative* skills to discern the use to which rhetoric is put.

What are the interpretative skills that help us to discern the use to which rhetoric is put in religious life?

Modern developments in theology have in many ways beckoned us to use language well, to weigh our words, and to examine and attend to *how* we use language.[14] This examination will show the peculiarities of religious discourse as language that at best only lets us speak of its object indirectly. Bad theology obfuscates and good theology ultimately commands silence as the most appropriate response in the presence of mystery and the Eternal.

But if modern theology has sometimes felt the need to resort to rhetoric and grammar (though not always under these names) as the tool through which we are to attain clarity, it has turned even more to hermeneutics. The reason for this may be that in matters relating to the Eternal we are more often the recipients than the instigators of genuine religious communication.

---

[13] Hence Plato's desire to rid himself of all poets from his ideal society in the *Republic* because they deceive the young with their lying stories.

[14] For example, a theologian might draw attention to the important differences between: 1) 'believing *someone*' – as in 'he believed her love for him' – and 'believing *things*' – as in 'he believed the bridge would hold him'; 2) 'believing *in*' – as in 'he believes in science' – and 'believing *that*' – as in 'he believes that the earth is flat', etc.

Hermeneutics focuses on the other aspect of the communication. It looks at the communication from the perspective of the hearer or reader. Hermes was the Greek god who transported the messages from the gods on Olympus to men on earth. Iconically, he is recognisable by the little wings attached to his shoes or feet, which carried him from the transcendent heights with the gods to men below. One might say that hermeneutics is on one level the systematic reflection on how language conveys meaning to the hearer or reader. On another level, it is the science that shows the meaning in language or, in the views of some, it is the science which attempts to disclose the 'real' world wrapped in our language. I prefer to see it simply as the thinking directed to understanding 'others' when they have committed themselves in a text, whether spoken or written.

One of the first to think through this art of a systematic approach to understanding texts was the so-called 'father of modern theology', F. D. E. Schleiermacher (1768–1834). Schleiermacher noted that communications had different natures and that misunderstandings were also of different kinds. Some forms of communication are rather automatic and language is almost idling, as when it is used in business or when we ask each other 'how are you?'. We respond predictably 'Fine, and you?' (even when we feel ill or miserable – the point of the original question is to greet the other, not to act as a request for a medical report). Predictable language is the language of the marketplace. The meaning is self-evident and the understanding is automatic. However, there are other forms of language which are deeper and which demand experience and careful observation to be understood. Finally, there are the creative uses of language (as in literature and poetry), the language of another culture or age, the language that discloses 'another world' or that seeks to convey the transcendent. All these forms of communication demand close attention to the rules through which understanding can be attained. This is in substance the sphere of hermeneutics, the investigation of rules that guide us towards the understanding of deep and alien communications.

How did Schleiermacher define the science of interpretation?

For Schleiermacher, the deepest form of linguistic communication required an investigation in which it was necessary to pay attention to some particular points.

Firstly, there was the psychological dimension. In order to understand a communication, it was essential to understand *people*, both as a totality (human nature, human psychology) and in their individuality with all their idiosyncratic peculiarities. This aspect of the task of understanding requires particular skills, notably 'comparative' skills and 'divinatory' skills. Comparative skills are essentially capacities to see the total nature of human life in all its diversity, enabling us to make generalisations and thus to provide the widest human context for the text. But Schleiermacher saw that there was also a need for divinatory skills, the capacity to make distinctions, to see an author's individuality and his distinctiveness, i.e. the unique individual who issued the text.

Secondly, it was essential to understand *grammar*. Again, it was vital to have an overview of the whole linguistic expression of humanity, the widest context for a particular text, which in turn made it necessary to make use of comparative skills. One language could be compared to another, and one text to another, in order to appreciate the different nuances that language might bear. On the other hand, it was also important to possess divinatory skills to appreciate the uniqueness and particularity of the specific text under investigation (such as that of a poetic expression in which every word counts).

Schleiermacher's structured approach to a text was such that he believed that one could actually understand a text better than its author. This was because the author of the text was himself or herself not always conscious of the total context, either of people or of language. A consequence of this was that much of the meaning an author conveyed might actually be subconscious and submerged in the text. In other words, there might be meanings in the text of which even the author might not be fully aware. It is perhaps a reason why we have critics who have the capacity to draw our attention to hidden depths in discourse and may also be a reason why, for example, one can never cease to interpret the Scriptures, for familiar texts may have meanings[15] yet to be disclosed. Of course, Schleiermacher lived before the age of modern psychology and was not alert to the possibilities opened up by depth psychology, the Freudian or Jungian unconscious. However, he did invite us to study human beings closely as part of the hermeneutical processes to which we become committed in the effort of coming to a better and deeper understanding of a text.

Do texts have a meaning on which in principle we might all agree?

Immersed in the hermeneutical process envisaged by Schleiermacher is a circular form of reasoning which we can only hope is not a vicious circle. To understand texts, we have to understand human beings; to understand human beings, we have to understand their texts.

There appears to be no end to the task of understanding human beings; in order to begin to gain a full picture, we must engage with our human past, we must explore human psychology, we must investigate human social life, we might need to know about human genes and so on – they are all open-ended disciplines. Similarly, there is no end to the enquiries we can make about language and about texts; to the writing of books there is no end, let alone to human chatter! How do we obtain the full picture of human language? Schleiermacher admitted that there was no end to hermeneutical investigations, not least because we can never make a full assessment of mankind or of language. On the other hand, he allowed for the fact that we can, and normally do, understand one another and he was also hopeful

---

[15] That one text might have multiple meanings was a common presupposition of the Church Fathers, in particular St Augustine, who refers to this feature in 2002, Bk. III, 27, 38 or 1982, 1.20–21.

that by attending to some basic rules, we can gain an ever more satisfactory understanding of creative and sacred texts which by their nature possess the more open texture that will inevitably puzzle us.

What he did not share with many of our contemporaries was the loss of faith in communication;[16] in other words, he did not share the utter cynicism about communication that we encounter in the modern world. In this rampant cynicism we are unwilling to take anything at its face value and we see everything either as part of a human will to power or as dissimulation. Christian theologians certainly see the sin of the will to power but they cannot or should not share the cynicism about communication; a failure to hear the sincerity of the other in the text is to condemn ourselves to the prison of our own imagination. The cynicism that does exist originates in part in that section of modern psychology that is not prepared accept at face value any human intentions. It inevitably led to a *hermeneutical suspicion* about the meaning of any and every text.

In the light of what we know about human beings, it may in fact be reasonable to adopt a *moderate* form of hermeneutical suspicion in which one questions the purpose of the communication and in which one is not wilfully and woefully blind to the author or speaker's own interest in creating the text. A more *extreme* form of hermeneutical suspicion supposes that the real meaning is always hidden[17] and that the text is constructed with the witting or unwitting purpose of *deceiving* the hearer or reader. This position is just that: extreme. The extreme suspicion eventually leads to bizarre interpretations[18] – those which normally begin by telling us that religion is 'nothing but …' – interpretations that supposedly expose the 'true' meaning. A good deal of recent theological and secular theorising suffers from this twisted hermeneutic.

Modern theology looked to rhetoric, grammar and hermeneutics as assured methods to understanding, but they are double-edged swords. Used rightly, they can indeed open up meanings that deepen life. Used wrongly, they can imprison one ever more securely within the walls of one's own imagination and thought, and, like the sophists, one can close oneself off from the truth. It is an imprisonment that can only lead to despair.

---

[16] Steiner discusses this loss of faith in communication (Steiner, 1997); Wittgenstein also states: 'Everybody is mistrustful (or most people are), perhaps more so to their relations than towards others' (Wittgenstein, 1980, 54e) and goes on to wonder why this might be so.

[17] G. Steiner refers to 'a dialectic of trust' (1997, p. 101) as essential to translation or the understanding of the other.

[18] Note e.g. the interpretations that view theology and religion as the tool of imperialism, or capitalistic exploitation, or as the deliberate tool for female oppression. It is not that theological and religious texts could not contribute to these evils. It is only the interpretation, which supposes that these faults are their essential meanings and that the texts are always like that, which is bizarre.

Chapter 18
Defining Theology

Looking back, what kind of discipline is theology?

To clarify the discipline of theology we have had to ask three very basic questions:

1. What is its subject matter?
2. What is its methodology?
3. What are the criteria to be used in making judgments about, and in, theology? In other words, how do we know the difference between good and bad theology, a deep and shallow religious life, an accurate or misleading sense of the God?

All three questions have separately led to long and involved discussions in theological literature. They are each the source of a good deal of dispute. The tangled web of discussions can certainly lead to confusion. However, it is possible to proceed with at least some cursory answers and some indications of what the choices are.

So what exactly is the subject matter of theology?

As we saw earlier, as regards the subject matter of *theology*, there are two very basic options: a) the *God*[1] and b) *human beings*, or at least some aspect of human beings and their life, for example, human faith, human religion and human spirituality.

What are the implications of choosing the God as the primary subject matter of theology?

The problem with 'the God' is that there may be no referent for 'the God' or, to put it more prosaically, it is possible, as we saw earlier, that it may not make sense to say that 'God exists'. This could imply that there is no *real* or *existing* subject matter for theology. As such, perhaps it is also possible to say that speech about the God is speech about nothingness, about absence or the void. This could be a deep observation, because the God may be a mystery. But the more cynical could

---

[1] Or some related descriptive term, for example, the Wholly Other, the Divine, the Eternal, the Sacred, the Supernatural, the Real, etc. It is itself a major theological discussion about which term (or terms) is to be preferred. Generally, it needs to be said that 'God' is not a proper name for some identified individual in the way that the word 'Johnny' might be.

equally well conclude that if the God is non-existent, then whatever is written or said under the aegis of theology is little more than empty fabrication. They will be words and thoughts about nothing[2] or nothing much.

What are the implications of choosing human beings as the primary subject matter of theology?

The problem with taking 'human beings' as the primary subject matter of theology is that it does not identify theology as a separate discipline from one of the many other sciences that investigate human life, such as history, psychology, sociology or anthropology. Theology would take the form of being little more than a subfield of one of these major disciplines. Certainly, fields such as the philosophy of religion, the psychology of religion, the sociology of religion, the history of religion, church history, the phenomenology of religion and comparative religion are all well recognised as proper fields of study and as being worthy in their own right. The objection to them is that none seem to take seriously religious categories in and for themselves; in short, these disciplines are not *theological* because they never really bring the God or the Eternal into play. Conversely, they think and write *etsi deus non daretur* (as if the God did not exist). Instead, religious conceptions are translated into another discourse and are subordinated to another order of categories, each appropriate to its field of study.

Nevertheless, the various forms of study to which we have just referred do have some purchase, regardless of whether one acknowledges the reality of the God. Simply by making human beings and human behaviour the key focus of study, there is an obvious subject matter that is properly located in this world and thus is in important respects available for examination and inspection. However, any theological preference of focusing solely on the human does generate suspicion. Is this choice of subject matter on the part of theologians sufficiently disinterested? After all, it offers theologians job security in a secular world! In the universities theology as a discipline is regarded with some suspicion because of its peculiar character. But by transforming it into a province of a more 'Kosher' discipline, such as psychology, sociology or history, there would always be a place for theology and a job for theologians to do in the university. Compare the *psychology of religion* to the *psychology of astrology*, i.e. the psychology of those who write and read astrological predictions, etc. In the latter case, it is human *behaviour* that is of interest, whilst there is no need to make decisions about the worth or otherwise of astrological predictions. Similarly, in the former, as a part of the psychology that examines human religiosity, one needs to make no judgments about the Divine so long as one sees it solely as a study of human nature. Scientifically, God is left out of the picture and methodologically there is every reason to do so. Scientifically, the introduction of the God has often brought the scientific investigations to an

---

[2] See D. Hume's conclusion at the end of his *An Enquiry Concerning Human Understanding* (2000).

abrupt, and possibly premature, conclusion, because one has clearly changed the key of the discussion and the intellectual investigation.

Are 'the God' and 'human beings' the only two choices of the designated subject matter for theology?

If 'the God' may leave theology without a subject matter, the focus on 'human beings' may have emptied theology of any distinctive content. Perhaps there is a third option. In his later writings, Barth canvassed one such alternative. In the *Humanity of God* he proposed a new name for theology. He wished to call it 'theanthropology'. Theanthropology, as the new name would indicate, dealt with the God-human. Perhaps we should interpret this as *the relationship* between the God and human beings. Therefore, both the God and human beings are brought within the scope of study, not as separate entities but as mutually interrelated realities.

There is then a human aspect to it all, but human beings and human activity alone cannot define the subject matter, nor is it entirely under human control. Recognition of the the lack of human control seems to sit rather uneasily with the idea that we are talking of human intellectual disciplines. Since we may think of theology as a systematic reflection about the God-human, we might conclude that as a form of reflection the subject matter must be under our control. After all, thinking is something that *we* do, mostly as a self-conscious activity. However, it is not thinking itself that either constitutes or authorises the God–human relationship, even from a human perspective; *thinking* is not the sole, or even the overriding, response in this relationship. Perhaps primacy should be given to love, to creativity and, on the part of human beings, to awe, obedience or thanksgiving. Unfortunately, as 'thinking' has so often been associated with mastery and control, to make this the overriding feature of the relationship smacks of blasphemy or at least of something that is religiously absurd. S. Kierkegaard suggested as much when he spoke scornfully of those thinkers who keep the God in the waiting room of life whilst they examine and pick over His credentials to see whether they will allow Him entry.

How does thinking relate to religious life with its implicit relationships?

The complexity surrounding the role of thought is shown by asking whether one can truly love or obey without at the same time giving or taking thought. The answer is clearly no, though there are situations where the form in which one takes thought can get in the way of love or obedience, for example, where we try to find reasons for loving someone when no reasons are needed or where taking thought becomes a form of disobedience. Examples of such disobedience may be discerned in finding ways around fulfilling a moral (or divine) command or by undermining the command's purpose, famously in misleading people by being 'economical with the truth'. We fulfil the moral command not to lie, yet the reflective way in which we fulfil it deceives people.

So, it is possible to ask the following question: can one truly think and reflect *coram Dei* (before the God) without at the same time loving or rebelling and obeying or disobeying? The answer is less clear, but I would suggest that it is also no. At a minimum, in order to think well, one must *love* the truth and *obey* the rules of logic, as well as take seriously any given facts and necessities – these are all implicit in the act of thinking. If, as Scripture states, in religious worship one must worship 'in spirit and in truth', one can do no less in theology, i.e. one must think 'in spirit and in truth'. If theological thought has to do with grappling with the sense to be found in the God–human relationship, it may be that this sense is not what *we* make but what is given; in this context, thought becomes acknowledgement and obedience. Thinking will take the form of worship and become an act of reverencing the truth by which we live.

It may be that these reflections on the subject of theology do not answer the objection first offered to having 'the God' as the subject matter. To take the subject of theology to be a Divine–human relationship may simply be presuming too much. If one discerns no command and finds no love, can one have a relationship with the Divine? Could one, in fact, still speak of a relationship that could become the focus of reflection? For the sake of one's humanity, one might leave the question of God's existence open. To live without a moral compass, to have no feeling for beauty, to have no intellectual passion for the truth and to have no sense that these might matter more than whatever might come to pass in our temporal world is not just to lose sight of a religious life but possibly to put our humanity at risk.

What is the methodology of theology?

There are various exemplary options that exist. So often, many think that the paradigm of *all* intellectual enquiry is provided by the natural sciences. All other disciplines are measured and judged by its practices and results. The method of the natural sciences namely, of devising theories to *explain* physical phenomena, setting up critical experiments and thus providing the *evidence* that either establishes or eliminates the theory as the certain, or the most probable, explanation – is seen as the ideal. These critical experiments ought to be repeatable so that others can verify the facts for themselves.

The social sciences are similarly seen by some to be like the natural sciences but somehow a little less rigorous. The supposed reason for the lack of rigour in the social sciences is sometimes attributed to one awkward fact, namely, the sheer complexity of human social organisation. It is nigh on impossible to identify or control all the factors that have a bearing on human social life. The consequence of this is that it is impossible to devise and conduct critical experiments. A further complication is that conducting experiments on human beings may be taken to be immoral unless this research scrupulously follows an approved set of rules, rules which may render the experiments impossible.

Another reason why the social sciences appear to be less rigorous may be due to the fact that human awareness of the act of study impacts on the character of the subject of study. In effect, the discipline changes the subject matter (society) being studied (Winch, 1990). Because of these considerations alone, the social sciences are perceived as producing less certain or less well-established 'explanations'.

To view the social sciences as a kind of natural science is probably mistaken, but the natural science paradigm is nevertheless very attractive and maintained by many as a kind of intellectual ideal to which all other disciplines ought to approximate as best they can. The problematical nature of this view becomes more evident when we consider not the social sciences but the human sciences, for there the paradigm of the natural sciences is even less workable. Take, for example, history as an intellectual enterprise: it is not in a position to formulate theories that are subject to critical experiments for the simple reason that history does not repeat itself. It deals effectively with what is singular and unique.

In contrast to the methods of science, the methods of the humanities and of philosophy take on a different character. Whereas the sciences are designed to meet a particular human interest, namely, the interest in causal *explanations* for natural events, the humanities are much more interested in gaining and developing *understanding*. Thus, art and art criticism do not provide *explanations* but are activities that should deepen one's appreciation of the world and that address and express human aesthetic interests. Literature and literary criticism show what it is to be human and *inter alia* the moral interests that people may have. I have tried to maintain that within religion and theology, the human interest in the Eternal predominates and it is love which best characterises this sphere of interest. Gaining and developing understanding within the humanities, particularly with their characteristic interests in mind, requires something other than critical experiments. They require methods that effectively lead to conceptual clarification, which helps us to see relationships or to see things differently and which enhances our skills in what to do to live well.

It would be a mistake to claim that the humanities ignore causal explanations; these have a place, but they do not comprise the whole or even the major concern. For example, when a mother weeps at the death of her child and asks 'why?', the answer cannot simply be couched in the terms of medical explanations. That particular answer alone would not satisfy her question. Her question is more concerned about the *sense* of human life. Fundamentally, she wants to *understand* it and is asking whether there is any aesthetic, moral or 'eternal' sense in a life cut off in its prime or before its full development. One possible method might be to attempt to understand it through art or the sculpture of a pieta and find the answer in the response it generates.

Theology has, it might be said, much more in common with philosophy, even if it cannot wholly ignore the studies of history, psychology, sociology or, for that matter, art, literature or music. Philosophy seeks to show the sense of things. Philosophical 'solutions' to major puzzles generally do not depend on finding out *more* facts or establishing causal connections. The facts and the causal connections are mostly taken as known, or taken for granted, because that is not where the prime philosophical difficulties are to be found. Theology, like philosophy, is more interested in expressing well and clearly matters pertaining to human life, finding solutions to situations where we may have been led into confusion or into incoherence. How, for example, do we reconcile our perceptions of causal connections with our sense of freedom? 'Facts' alone could not solve this problem until we understand what facts would have a bearing on the issue and how. Could the question concerning eternal life be solved, in principle, by factual evidence? There are at least some philosophers who think that it cannot, or at least not without clarifying the kind of question it is and what *kind* of 'facts' could have a bearing on it.

Theology's method is to find stories, arguments and practices that show the character and nature of religious life, that is, to show how we as human beings exist *coram dei* (before the God) and, indeed, how we *ought* to exist before the God.

What are the criteria to be used in and about theology?

Inevitably, one must make judgments in and about theology. The problem is to know how one is to make such judgments. There are certain requirements that one can readily expect any theology to meet.

Some Logical Requirements
Does the theology exhibit the following qualities?:
1. freedom from contradiction;
2. coherence/unity;
3. scope/universality/catholicity;
4. relevance and applicability (Brummer, 1981, pp 139–43).

Some Aesthetic and Moral Criteria
Is the theology:
1. impressive?;
2. poetic?;
3. simple or convoluted?;
4. elegant?;
5. good or just?

Some Religious Criteria
1. Does the theology do justice to, and facilitate or renew, religious life? (Note Augustine's observation [Augustine, 1996, p. 124]:

> So if it seems to you that you have understood the divine scriptures, or any part of them, in such a way that by this understanding you do not build up this twin love of God and neighbour, then you have not understood them. If on the other

hand you have made judgements about them that are helpful for building up of this love, but for all that have not said what the [scriptural] author you have been reading actually meant in that place, then your mistake is not pernicious, and you certainly cannot be accused of lying. Being a liar, of course, means having the intention of saying what is false; and that is why we find many people intending to lie, but intending to be mistaken, none.

What Augustine says here about the study of Scripture might equally well apply to theology.)
2. Is it profound or deep?
3. Is it fruitful? Is it helpful in giving direction of an aesthetic, ethical or religious nature?

Are there any other considerations?

Theology is above all an act of *communication*, so it is important to ask whether it does in fact communicate. However, in order to ask that question and to answer it, we need to attend to the audience of the communication and to the person responsible for the communication. So, in making judgments about theology, particularly as an act of communication, we should ask two further questions: firstly, to whom is the theology addressed?; and, secondly, who is responsible for the theology?

The former question is asked because theology is *not* written, spoken, lived, painted, sung, confessed or prayed in a vacuum. It is always done with a certain audience in mind. As an act of communication, we can always ask: is it effective? If the audience does not understand it, or if the theologian consciously or unconsciously deceives the audience or is insincere, then we would be inclined to say that the communication is seriously flawed or inhuman.[3] We must therefore identify the audience to appreciate the full character of theology and to evaluate it properly for each makes its own demands. Thus, we might have a theology that is addressed to audiences with very different needs. There is the academy, the church, the un-churched; there are people of faith but of another tradition. We can probably think of as many audiences as there are groups of people; as such, we could identify the poor, the rich, a particular gender, children (remember what Scripture says about those who deceive the young and mislead them) or people of another period of time or place. All make their own demands on the theologian, as one who speaks to them about the Divine. It is the character of the audience which has led to some characteristic forms of theology, for example, liberation theology

---

[3] H. Arendt writes: 'Whatever cannot become the object of discourse – the truly sublime, the truly horrible or the uncanny – may find a human voice through which to sound into the world, but it is not exactly human. We humanise what is going on in the world and in ourselves only by speaking of it, and in the course of speaking of it we learn to be human' (1973, pp. 24–5).

or feminist theology, because the intention was to liberate or engage women in reflection.

There are also two other categories of audiences that must be considered but which are not often mentioned. These are the self and the God. To be honest, much of our thinking, writing and speaking are done as much for the sake of our own understanding as for those of others. Further, there are also some theologies that consciously address the Divine. St Augustine did so in his confessions. As such, Augustine's theology in that text is strictly a prayer in which the whole of human life is put under the microscope. In effect, he is saying: this is how I understand our life before you, the God. Another notable example of a theologian addressing God is St Anselm in his *Proslogion*, when he devised the ontological argument whilst in prayer. In addition to asking whether his argument is sound, we might appropriately ask whether it is a good prayer. Has he made himself transparent before the Divine? At the very least, we should ask the following question: how does the fact that it is a prayer affect the status and meaning of the argument? To be honest, we always do our theology before the God who is Truth and who knows the innermost secrets of the heart. There is no scope for deception and we will be convicted for what we say.

How is it that the theologian comes into focus in the effort to evaluate a theology?

People will always ask who is responsible for this theology. Today people know that it is nigh on impossible for anyone to see the world except through his or her own desires and wishes. The interests people have can blind them to what is unreservedly true. If human understanding is shaped unwittingly by self-serving interests, then it is public conversation with others that provides the appropriate correction and cure. Theology by nature is self-involving. This is what gives theology its characteristic voices, so that one might recognise it as black theology or post-colonial theology. However, being self-involving does not mean that it does not seek to be impartial, disinterested (in the proper sense of not being self-serving) and truthful. We shall always struggle to be honest with ourselves and with others.

Appendix
Christological Glossary

The creative thinking of the church is evident from the following.

Ebionism: a position of Jewish-Christian circles which stressed the centrality of the Torah. Jesus was considered to be the messiah through his perfect obedience to the Law. Its radical monotheism excluded the ascription of divinity to Christ and as a consequence the mission of Jesus was primarily seen in prophetic rather than redemptive terms. It also followed that the death of Jesus had no particular significance other than as a sign of his unconditional faithfulness.

Gnosticism: a redemptive view of life but one which involved salvation *from* the world. The material world is essentially evil and a prison to human souls, which are redeemed through elaborate rituals and secret, esoteric knowledge. In Christian circles it tended towards docetism, i.e. Jesus only appeared to be human and was not really human because of the evil nature of the material world. Jesus is one of many spiritual beings.

Origen (185–255 AD): developed the Trinitarian doctrine of Tertullian under the influence of Neoplatonic philosophy. Tertullian identified the Son with the Neoplatonic logos, finding a precedent in John's Gospel; in so doing he brought together both Christ's distinct personality and divinity. The Word (logos) is personal but intrinsically and eternally divine; the Son proceeds from the Father by an 'eternal generation'; it is not true that 'there was time when the Son was not'. Yet in Origen's view the Son was both mutable and morally subordinate to the Father. Thus, on this view the Son holds some intermediate status which is attributable to the fundamentally pantheistic framework of neo-platonism where the logos is one step in the process of God, the One, becoming the world, the many. In this respect, Origen's position savours of Arianism.

Monarchianism: a position which stressed the unity between Christ and God to the point where Jesus Christ lost any distinct personality.

Arianism: a position which stressed the distinct personality of Christ to the point of sacrificing his unity with God. The consequence is that Christ was regarded as a superhuman being or derivative deity, but not as one with God. Arius could say: 'There was a time when he was not.' Christ is clearly a mediator between humans and God through his status as an intermediate being.

Tertullian (d. 220 AD): the man who provided the first intermediate position between Monarchianism and Arianism, but only at the level of bare affirmation: '*Una substantia, tres personae*' – one substance, three persons ('persona' used to refer to masks worn by actors in the theatre).

Dynamic Monarchianism: apart from his supernatural birth, Jesus was fully human but was divine insofar as he was imbued with a divine power (Greek: *Dynamis*) at his baptism. This fits in well with the 'adoptionist' view of Jesus expressed in Mark's Gospel, where Christ is adopted the Son of God at his baptism by John.

Modalistic Monarchianism: the Son is a mode or form of God's appearing (theophany). The implications are that the Son did not exist prior to the incarnation, i.e. it denies pre-existence. The other implication is that God, the Father, suffered when He appeared in the form and life of Jesus, i.e. patripassionism – condemned as a heresy by the early church but recently re-asserted by J. Moltmann.

Sabellianism: a position that takes the modalistic form of Monarchianism one stage further: the Father, Son and Holy Spirit are consecutive modes of God's appearing, corresponding with the periods of the Old Testament, New Testament and church. This was specifically condemned at the Council of Constantinople in 381 AD.

Apollinarianism: a 'heresy' condemned at the Council of Constantinople (381 AD) where the humanity of Christ was obscured by his divinity. It had two stages which correlated to differences in Greek psychology (human beings were regarded as being constituted of either two or three parts – dichotomists or trichotomists): 1) Christ was said to have had a human body but a divine soul; 2) Christ had a human body, a human animal soul but a divine rational soul. It is a position that implicitly devalues the body and the physical world as if human beings are to be saved *from* the world, rather than that the world (with human beings) is saved.

Eutychianism: this stressed the unity of the human and the Divine in Jesus Christ to the point where there is no plurality – even the human body is changed by its unity with the deity. The humanity is absorbed and lost in the divinity 'like a drop of honey in the sea'.

Nestorianism: this emphasised the plurality of natures (human and divine) to the point where the unity of the person is lost. The unity which does exist is a moral, rather than a metaphysical, one. There is a 'concord of will and purpose, not the oneness of a single personal life'. There was the suggestion of a possible metaphysical unity after the resurrection when Jesus shared in the inherent position of the logos. It was generally anti-docetic but stressed the humanity of Christ so that Jesus, as man, is only an ethical teacher. The position was condemned at the Council of Ephesus (431 AD).

Cyril of Alexandria: Cyril was anxious to avoid Nestorianism and hence tended toward Eutychianism, but should not be identified with it. He said that the divine Logos took on an impersonal but complete human nature (thus giving a unity of person with a plurality of natures). There are effectively two natures in a single subject of whom the qualities of either natures may be predicated.

Leo's Tome: in this text Leo was anxious to avoid Eutychianism and therefore tended toward Nestorianism with a Christology of two natures in one subject. The two natures are quite separable, though neither stands apart from what the other does, so there is some ground for an interchange of qualities.

These early Christological accounts and controversies were briefly summarized by R. Hooker in the seventeenth century (*Eccl. Politics*, V, 54, p. 195). He wrote: 'There are but four things which concur to make complete the whole state of our Lord Jesus Christ – his deity, his manhood, the conjunction of both, and the distinction of one from the other. Four principle heresies there are which in these things withstood the truth: Arius by bending himself against the deity of Christ, Apollinaris by maiming and misinterpreting that which belongs to his human nature, Nestorius by rending asunder and dividing him into two persons, Eutyches by confounding in his person those natures which should be distinguished.'

Bibliography

Adam, A. K. M., *What is Post-Modern Biblical Criticism?*, Fortress (Minneapolis, 1995)

Al-Ghazali, *The Ninety-Nine Beautiful Names*, trans. D. B. Burrell and N. Daher, The Islamic Texts Society (Cambridge, 1992)

Anselm, *Cur Deus Homo?* Griffith, Farran, Okeden & Welsh (London, 1989)

Aquinas, St Thomas, *Summa Theologiae*, ed. T. McDermott, Eyre and Spottiswoode (London, 1989)

Arendt, H., *The Human Condition*, University of Chicago Press (Chicago, 1958)

Arendt, H., *Men in Dark Times*, Penguin (Harmondsworth, 1973)

Aristotle, *Magna Moralia*, Heinemann (London, 1935)

Augustine, *City of God*, OUP (London, 1963)

Augustine, *De Genesi ad Litteram, The Literal Meaning of Genesis*, vols 1 and 2, Newman Press (New York, 1982)

Augustine, *Confessions*, trans. H. Chadwick, OUP (Oxford, 1991)

Augustine, *De Doctrina Christiana (Teaching Christianity)*, trans. E. Hill, New City Press (New York, 2002)

Augustine, *De Magistro*, trans. Garry Wills, in *St. Augustine's Childhood, Confessiones*, Bk. 1, pp. 126–91, Continuum (London, 2001)

Augustine, *On the Free Choice of the Will, On Grace and Free Choice, and Other Writings*, ed. P. King, CUP (Cambridge, 2010)

Aulen, G., *Christus Victor*, SPCK (London, 1970)

Austin, J. L., *Logic and Language, Essays, 2nd Series*, Blackwell (Oxford, 1953)

Austin, J. L., *Sense and Sensibilia*, OUP (Oxford, 1962)

Austin, J. L., *How to Do Things with Words*, OUP (Oxford, 1976)

Baillie, D. M., *The Theology of the Sacraments and Other Papers*, Faber & Faber (London, 1957)

Baillie, D. M., *God was in Christ*, Faber & Faber (London, 1961)

Baillie, J., *And the Life Everlasting*, OUP (London, 1941)

Bailie, J., *The Idea of Revelation in Recent Thought*, Columbia University Press (New York, 1964) (first published in 1956)

Baillie, J., *Baptism and Conversion*, OUP (London, 1984)

Barclay, W., *Introducing the Bible*, Bible Reading Fellowships, Denholm House Press (London, 1972)

Barnes, L. P., 'Forgiveness, the Moral Law and Education: A Reply to Patricia White', *Journal of the Philosophy of Education*, 36(4): 529–44 (2002)

Barr, J., *Old and New in Interpretation*, SCM (London, 1966)

Barr, J., *The Bible in the Modern World*, SCM (London, 1973)

Barr, J., *Fundamentalism*, SCM (London, 1977)

Barrett, J. L., *Why Would Anyone Believe in God?* Altamira Press (Walnut Creek, 2004)
Barrett, W., *Death of the Soul*, OUP (Oxford, 1986)
Barrett, W., *The Illusion of Technique*, Kimber (London, 1979)
Bartsch, H. W., ed., *Kerygma and Myth*, SPCK (London, 1953)
Barth, K., *Church Dogmatics, The Doctrine of the Word of God*, vol. 1/1, T&T Clark (Edinburgh, 1975) (first published in 1936)
Barth, K., *Church Dogmatics*, vol. 1/2, T&T Clark (Edinburgh, 1978) (first published in 1956)
Barth, K., *Dogmatics in Outline*, SCM (London, 1960)
Barth, K., *The Humanity of God*, Collins (London, 1967)
Becket, S., *Waiting for Godot*, Faber & Faber (London, 1965)
Benedict XVI, *Spe salvi*, papal encyclical, Vatican,
Berkhouwer, G. C., *Holy Scriptures*, Eerdmans (Grand Rapids, 1975)
Bigg, C., *The Church's Task under the Roman Empire*, Clarendon (Oxford, 1905)
Blamires, David, trans. and introduction, *The Book of the Perfect Life (Theologia Germanica)*, Alta Mira Press (Walnut Creek, CA, 2003)
Boethius, *The Consolation of Philosophy*, Penguin (London, 1999)
Bolton, D., *An Approach to Wittgenstein's Philosophy*, Macmillan (London, 1979)
Bonhoeffer, D., *Christology*, Collins (London, 1966)
Bonhoeffer, D., *Ethics*, SCM (London, 1971)
Bourdieu, P., *Outline of a Theory of Practice*, CUP (Cambridge, 1977)
Braaten, C., *History and Hermeneutics*, Westminster (London, 1966)
Bray, G., *Biblical Interpretation Past and Present*, Apollos (Leicester, 1996)
Brown, R. E., *The Critical Meaning of the Bible*, Paulist Press (New York, 1981)
Brummer, V., *Theology and Philosophical Enquiry: An Introduction*, Macmillan (London, 1981)
Brummer, V., *What Are We Doing When We Pray?* SCM (London, 1984)
Brunner, E., *Man in Revolt*, Lutterworth (London, 1947)
Brunner, E., *The Misunderstanding of the Church*, Lutterworth (London, 1952)
Bultmann, R., 'New Testament and Mythology; The Mythological Element in the New Testament and the Problem of its Re-interpretation', in H. W. Bartsch, ed., *Kerygma and Myth*, pp. 35–6, SPCK (London, 1953)
Burnaby, J., *The Belief of Christendom*, SPCK (London, 1959)
Burrell, D., 'The Spirit and the Christian Life', in P. Hodgson and R. King, eds., *Christian Theology, an Introduction to its Traditions and Tasks*, SPCK (London, 1983)
Burrows, M. ed, *Biblical Hermeneutics in Historical Perspective*, Eerdmans (Grand Rapids, 1991)
Byrne, P., *The Moral Interpretation of Religion*, Edinburgh University Press (Edinburgh, 1998)
Calvin, J., *Institutes of the Christian Religion*, vols. 1 and 2, T&T Clark (Edinburgh, 1899)
Cairns, D., *The Image of God in Man*, London, SCM (London, 1953)

Childs, B. S., *Biblical Theology in Crises*, Westminster (Philadelphia, 1970)
Childs, B. S., *Introduction to the Old Testament as Scripture*, SCM (London, 1979)
Church of England, Commission on Doctrine, *The Mystery of Creation* (1995)
Coleridge, S. T., *Confessions of an Inquiring Spirit*, Scolar Press (Menston, 1971)
Collins, A., *Feminist Perspectives on Biblical Scholarship*, Scolar Press (Menston, 1985)
Copleston, F. C., *A History of Philosophy*, vol. 3, Pt. 2, Doubleday (New York, 1963)
Cupitt, D., *The Nature of Man*, Sheldon Press (London, 1979)
D'Costa, G., *Christian Uniqueness Reconsidered*, Orbis (Maryknoll, NY, 1990)
Davies, J. G., ed., *A Dictionary of Liturgy and Worship*, SCM (London, 1972)
Davis, F., Paulhus, E. and Bradstock, A., *Moral, But No Compass, Government, Church and the Future of Welfare*, Matthew James Publishing Ltd. (Chelmsford, 2008)
Dawkins, R., *The Selfish Gene*, OUP (Oxford, 1989)
Dawkins, R., *River out of Eden*, Phoenix (London, 1995)
Dictionary of Liturgy and Worship, ed. J. G. Davies, SCM (London, 1972)
Dillistone, F. W., *The Christian Understanding of Atonement*, James Nisbet & Co. (Welwyn, 1968)
Dodd, C. H., *The Bible Today*, CUP (Cambridge, 1951)
Dodd, C. H., *The Authority of the Bible*, Fontana (London, 1956)
Dostoyevsky, F., *The Brothers Karamazov*, Penguin (Harmondsworth, 1958)
Downie, R. S., 'Forgiveness', *Philosophical Quarterly*, 15: 128–34 (1965)
Ebeling, G., *The Word of God and Tradition*, Collins (London, 1968)
Eckhart, Meister, *Meister Eckhart*, Fontana Library (London, 1963)
Eckhart, Meister, *The Essential Sermons, Commentaries, Treatises and Defense*, trans. and intro. by E. Colledge and B. McGinn, Paulist Press (New York, 1981)
Farmer, H. H., *Revelation and Religion*, James Nisbet & Co. (London, 1954)
Felderhof, M. C., 'Evil: Theodicy or Resistance?', *Scottish Journal of Theology* 57(4): 397–412 (2004)
Fénélon, Francois *The Inner Life*, available at the Internet Encyclopaedia of Philosophy, http://www.passtheword.org/DIALOGS-FROM-THE-PAST/innerlife.htm (date accessed 9 June 2011)
Feuerbach, L., *The Essence of Christianity*, trans. G. Eliot, introductory essay by K. Barth, foreword by H. Richard Niebuhr, Harper & Row (New York, 1957)
Feuerbach, L., *Lectures on the Essence of Religion*, Harper & Row (New York, 1968)
Feuerbach, L., *Principles of the Philosophy of the Future*, Hackett Pub. Co. (Indianapolis, 1986)
Fiddes, P. S., *The Promised End: Eschatology in Theology and Literature*, Blackwell (Oxford, 2000)
Fletcher, J., *Situation Ethics*, SCM (London, 1966)

Flew, A. and MacIntyre, A., *New Essays in Philosophical Theology*, SCM (London, 1955)
Fox, A., *Plato and the Christians*, SCM (London, 1957)
Frank, S. L., *God with Us*, Jonathan Cape (London, 1946)
Franks, R. S., *The Atonement*, OUP (Oxford, 1937)
Frei, H. W., *The Eclipse of Biblical Narrative*, Yale (New Haven, CT, 1974)
Freud, S., *Introductory Lectures on Psycho-Analysis*, Penguin (London, 1974)
Freud, S., *Civilization and its Discontents*, Hogarth Press (London, 1963)
Gaita, R., *A Common Humanity*, London, Routledge (London, 2000)
Gilkey, L., *Naming the Whirlwind, The Renewal of God-Language*, Bobbs-Merrill (Indianapolis, 1969)
Gray, J., *Straw Dogs*, Granta Books (London, 2002)
Greene, G., *The Power and the Glory*, Penguin (Harmondsworth, 1962)
Gunneweg, A. H. J., *Understanding the Old Testament*, SCM (London, 1978)
Gunton, C., *The Christian Faith*, Blackwell (Oxford, 2002)
Haering, T., *The Christian Faith, a System of Dogmatics*, Hodder & Stoughton (London, 1915)
Haldane, J., *Reasonable Faith*, Routledge (Abingdon, 2010)
Hamilton, K., *Words and The Word*, Eerdsman (Grand Rapids, 1971)
Harvey, Van, *The Historian and the Believer*, Macmillan (London, 1966)
Hauerwas, S., *With the Grain of the Universe*, SCM (London, 2002)
Hawkins, P. S., *Undiscovered Country*, Seabury (New York, 2009)
Heiler, F., *Prayer, a Study in the History and Psychology of Religion*, ET Galaxy Book, OUP (New York, 1958) (first published in 1932)
Hengel, M., *Between Jesus and Paul*, SCM (London, 1983)
Hermann, W., *The Communion of the Christian with God*, ed. and intro. by R. T. Voekel, SCM (London, 1971)
Hick, J., *Death and Eternal Life*, Collins (London, 1976)
Hick, J. and Hebblethwaite, B., eds., *Christianity and Other Religions*, Fount Paperbacks (London, 1980)
Hobbes, T., *Leviathan*, CUP (Cambridge, 1991)
Hodgson, P. and King, R., *Christian Theology, An Introduction to its Traditions and Tasks*, ch. 6, SPCK (London, 1983)
Holmes, E. E., *Prayer and Action*, Longmans, Green and Co. (London, 1911)
Hooker, R., *Eccl. Politics*, V, 54, p. 195, http://books.google.com/books?id=fKI-AAAAcAAJ&pg=PR18&dq=R.+Hooker,+of+the+Laws+of+Ecclesiastical+Politics&hl=en&ei=uc70TbCjEIOv8QOg7KS2Bw&sa=X&oi=book_result&ct=result&resnum=3&ved=0CDIQ6AEwAjgK#v=onepage&q&f=false (date accesed 11 June 2011)
Hume, D., *An Enquiry Concerning Human Understanding*, Clarendon (Oxford, 2000)
James, W., *The Varieties of Religious Experience*, Fontana (London, 1974) (Gifford Lectures, first given 1901–1902)

Jeanrond, W., *Theological Hermeneutics: Development and Significance*, Macmillan (Basingstoke, 1991)
Johnston, M., *Saving God, Religion after Idolatry*, Princeton University Press (Princeton, 2009)
Jones, O. R., *The Concept of Holiness*, George Allen & Unwin (London, 1961)
Kahler, M., *The So-called Historical Jesus and the Historic Biblical Christ*, Fortress Press (Minneapolis, 1964)
Kant, I., *Critique of Judgment*, Dover (New York, 2005)
Kaufman, G. D., *God, The Problem*, Harvard University Press (Cambridge, MA, 1972)
Keck, L., *Taking the Bible Seriously*, Abingdon Press (Abingdon, 1962)
Kelsey, D. H., *The Uses of Scripture in Recent Theology*, SCM (London, 1975)
Kierkegaard, S., *The Journals of Soren Kierkegaard*, ed. and trans. by A. Dru, Oxford University Press (London, 1938)
Kierkegaard, S., *Works of Love*, OUP (London, 1946)
Kierkegaard, S., *The Gospel of Suffering*, James Clarke & Co. (Cambridge, 1955)
Kierkegaard, S., *Purity of Heart*, Harper & Row (New York, 1956)
Kierkegaard, S., *The Journals of Soren Kierkegaard*, Collins (London, 1958)
Kierkegaard, S., *Journals and Papers*, Indiana University Press (Bloomington and London, 1967)
Kierkegaard, S., *Journals and Papers*, vol. 3, L–R, ed. Howard V. Hong and Edna H. Hong, Indiana University Press (Bloomington and London, 1975)
Kierkegaard, S., *The Sickness unto Death*, Princeton University Press (Princeton, 1980)
Kierkegaard, S., *Philosophical Fragments*, Princeton University Press (Princeton, 1985)
Kierkegaard, S., *Either-Or*, Pts. 1 and 2, Princeton University Press (Princeton, 1987)
Kierkegaard, S., *Concluding Unscientific Postscript*, Princeton University Press (Princeton, 1992)
Kierkegaard, S., *A Literary Review*, Penguin (Harmondsworth, 2001) (first published in 1846)
Kirk, K. E., *The Vision of God*, 2nd edition, Longmans, Green and Co. (London, 1932) (1941 impression)
Knitter, P., *Introducing Theologies of Religions*, Orbis (Maryknoll, NY, 2002)
Kummel, W. G., *The New Testament: The History of the Investigation of its Problems*, SCM (London, 1973)
Kung, H., *The Church*, Burns and Oates (London, 1976)
Kung, H., *Art and the Question of Meaning*, SCM (London, 1981)
Lash, N., *Believing Three Ways in One God*, SCM (London, 1992)
Lash, N., *Theology for Pilgrims*, Darton, Longman and Todd (London, 2008)
Linzey, A., *Animal Theology*, SCM (London, 1994)
Lorenz, K., *King Solomon's Ring*, Methuen (London, 1952)
Lorenz, K., *On Aggression*, Methuen (London, 1966)

Lucas, J. R., *Freedom and Grace*, SPCK (London, 1976)
Lyotard, J-F., *The Postmodern Condition: A Report on Knowledge*, Manchester University Press (Manchester, 1984)
Mackintosh, H. R., *The Christian Experience of Forgiveness*, Fontana (London, 1961) (first published in 1927)
Macquarrie, J., *God-Talk, An Examination of the Language and Logic of Theology*, SCM (London, 1967)
Mander, W., 'A Philosophical Discussion of Eternal Life', *Farmington Papers*, PR13, 2003
Marx, K., *Selected Writings in Sociology and Social Philosophy*, eds. T. D. Bottomore and M. Rubel, Penguin (London, 1963)
Maxwell, W. D., *An Outline of Christian Worship, its Development and Forms*, OUP (London, 1936)
McIntyre, J., *The Shape of Christology*, SCM (London, 1966)
McTaggart, J. and McTaggart, E., *Some Dogmas of Religion*, Edward Arnold (London, 1906)
Midgley, M., *Beast and Man: The Roots of Human Nature*, Methuen (London, 1980)
Midgley, M., *Wisdom, Information and Wonder*, Routledge (London, 1989)
Midgley, M., *Science as Salvation, A Modern Myth and its Meaning*, Routledge (London, 1992)
Miles, T. R., *Speaking of God, Theism, Atheism and the Magnus Image*, William Sessions Ltd (York, 1998)
Miller, A., 'Rhetoric Paideia and the Old Idea of a Liberal Education', *Journal of Philosophy of Education*, 41(2): 183–206 (2007)
Moltmann, J., *Man*, SPCK (London, 1974)
Moltmann, J., *The Crucified God*, SCM (London, 1974)
Moltmann, J., *The Trinity and the Kingdom of God*, SCM (London, 1981)
Moltmann, J., *On Human Dignity, Political Theology and Ethics*, SCM (London, 1984)
Moran, G., *Theology of Revelation*, Burns & Oates (London, 1967)
Morris, D., *The Naked Ape*, Cape (London, 1967)
Moyisse, S., *Introduction to Biblical Studies*, Cassell (London, 1998)
Mukonyora, I., ed., *'Rewriting' the Bible*, Mambo (Gweru, Zimbabwe, 1993)
Murdoch, I., *The Sovereignty of the Good*, Routledge & Kegan Paul (London, 1970)
Newbigin, L., *The Finality of Christ*, SCM (London, 1969)
Newman, J. H., *Oxford University Sermons* (London, 1880)
Niebuhr, H. R., *The Responsible Self*, Harper & Row (New York, 1963)
Niebuhr, H. R., 'The Idea of Original Sin in American Culture' in W. S. Johnson, ed., *Theology, History and Culture*, pp. 174–91, Yale University Press (New Haven, CT, 1996)
Niebuhr, R., *The Nature and Destiny of Man*, vols. 1 and 2, James Nisbet & Co. (London, 1941)

Niebuhr, R., *Moral Man and Immoral Society*, SCM (London, 1963)
Nietzsche, F., *The Genealogy of Morals*, Doubleday (London, 1990)
Nietzsche, F., *Twilight of the Idols/The Anti-Christ*, Penguin (London, 1990a)
Nietzsche, F., *The Birth of Tragedy*, Penguin (London, 1993)
Nineham, D., *The Church's Use of the Bible*, SPCK (London, 1963)
Nineham, D., *The Use and Abuse of the Bible*, SPCK (London, 1976)
Nygren, A., *Essence of Christianity*, Epworth (London, 1960)
Ong, W., *Orality and Literacy: The Technologizing of the Word*, Methuen (London, 1982)
Origen, *Treatise on Prayer (De Oratione)*, trans. E. G. Jay, SPCK (London, 1954)
Otto, R., *The Idea of the Holy*, Penguin (Harmondsworth, 1959)
Pannenberg, W., *Jesus: God and Man*, SCM (London, 1968)
Pannenberg, W., *What is Man?*, Fortress Press (Philadelphia, 1972)
Pannenberg, W., *Anthropology in Theological Perspective*, trans. M. J. O'Connell, T&T Clark (Edinburgh, 1985)
Pannenberg, W., Rendtorff, R., Rendtorff, T. and Wilken, U., eds., *Revelation as History*, Macmillan (New York, 1968)
Passmore, J., *The Perfectibility of Man*, Duckworth (London, 1970)
Patte, D., *Ethics of Biblical Interpretation*, Westminster John Knox Press (Louisville, Ky., 1995)
Pattison, S., 'The Emperor's New Verbs', *Local Government Studies*, 21(4): 539–45 (1995)
Phillips, D. Z., *The Concept of Prayer*, Routledge & Kegan Paul (London, 1965)
Phillips, D. Z., *Death and Immortality*, Macmillan (London, 1970)
Phillips, D. Z., *Religion and the Hermeneutics of Contemplation*, CUP (Cambridge, 2001)
Phillips, D. Z., *Religion and Friendly Fire*, Ashgate (Aldershot, 2004)
Phillips, D. Z. (ed), *Whose God? Which Tradition? The Nature of Belief in God*, Ashgate (Aldershot, 2008)
Pieper, J., *Faith and Belief*, Faber & Faber (London, 1963)
Plato, *Apology*, trans. H. N. Fowler, Heinemann (London, 1914)
Plato, *Euthyphro*, trans. H. N. Fowler, Heinemann (London, 1914)
Plato, *Phaedrus*, trans. H. N. Fowler, Heinemann (London, 1914)
Plato, *Gorgias*, trans. E. R. Dodds, Clarendon (Oxford, 1959)
Plato, *Charmides*, in *Early Socratic Dialogues* ed. T. J. Saunders, Penguin (Harmondsworth, 1987)
Plato, *Phaedo*, ed. C. J. Rowe, CUP (Cambridge, 1993)
Plato, *The Republic*, trans. R. W. Sterling and W. C. Scott, W. W. Norton (London, 1996)
Plotinus, *The Enneads*, trans S. Mackenna, Faber & Faber (London, 1956)
Polanyi, M., *Personal Knowledge*, Routledge & Kegan Paul (London, 1956)
Popper, K., *The Logic of Scientific Discovery*, Hutchinson (London, 1959)
Popper, K., *The Poverty of Historicism*, Routledge & Kegan Paul (London, 1961) (first published in 1957)

Race, A., *Christians and Religious Pluralism*, SCM (London, 1983)
Rahner, K., *Theological Investigations*, vol. 5, Darton Longman & Todd (London, 1966)
Rahner, K., *Inspiration in the Bible*, Herder & Herder (London, 1961)
Ramsey, I. T., *Freedom and Immortality*, SCM (London, 1960)
Ramsey, I. T., *On Being Sure in Religion*, University of London, Athlone Press (London, 1963)
Ramsey, I. T., *Religious Language*, SCM (London, 1957)
Reid, J. K. S., *The Authority of the Scripture*, Methuen (London, 1957)
Reid, T., *Essays on the Powers of the Human Mind*, vol. 1, Richardson and Co. (London, 1822)
Reimarus, H. S., *Fragments*, ed. C. H. Talbert, trans. R. S. Fraser, SCM (London, 1971)
Reynolds, B., *Dante, The Poet, the Political Thinker, the Man*, I. B. Tauris (London, 2006)
Rhees, R., *On Religion and Philosophy*, ed. D. Z. Phillips, CUP (Cambridge, 1997)
Richardson, A. R., *The Bible in the Age of Science*, SCM (London, 1961)
Rilke, R. M., *The Notebooks of Malte Laurids Brigge*, trans. B. Pike, Dalkey Archive Press (London, 2008) (first published in 1910)
Rose, G., *Mourning Becomes the Law*, CUP (Cambridge, 1996)
Rose, G., *Judaism and Modernity*, Blackwell (Oxford, 1993)
Rowland, C., *Liberating Exegesis*, Westminster (Louisville, KY, 1989)
Rowley, H. H., *The Relevance of the Bible*, James Clarke & Co. (London, 1941)
Sawyer, J. F. A., *From Moses to Patmos*, SPCK (London, 1977)
Sartre, J. P., *Existentialism and Humanism*, Eyre Methuen (London, 1958)
Schaff, P., ed., *A Select Library of the Nicene and Post Nicene Fathers of the Christian Church*, vol. 1, Eerdmans (Grand Rapids, 1979)
Schleiermacher, F. D. E., *The Christian Faith*, trans. and ed. by H. R. Mackintosh and J. S. Stewart, T&T Clark (Edinburgh, 1928)
Schleiermacher, F. D. E., *On Religion, Speeches to its Cultured Despisers*, trans. J. Oman, Harper & Row (New York, 1958)
Schleiermacher, F. D. E., *Servant of the Word, Selected Sermons of Friedrich Schleiermacher*, Fortress Press (Philadelphia, 1987)
Schillebeeckx, E., *Revelation and Theology*, Sheed and Ward (London, 1967)
Schillebeeckx, E., *Jesus, an Experiment in Christology*, Collins (London, 1979)
Schillebeeckx, E., *Interim Report on the Books Jesus & Christ*, SCM (London, 1980)
Segal, R. A., ed., *The Myth and Ritual Theory*, Blackwell (Oxford, 1998)
Smith, W. Cantwell, *The Meaning and End of Religion*, Macmillan (New York, 1962)
Smart, J. D., *The Interpretation of Scripture*, SCM (London, 1961)
Smart, J. D., *The Strange Silence of the Bible in the Church*, SCM (London, 1970)
Steiner, G., *Errata: An Examined Life*, Phoenix (London, 1997)
Stevenson, L., *Seven Theories of Human Nature*, OUP (Oxford, 1974)

Stevenson, L., *The Study of Human Nature*, OUP (Oxford, 1981)
Stuhlmacher, P., *Historical Criticism and Theological Interpretation of Scripture*, SPCK (London, 1979)
Sutherland, S. R., *God, Jesus and Belief*, Blackwell (Oxford, 1984)
Taylor, C., *Sources of the Self, the Making of the Modern Identity*, Harvard University Press (Cambridge, MA, 1989)
Thomas, O. C., *Attitudes Toward Other Religions*, SCM (London, 1969)
Tillich, P., *Systematic Theology*, James Nisbet & Co. (London, 1953)
Tillich, P., *The Protestant Era*, abridged edition, University of Chicago Press (London, 1957)
Tolstoy, L., *A Confession and Other Religious Writings*, Penguin (London, 1987)
Turner, D., *Faith Seeking*, SCM (London, 2002)
Turner, H. E. W., *The Patristic Doctrine of Redemption*, Mowbray (London, 1952)
Twerski, A. J., *Generation to Generation*, Traditional Press (New York, 1985)
Underhill, E., *Worship*, Collins (London, 1962)
Vickers, B., *In Defence of Rhetoric*, Clarendon (Oxford, 1998)
Wainwright, A., *Beyond Biblical Criticism*, SPCK (London, 1982)
Watson, F., *Text, Church and World*, T&T Clark (Edinburgh, 1994)
Wardy, R., *The Birth of Rhetoric*, Routledge (London, 1996)
Weber, M., *Sociology of Religion*, Beacon Press (Boston, Mass., 1964)
Webster, J., *Holiness*, SCM (London, 2003)
Weil, S., *The Need for Roots*, Routledge & Kegan Paul (London, 1952)
Weil, S., *Waiting on God*, Fontana (Glasgow, 1959)
Weil, S., *Gravity and Grace*, Routledge & Kegan Paul (London, 1972)
Weil, S., *Letter to a Priest*, Routledge (London, 2002) (first published in 1951)
White, J. F., *Introduction to Christian Worship*, Abingdon Press (Nashville, 1980)
White, P., 'What Should We Teach Children about Forgiveness?', *Journal of the Philosophy of Education*, 36(1): 57–67 (2002)
Whitehead, A. N., *Process and Reality, an Essay in Cosmology*, Gifford Lectures 1927–1928, CUP (Cambridge, 1929)
Wiles, M., 'Worship and Theology', in D. W. Hardy and P. H. Sedgwick, eds., *The Weight of Glory*, pp. 69–78, T&T Clark (Edinburgh, 1991)
Wilken, R. L., 'Christian Formation in the Early Church', in J. van Engen, ed., *Educating People of Faith*, Eerdmans (Grand Rapids, 2004)
Williams, D. D., *The Spirit and the Forms of Love*, James Nisbet & Co. (Welwyn, 1968)
Wills, G., *St. Augustine's Childhood*, Continuum (London, 2001)
Williams, B., *Moral Luck*, CUP (Cambridge, 1981)
Winch, P., *The Idea of a Social Science*, 2nd edition, Routledge (London, 1990)
Wittgenstein, L., 'Lectures on Religious Belief', in C. Barrett, ed., *Lectures and Conversations on Aesthetics, Psychology and Religious Belief*, Blackwell (Oxford, 1970)
Wittgenstein, L., *Culture and Value*, Basil Blackwell (Oxford, 1980)
Wolf, W. J., *No Cross, No Crown*, Doubleday (New York, 1957)

Wolterstorff, N., *Reason within the Bounds of Religion*, 2nd edition, Eerdmans (Grand Rapids, 1984)
World Council of Churches, *Baptism, Eucharist and Ministry*, Faith and Order Paper No. 111, WCC (Geneva, 1982)
Young, F. M., *Sacrifice and the Death of Christ*, SPCK (London, 1975)
Young, F. M., *The Art of Performance*, Darton Longman & Todd (London, 1990)

Index

action
    human identity in 75
    sacraments as 54, 59–60
Age of Reason 126
aggression, and the human condition 89–90
agnosticism 17
anarchy, and spontaneity 77–8
animals, cruelty to 71
Anselm, St 162
    Cur Deus Homo? 140
        satisfaction theory 143–4
    on existence of God 163
    Proslogion 202
Apollinarianism 150, 204
apologetics 11
aporia, Plato's dialogues 2, 78fn7
Aquinas, Thomas St
    on existence of God 163–4
    on prayer 49
    Summa Theologiae 8
    on virtues 84–5, 99
Arianism 150, 203
Athanasius, St 150
attention
    and Christian faith 4, 5
    need for 88
    theological 131
    to language 185, 187fn7, 188
    Weil on 169fn2
Augustine, St 185
    on evil 95
    on the human condition 94
    on the Scriptures 200–1
    on silence 156
    on sin 83, 92
    on speaking of God 157
    on the Trinity 156
    works
        Confessions 4, 94
        The City of God 95

Aulen, G. 140
autonomy, Tillich on 79

Babel, Tower of 137
Baillie, D.M. 101
baptism
    practice of 62–3
    purpose 61–2
    and water 62
Barth, Karl 72, 111, 134, 147, 176
    Humanity of God 197
believers, unbelievers, differences 132–3
betrayal, and kissing 60
Bible
    King James Version 178
    role in worship 175
Bonhoeffer, D. 145–6
Brunner, Emil 72
    The Misunderstanding of the Church 115

Calvin, John 63
    on the church 116, 119, 120
    Institutes 8
causes
    Aristotelian 21
    Thomistic 21
Chalcedon, Council of (451) 149, 150–1
Chekov, Anton, *The Death of an Official* 106
Christian faith, and attention 4, 5
Christian year
    and cycle of nature 38
    and the Eternal 37
    and Jewish practice 37–8
    and life of Christ 37
Christianity
    and context 4
    expression of 133
    insiders/outsiders 6–8
    interest in 5

revisiting
beginning 8
    purpose 3
    rules, ambiguous status of 133–4
    transformations 1–3
    understanding of 6
Christology
    controversies 205
    from above 147
        critique of 147–8
    from below 147
    glossary 203–5
church, the
    apostolicity 110
    authority, claimed 110
    Calvin on 116, 119, 120
    as community of love 110
    conservatism 113
    as divine society 111, 116–17
        critique of 112–13
    as fallible institution 152
    as human institution 113–14
    invisible 116, 117, 119, 120
    nature of 114–15
    reforming agenda 112
    role of 110
    and salvation 124
    sociality 115
    visible 116, 119, 120
communication
    and grammar, importance of 192
    and hermeneutics 191–3
    psychological dimension 191
    Schleiermacher on 191–2
    and structure 188
    in theology 185–6, 201
    see also language
community of love, the church as 110
Constantinople, Council of (381) 150, 204
Creator, God as 159, 160–61
cultus 55
    definitions 31
    religion as 31
Cyprian, St 124
Cyril of Alexandria 205

Dante, on language 186
Darwinism, and human beings 71

Dawkins, Richard 67
The Selfish Gene 68
democracy, limitations of 81
Dillistone, F.W., *The Christian
    Understanding of Atonement* 140
disinterestedness 33–4
divine law 82
divine love, ubiquity of 125–6
docetism 149
dogmatics
    formal 11
    material 11
Dostoyevsky, Fyodor, *The Brothers
    Karamazov* 102
Durkheim, E. 80

Ebionism 203
Ebionites 149
Eckhart, Meister 49, 53, 161
Ephesus, Council of (431) 205
eternal
    in the ancient world 25–6
    meanings 24–5
eternal happiness
    Kierkegaard on 73
    possibility of 74
eternal life 10, 11, 15–27
    causal explanations 22
    as final cause 23–4
    as hypothesis 23
    knowledge of 21–3
    and religious life 18
    significance 15–16
    and timeless concerns of life 18
eternal love, and romantic love 26
Eternal, the
    and the Christian year 37
    cultivation of 33–4
    human alienation from 90
    and human beings 72
    human interest in 145
    human relationship to 57
    individual relationship to 126
    omnipotence 117
    paradoxical presence 30
    and religion 53
    as *sui generis* category 148
    symbolic presence 36

unknowability 29
   and worship 33, 41
eternity, and love 26
ethics 11
Eucharist, meaning 63–4
Eutychianism 204, 205
evil
   Augustine on 95
   origins of 95
   see also sin

faith
   components 9fn19
   people of 120
   social nature of 121
faiths
   diversity of, need for 126–7
   other, attitudes to 123
   relationships between 122–3
forgiveness
   alternatives to 103
   concept 101
   cost of 105
   critiques of 101–4
   and divine love 109
   inappropriateness of 105–6
   injustice of 102–3, 104
   inner levels 107–8
   Kierkegaard on 107fn13
   and love 109
   'no problem' attitude 103, 105
   re-descriptions 106
   and repentance 104
   and self-indulgence 106
   and trivial wrongs 105, 106–7
   White on 103–4
      critique of 104–6
Frank, S.L.
   on prayer 50–1
   on the sacraments 54
free will, and human beings 76–7
freedom, of God 161
Freud, S., *Civilization and its Discontents* 89

Galton, Francis, Sir 43
glossary, Christological 203–5
Gnosticism 70, 203

Gnostics 149–50
God
   abuse of His name 158
   acting in us 136
   as Creator 159, 160–1
   existence of 158–60, 162–7, 195–6
      Aquinas' axiological argument 164
      Aquinas' cosmological arguments 163
      Kant's moral argument 164
      ontological argument 163
   freedom of 161
   goodness of 161–2
   as love 26
   oneness of 134
   silence about 157–8
   speaking about 155–6, 157, 165–6
      analogy 165–6
      metaphor 166
      mythological 166
      via negativa 165
      via positiva 165
   as subject of theology 195–6
   use of concept 162
   and the world, distinction 165
   worship as activity of 32
God-human relationship 197
good life, the, as well-ordered life 77–8
goodness, of God 161–2
Gray, John, *Straw Dogs* 68
guilt
   collective, rejection of 95
   and responsibility 94–5

Haering, T., *The Christian Faith* 8
Hegel, G.W.F. 9
Heine, H. 141–2
Hermann, W. 117
hermeneutics, and communication 191–3
Hobbes, Thomas, *Leviathan* 80
Holocaust, the 81fn15, 82
Hooker, R. 205
human beings
   animal nature of 70–1
   Christian account of 69–70
   and Darwinism 71
   and the Eternal 72
   eternal quality 73

and free will 76–7
in Genesis 70
identity, in action 75
imago Dei 70, 72–3
interdependency 93
and language 71
and moral categories 72
in Psalm 8 69–70
self-understanding 65–6
as subject of theology 196–7
as theological topic 65–9
human condition
and aggression 89–90
Augustine on 94
diagnoses 89–90, 99
improvement 91–2
Plato on 94
responsibility for 92, 94–5
human control, and science 167–8
human institution, the church as 113–14

ideas, Popperian falsification of 2
imago Dei, human beings 70, 72–3
injustice, of forgiveness 102–3, 104
insanity, and ritual 56
intellect
in religious life 3
suspicion of 2
intellectual life, and lack of certainties 2
interests 17–19
connections 19–20
Islam 133

Jesus Christ
Christological debates 151, 152–3
dual nature, debates 150–1
in early church thinking 148–9, 151–2
historical approach 146, 147
identity, search for 146, 147
models of 152
in the New Testament 149
objective theories 141
patristic view of 149–50
recapitulation theory 141, 142
role 139–40
as role model 142–3
and sacraments 60
as second Adam 142

subjective theories 141
titles 149
and the Word 139
Jewish Christians 149
Judaism 133
judgment
autonomous 82
moral 82–3

Kant, I. 82, 162
on existence of God 164
Kierkegaard, S. 9, 104, 153, 162, 197
on eternal happiness 73
on existence of God 164
on forgiveness 107fn13
on prayer 48
Kirk, K. E. 47, 50
kissing, and betrayal 60
knowledge
nature of 123, 169
pluralism 123–4
and practice, balance 4
scientific, narrative, distinction 21fn15
tacit 4
Kung, Hans 111

language
attention to 185, 187fn7, 188
and context 4
Dante on 186
and human beings 71
see also communication
language-game 7
Leo's Tome 205
Linzey, Andrew, *Animal Theology* 70–1
living
with confidence 3–4
and the religious life 2
and uncertainty 3
living well 77
meaning 84
obstacles to 88–9
and self-examination 87
and virtues 87–8
see also good life, the
Logos see Word, the
Lorenz, K. 89
love

divine
- constancy of 109
- and forgiveness 109
- and eternity 26
- failure of 93
- and forgiveness 109
- God as 26
- as key virtue 85–6

Luther, Martin 55

McIntyre, John 152
Mackintosh, H.R. 115
McLuhan, Marshall 185
Manichaeism 91
Martell, Yann, *The Life of Pi* 69
Marx, Karl, *Das Kapital* 89
materialism 15, 16–17
Maurice, F.D. 183
miracles, definition 22
Monarchianism 150, 203
- Dynamic 204
- Modalistic 204

moral failure 101
moral law, obedience to 100
Morris, Desmond 71
- *The Naked Ape* 68

music, sound as 58–9

natural law 81, 87
natural theology, examples 172
Nestorianism 204–5
Nicea, Council of (325) 149, 150
Niebuhr, Reinhold 72
Nietzsche, G.W.F.
- on Socrates 2fn5
- works
    - *Genealogy of Morals* 89
    - *The Birth of Tragedy* 90

Origen 203
- *De Oratione* 47
- on prayer 49

paganism 36
Pannenberg, W. 67, 148
- *Jesus: God and Man* 147
Pardes, biblical interpretation 183fn14
Paul, St, on sin 92

Pelagianism 63, 91
Pentecost, significance 136, 137
philosopher-kings rule 80–1
Pieper, J. 156
Plato
- dialogues, aporia 2, 78fn7
- on the human condition 94
- philosopher-kings rule 80–1
- works
    - *Euthyphro* 161
    - *Gorgias* 189, 190
    - *Republic* 80

prayer 41–51
- Aquinas on 49
- disagreement about 42
- efficacy of 43–7
- experiments 43–4
- Frank on 50–1
- and God's omniscience 47
- and God's will 48
- Kierkegaard on 48
- Origen on 49
- reasons for 42–3
- results 43
- in Scripture 41
- theological issues 47–8
- types of 48–50
- and worldly perspective 42
- and worship 41

Prometheus myth 90
Protestantism, sacraments in 55, 57, 60, 61
purity, and sacred spaces 38

quadrivium 186, 187
- *see also trivium*

Ramsey, I.T. 183
reason
- law of 79
- limitations of 100
- use of 82

recapitulation theory, Jesus Christ 141, 142
reductionism 16–17
Reimarus, H.S. 179
religion
- as *cultus* 31
- and the Eternal 53
- and the ethical life 164

as public activity 54
science, relationship 20–1, 168–70
Weber on 44fn2
religionism 95
religious discourse
and language 190–1
and truth 190
religious life 137
and eternal life 18
intellect in 3
and living 2
and worship 34–5
religious traditions 122
repentance, and forgiveness 104
repetition, and ritual 56–7, 60
responsibility, and guilt 94–5
revelation 170–71
general 172–3
special 173
rhetoric 188–9
and truth 189
Richardson, A., *A Dictionary of Christian Theology* 136
ritual
and insanity 56
and repetition 56–7, 60
sacraments as 56
uneasiness about 56, 57
and worship 35–6

Sabellianism 150, 204
sacraments
as action 54, 59–60
contested nature of 55
Dominical 61
Frank on 54
and Jesus Christ 60
meaning of 57
number of 60–61
in Protestantism 55, 57, 60, 61
as ritual 56
sacred spaces
organization of 38
and purity 38
Saddam Hussein 94
salvation 121, 123
and church, the 124
and non-Christians 124fn7
satisfaction theory, Anselm's 143–4
Schleiermacher, Friedrich 44, 162
on communication 191–2
The Christian Faith 8, 185
science
amorality of 20
and human control 167–8
nature of 169
religion, relationship 20–21, 168–70
theology
differences 170–1
relationship 169–70
Scriptures
Augustine on 200–1
authority of 175–6, 182
confidence in 178–9
inerrancy of 179–80
interpretations 183
role 175
and tradition 177–8, 180–1, 182
vernacular translations 178
and the Word of God 176–7
secularisation 56
self-examination, and living well 87
self-indulgence, and forgiveness 106
silence
about God 157–8
Augustine on 156
importance of 156–7
sin
Augustine on 83, 92
meaning 90–1
and perversity of will 94
positive aspects of 96–7
St Paul on 92
the unforgivable 105
Weil on 96–7
see also evil
smile, human meaning of 58
social contract, concept 80
social sciences, rigour in 198–9
Socrates
Nietzsche on 2fn5
and the sophists 189–90
sound, as music 58–9
Spirit, the 136–7

spontaneity, and anarchy 77–8
Strauss, D.F. 179
Tertullian 203, 204
theology
    branches 11
    communication in 185–6, 201
    criteria 200–1
    definition 10–11
    encounter 146
    God as subject of 195–6
    and human beings 65–9, 196–7
    methodology 199–200
    science
        differences 170–1
        relationship 169–70
    scope 195
    sources 175
    subject matter 8–9, 195–8
    and the theologian 202
    writers on 8
theonomy, Tillich on 79
theophanies 32
Thirty-Nine Articles 152
Tillich, Paul 55, 56
    on autonomy 79
    Systematic Theology 8
    on theonomy 79
tradition, and the Scriptures 177–8, 180–81, 182
Trinity
    Augustine on 156
    in Christianity 134–6
    economic 135
    essential 135
trivium 186, 187
    see also quadrivium
truth
    cultivation of 33
    and religious discourse 190
    and rhetoric 189
Turner, D. 49
Turner, H. E. W., 'Doctrine of the Trinity' 136

uncertainty, and living 3
Unitarianism 134
universe, sacramental meaning 59

virtues
    Aquinas on 84–5, 99
    key 84–6
    and living well 87–8
    and love 85–6

water, and baptism 62
Weber, Max, on religion 44fn2
Weil, S. 153
    on attention 169fn2
    on sin 96–7
Westminster Confession 152
White, Patricia
    on forgiveness 103–4
    critique of 104–6
will, the
    perversity of, and sin 94
    weakness of 100
Wittgenstein, L. 33
Word, the (*Logos*)
    and Jesus Christ 139
    manifestations 57
    and the Scriptures 176–7
worship
    as act of honouring 32
    as activity of God 32
    Christian, features 36–7, 39
    and the Eternal 33, 41
    as human activity 32
    practice 35
    and prayer 41
    purpose of 31–3
    Quaker 36–7
    and religious life 34–5
    and ritual 35–6
    role of Bible in 175

Xenophanes 67

For Product Safety Concerns and Information please contact our EU representative GPSR@taylorandfrancis.com
Taylor & Francis Verlag GmbH, Kaufingerstraße 24, 80331 München, Germany

www.ingramcontent.com/pod-product-compliance
Lightning Source LLC
Chambersburg PA
CBHW062216300426
44115CB00012BA/2084